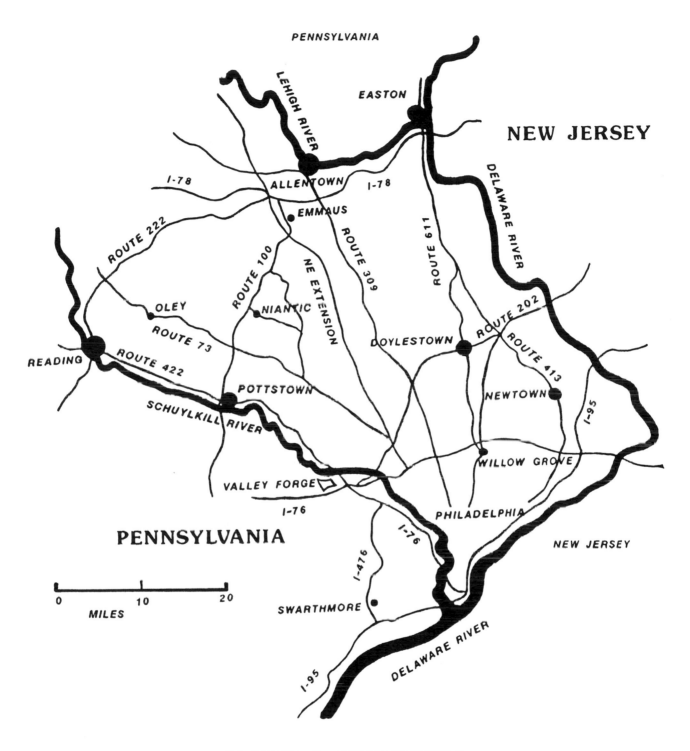

JAMES A. MICHENER

THE BEGINNING TEACHER AND HIS TEXTBOOKS

JAMES ALBERT MICHENER, A.B.

SWARTHMORE COLLEGE, '29

Came to The Hill in 1929 in the Department of English; Phi Beta Kappa.

The Hill School *Dial* 1930 and 1931 Yearbooks

JAMES A. MICHENER

THE BEGINNING TEACHER AND HIS TEXTBOOKS

BY

G. L. DYBWAD AND JOY V. BLISS

WITH

NOTES AND REMINISCENCES

BY

JAMES A. MICHENER

LIMITED EDITION

The Book Stops Here
Albuquerque, New Mexico
1995

Books by G. L. Dybwad and Joy V. Bliss

Annotated Bibliography: World's Columbian Exposition, Chicago 1893.

Dybwad, G. L. and Joy V. Bliss
James A. Michener : The Beginning Teacher and His Textbooks

ISBN: 0-9631612-1-0
Library of Congress Catalog Card Number: 95-79641

For information contact: The Book Stops Here, Publisher
1108 Rocky Point Court NE
Albuquerque, NM   87123-1952

FIRST EDITION LIMITED TO 800 COPIES FOR SALE

Jacket front illustration: Sentence diagrams from the Edgar textbook used by James A. Michener
Jacket back illustrations: James A. Michener, portrait by John Kings, and James A. Michener with
                Joy V. Bliss and G. L. Dybwad, 1993 interview
Frontispiece illustration: James A. Michener, Hill School, *The Dial*, 1930 and 1931

Printed in the United States of America

TABLE OF CONTENTS

Page

Introduction   7

Foreword: "The Old Schoolbooks" by James A. Michener   9

Purchase of the Michener Textbooks   11

The Doylestown High School Years: 1921–1925   15

The Swarthmore College Years: 1925–1929   23

The Hill School Teaching Years: 1929–1931   33

The Hill School Textbooks: Teaching and Learning   55

    Notes on the Textbooks by James A. Michener:

        "The Missing Jewel"   55
        "The Essential Dickens"   57
        "Analyzing a Sentence by Diagramming"   62
        "Graduate Course"   63
        "The Bonus Books"   65
        "My Failure"   68
        "Reading Should Be Fun"   72

The George School Teaching Years: 1933–1936   73

Postlude: Colorado State College, Harvard, Macmillan, WW II   85

Afterword   89

Acknowledgments   92

Reference List   93

Source Bibliography   98

Bibliography of the Hill Textbooks   100

Index   101

INTRODUCTION

This is the story of a young Pennsylvania prep school teacher—a teacher who became the celebrated writer James A. Michener. The biography of this portion of Michener's life was launched by the discovery of the textbooks he used at Hill School and was developed by the many letters he wrote and received, news articles about him, the memories of others, and his own written and verbal reminiscences about teaching in general and the textbooks in particular. As the narrative unfolds, the unquestionable importance of these early teaching years to his later writing career becomes apparent.

The title derives from "The Beginning Teacher," an essay by Michener, chosen by the National Council of Social Studies to introduce their 1939 yearbook. He wrote it ten years after he began his teaching career.

This book evolved and expanded slowly. After purchasing the Michener textbooks in 1987, our desire was to determine the origin of the books and then put them up for sale. As the investigation continued, an idea developed to publish a small pamphlet listing the books in the form of an illustrated annotated bibliography, which would make their background and content, including Mr. Michener's notes inscribed on their pages, available to a wider audience. The illustrated bibliography then expanded into a full book on these formative years when we found a lack of detail on Mr. Michener's early teaching career in three major biographies[1] by A. Grove Day, John P. Hayes, and George J. Becker, as well as in Michener's autobiography.[2] Now, the value of those early years in launching his independent writing career can more easily be weighed against the many other key events in his life.

The format solidified when Mr. Michener enthusiastically agreed by letter and telephone conversation to participate in the project by writing reminiscences and discussing his teaching years based upon the textbooks he had used at Hill School in Pottstown, Pennsylvania. Many have written about Mr. Michener, but to our knowledge, this is the first time he has contributed written segments to a biography about himself and then further authenticated the work by subscribing his signatures and appending his special rubrics in the oriental style denoting "finished." We feel honored.

Although the time frame is between 1921 and his ultimate professional writing career, which began in 1947 with *Tales of the South Pacific*,[3] the focus of this book is on the years of teaching: 1929–1931 and 1933–1936. Illustrations from his textbooks as well as pertinent photographs, news clippings, and correspondence help tell the story. The material is organized into three segments: Prelude at Doylestown High School and Swarthmore College—1921 to 1929; Teaching at The Hill—1929 to 1931 and George School—1933 to 1936; and Postlude summary—1936 to 1947. Taken together, the breadth of Mr. Michener's activities and experiences during these 26 years formed a very distinctive platform from which he was able to launch an innovative literary expression of our times which appeals to large numbers of people worldwide. The early teaching years are an integral and invaluable part of that platform.

We finish with some observations that grew out of the document search, our visit with Mr. Michener, and visits to eastern Pennsylvania where he grew up and learned as he taught.

The Old Schoolbooks

THE OLD SCHOOLBOOKS

Foreword by James A. Michener

In the winter of 1993, while I was working in Florida, a bulky letter reached me after having traveled to Pennsylvania, Maryland, Texas, and Maine. It was perhaps the most amazing correspondence I have ever received as a writer. It came from two men I had never heard of—they turned out to be husband and wife—and, considering its contents, from the unlikely hometown of Albuquerque, New Mexico.

It said that the authors had, by some extraordinary device they did not explain, come into possession of eighteen high school textbooks from which I had taught English in 1929, sixty-four years ago. My name appeared in ink in the books, plus notes about teaching, and several poems I had composed regarding the subjects being taught. I recognized every book and remembered its significance to me long ago. The handwriting of the notes and poems was certainly mine and this reunion of text and teacher after such a long span of years moved me deeply.

How had this cache of books left my rooms at The Hill School in Pottstown, Pennsylvania? By what accident had they been put up for sale years later? How did they fall into the hands of the Albuquerque couple who were already captivated by my novels? And what did the owners propose doing about their find?

When a follow-up phone call, made by my secretary, informed us that the New Mexico team was eager to publish the story in some form and gave evidence that they knew what they were doing and were confident that they could do a first-rate job, I explained that they had title to the books, they were free to utilize them in any way they deemed fit; and I could not stop them from publishing. But I also assured them that if they found some sensible way to present the books and my relation to them, with my notes, I would cooperate with no royalty from me in what could prove an interesting portrait of a professional writer at the very birth date of his career in books. I added that if they were not professionally oriented and if they did not aspire to do a significant presentation, I was not interested.

In closing I said that all things considered, I'd like to see the story in print and would cooperate insofar as I could to make the book come to pass. In fact, I'd add a few explanatory notes and give them permission to publish the poems.

I still knew nothing about the couple, nor how they and the books got to Albuquerque, or who at The Hill had picked up after me when I left in 1931 to travel abroad in Europe.

This is the book that these two imaginative people put together to show how a future writer got started in the book business.

James A. Michener

May 1993
Austin, Texas

9

PURCHASE OF THE MICHENER TEXTBOOKS

by G. L. Dybwad

Purchasing the Textbooks

Reading and books are my hobbies. After completing graduate work, I moved to Emmaus, Pennsylvania. Soon I began to appreciate the colonial heritage there and marvel at the ease of seeing our country's history in three dimensions. History learned by reading textbooks suddenly became palpable by living near it and being able to visit original sites. As a physical residue of history, old books soon lured me to local auctions and flea markets that abounded in the Lehigh Valley area. A chance purchase of a batch of old and valuable books for very little money in the late 1970s totally captured me.

My hobby developed to the point where I soon became heavily involved in buying and selling books and ephemera on weekends. On May 29, 1987, as was my Friday custom, I read through the auction section of the Allentown *Call Chronicle* newspaper to plan my auction schedule for the weekend. No local sales seemed promising, but I did notice an advertisement for an auction the next day in Oley, Pennsylvania. It listed books.

Most auctions never list books. The mention of books in the advertisement implied there were quite a number of them. That prospect appealed to me as a book dealer, since box lots of books are generally cheaper than books sold one at a time. I love box lots.

Consulting a map, I found that Oley was on Route 73, approximately 40 miles southwest of Allentown. Because that was farther than I normally had to drive to satisfy my passion for the hunt, my interest waned. However, the next morning was such a beautiful spring Saturday that I wanted to do something. So, while leisurely drinking coffee, I decided to see what a new auction house might have to offer.

This was my first and only auction trip to Oley. When I reflect on how close I came to skipping the trip, I believe I was destined to buy history that day. As I drove along Main Street, I found a charming rural Pennsylvania village steeped in local history. The well-kept Victorian houses on either side of the street spoke of a strong local pride in maintaining Oley's past. I turned in at the stately old brick firehouse and drove up the side road into the fairgrounds shaded by sycamore trees. The long, white auction house was, and still is, just past the band shell at the Carnival Grounds.

At the auction nearly everyone was seated indoors where David S. Allgyer, owner and auctioneer, sold the better merchandise. Outside in the morning sun arrayed against the wall of the auction house on the grass were long rows of lesser merchandise and box lots of books. Before the sale, I reviewed the books by glancing at their spines, which were up. The spine alone tells a great deal: the title, author, and publisher (original or reprint), the craftsmanship, the book age from the font and binding style, and something about the condition. Although there were many boxes, and hence many books, they all appeared to be textbooks, religious books, and business books. Because these had little or no resale value for me, my hopes evaporated.

G. L. Dybwad at the Oley Auction House in 1994

Only one spine caught my eye as belonging to a salable book—*The Story of Roland*—a 1930s color-illustrated storybook. In looking it over for condition, which was excellent, I noticed the signature "James A. Michener" on the fly leaf. This puzzled me since I certainly knew of a James A. Michener, writer and Pennsylvania resident. How *the* James A. Michener could have owned this early storybook was a mystery. I assumed it was a relative or merely a coincidence, so the signature did not excite me—but I remembered it. I signed up for a bidder number card in the main building and stayed for the sale. I bought some odds and ends outside before the auctioneer got to the books.

Since the boxes, or groups of boxes in some cases, typically sold from 25 to 50 cents each, the books did not interest the other bidders. I bought most, but not all, of them—19 boxes in all. The box with *The Story of Roland* had also caught the eye of my lone competitor—a woman who owned a book barn outside Reading, Pennsylvania. The box sold for $21—just short of the retail value of books like *Roland* in 1987. This means that neither one of us put any monetary value on the signature.

Uncharacteristically, the book part of the auction was over early— before noon. I loaded the boxes of books into my station wagon and headed home. Back in Emmaus, I unloaded and leisurely began sorting through the boxes looking for salable books. To my astonishment, several additional school textbooks surfaced signed in the same hand by James A. Michener. Their common subject was either English grammar or literature. The Michener books were scattered throughout the boxes. By then I realized with growing elation that this was not a coincidence, and the books were all somehow related. This compelled me to go through every book in every box very carefully, looking for additional books that were literary in nature and contained signatures, initials, or notes in the same hand. In total I found 18 related books randomly distributed in the 19 boxes. I carefully saved the sales slips from the auction and

THE STORY OF ROLAND

Michener's Signature in *The Story of Roland*

clipped out the newspaper advertisement to give my purchase extra provenance. Not all the English grammar and books of literature had Michener entries; a "Mr. Rolfe" had signed two books. I wondered who Mr. Rolfe was. Did he have a connection with English or with Michener?

Then I needed to establish if these James A. Michener signatures were indeed those of the author. A tentative answer came by comparing the textbook signatures with his autograph in his 1961 book, *Report of the County Chairman*, bought at auction a few years before.[1] I had a second reference signature, since my copy of the *County Chairman* also contained a letter on campaign stationery signed by Michener in 1962. That signature matched well also. In spite of a lapse of 30 years, the signatures from the 1960s were amazingly similar to those in the textbooks from the 1930s. I couldn't believe it.

Oley Auction Stubs and Receipt

I then had to ask Mr. Michener directly about this puzzling find. I called Random House in New York, publisher of several of Michener's books, and obtained his then current office address at the English Department of the University of Miami. I wrote to Mr. Michener on August 10, 1987, and asked if he recognized the books in question. My letter contained photocopies of signatures from four of the books. His affirmative reply came in an enthusiastic letter dated October 16, 1987.[2] My find was serendipitous. His reply raised a new question: What was George School?

Between 1987 and 1991, my wife and I toyed with the idea of writing a story based upon the textbooks. By July of 1992, we wanted Mr. Michener's help with our ever-expanding project, and we sent a complete set of photocopies of relevant pages from his former textbooks to his Austin office. These are the copies Michener describes in his foreword.

Report of the
County
Chairman
by
JAMES A.
MICHENER

The Text Fair
—1962—

James A. Michener

Michener's 1962 Signature in *County Chairman*

---

741 Levittown Shopping Center
Levittown, Penna.—WIndsor 3-1225
P.O. Box 620
Doylestown, Penna.

Charles Happ, Treasurer

MICHENER FOR CONGRESS COMMITTEE

Vote Democratic Nov. 6, 1962 — Elect James A. Michener To Congress

ALLENTOWN, PA.
924 HAMILTON ST.
SEPTEMBER 15, 1962

MR. HENRY NEIMEYER
203 MAIN ST.
EMMAUS, PA.

DEAR MR. NEIMEYER:

IT WAS A REAL PLEASURE MEETING YOU AT THE BAER
HOME ON AUGUST 31ST. MY WIFE AND I ENJOYED OURSELVES
IMMENSELY. WE CERTAINLY WELCOME SUCH OPPORTUNITIES TO
TALK WITH THE VOTERS OF THE EIGHTH CONGRESSIONAL DISTRICT.

YOUR SUPPORT OF MY CANDIDACY IS BOTH VALUED AND
APPRECIATED.

SINCERELY,

James A. Michener
JAMES A. MICHENER

JAM/s

Michener's 1962 Signature on Campaign Stationery

UNIVERSITY OF
Miami

Department of English
P.O. Box 248145
Coral Gables, Florida 33124

October 16, 1987

G. Dybwad
Box 258, RD 2
Emmaus, PA 18049

Dear Mr. Dybwad,

How astonished I was to see those old pages with their signatures, and especially the very old bookplate which I had attached
to so many of my books.

The books in question were a portion of those I used in teaching
at The Hill School in Pottstown and at the George School in
Newton, both in Pennsylvania. I am most happy that they have
fallen into the hands of someone who appreciates them. They left
my possession when I had to go off to war in 1942 or 1943 and I
often wondered what had happened to them.

Sincerely,

James A. Michener
James A. Michener
Distinguished Visiting Professor

JAM/tmp

Michener Acknowledges the Textbooks, 1987

Determining the History of the Textbooks

At our interview in 1993, we agreed with Mr. Michener that finding his 1929–1931 Hill School textbooks largely intact and in excellent condition after 56 years is incredible. Consequently, we tried to determine their history by contacting the Allgyer Auction house in Oley, Pennsylvania. Hazel Allgyer, wife of the auctioneer, told us that they had sold the auction business, but it still operates at the Oley fairgrounds. She had been the bookkeeper for the business and was glad to help us. We sent her a copy of the lot stubs. I had been bidder #193. The stubs show that there were two consignors for the books: #2 and #8. Mrs. Allgyer identified them from the 1987 auction records.[3]

Both consignors were contacted and asked if they or any relatives had ever gone to or been associated with Hill School in Pottstown, Pennsylvania. Neither family had a background at The Hill. However, one was a book collector, and he remembered buying a large number of books at a Niantic, Pennsylvania, auction just before the Oley auction. He kept the books he wanted (not English or literature textbooks) and consigned the remainder to the Oley auction. Hence, the textbooks used by Michener at Hill School probably lay in a Niantic book barn for many years before the Oley auction and had not been in the possession of a Hill family.

How did the textbooks find their way to Niantic? We learned from Hill School that they often deaccession old or unused books from the library to make room for new and more popular books. Credence for a Hill School library deaccession came from Mr. Michener when we asked him who originally owned the textbooks. He said, "They belonged to the Hill School."[4] Hence, the Michener textbooks could have been given away, then bought in a batch long ago, and stored together. Perhaps the buyer was the now deceased owner of the Niantic book barn.

Mr. Michener's 1987 letter implied that he had kept the books until he went off to the South Pacific. But after looking over the actual textbooks during our interview in 1993, he was sure that he left them at Hill School when he went to Europe in the spring of 1931. He said, "I can't remember teaching from any of these books at George School. So I would almost affirm that none of these books ever got to George School. I had no permanent address, as it were; and I was going to Europe for two years and so there is no way I could have taken these books with me. I may have just abandoned them at Hill School, and somebody picked them up."[5] He said that he, or his students in their classroom work, used all the textbooks except *The Facts and Background of Literature*, *Mr. Rolfe of The Hill*, and *Marching On*.

Since Mr. Rolfe's name appears in *Marching On*, he may have saved and used the Michener textbooks before turning them in to the library. The following students' names are found in three of the books: "John J. Weinberger" (listed in the 1931 Hill School yearbook, *The Dial*), "W. H. Nalty" (also listed in the 1931 yearbook, *The Dial*), and "Paul Reigner, Pennsburg" (no Hill graduates have come from Pennsburg, Pennsylvania). We may owe thanks to these students, or Rolfe, for preserving the Michener textbooks.

We may never know exactly how the books got to Niantic, Pennsylvania; but we are glad for their preservation so that we can add another historical dimension to a famous writer and get a glimpse at the style of education of the times.

THE DOYLESTOWN HIGH SCHOOL YEARS: 1921–1925

James A. Michener's preparation for a high school teaching career and the consequences of his early teaching years had a dramatic effect upon his lifework. It is intriguing to look back at his own high school days and compare his writings and activities with his expectations for students just a very few years later. Michener's progression through high school shows how quickly he blossomed and how early the way was paved for two consuming activities in his life—writing and physical fitness. The school that Michener attended, Doylestown (Pennsylvania) High School, has since been expanded and renamed Central Bucks West.

Freshman Year: 1921–1922

On the morning of August 30, 1921, all applicants for Doylestown High School reported; classes began one week later.[1] James Michener, 14 years old, was one of the freshman students. He was just back from a summer of travel: he had hitchhiked to his Aunt Laura's in Detroit and returned home by way of Iowa.[2] He had started a life of travel with short trips along the eastern states the previous year and expanded the scope of his adventures the summer before starting high school. Walking remained a major physical activity throughout his life; by his mid-eighties, he had "neither stopped nor slowed down."[3]

The Doylestown newspaper, *Bucks County Intelligencer*, printed the usual small town news of the day, which included rather comprehensive coverage of local sporting events. Michener's name first appeared in conjunction with sports in March 1922; he was a substitute guard on the Boy's Brigade basketball team. In his first game, he did not score.[4] When the nine-game season ended that month, Commander Murray "and his Boy's Brigade basketball five laid claim to the Doylestown junior championship."[5] With 37 total points, Michener was third in the point standings.

In his memoir, *The World Is My Home*, Michener pays warm tribute to George Murray—a placid, uneducated, unmarried roofer who used his small salary to run the local branch of the Boy's Brigade. Murray, a role model, rescued many underprivileged Doylestown boys through sporting activities.[6] Michener was one of Murray's boys for four or five years—until Murray's influence waned with the coming of Boys Scouts.[7]

Sophomore Year: 1922–1923

When the Doylestown public schools opened on September 5, 1922, for Michener's sophomore year, 936 students reported. Thirty teachers made up the entire school faculty; 15 were new, and 25 were women. Eight teachers taught high school; all but one were from Pennsylvania.[8]

In this second year of high school, Michener played tennis and basketball. He was too young to be on the football roster in 1922, and he was not included in the baseball team's photograph for the year, implying he was not on the team. Although he would later become an active member of *The Torch*—the student monthly magazine, he was not on the staff during this year.

Sports

Shortly after the school year was underway, the *Intelligencer* reported the results of the first match of the boys' championship tennis tournament: James Michener easily defeated classmate Edward Twining, 6-3 and 6-0. "Michener's fast serve carried him through a winner."[9] Later in life Michener played a tremendous amount of tennis, continuing until he was well into his seventies.[10]

The faculty roster did not list a coach when the school year began,

BASKETBALL TEAM, 1922–'23

Standing—F. Kolbe, Manager; R. McNealy, F.; E. Twining, C.; J. Michener, F.; J. A. Gardy, Coach. Sitting—D. Tomlinson, G.; H. Bigley, F.; D. Hodgins, C., Captain; L. Nash, F.; A. Tomlinson, G.

15

but Michener remembered that Coach J. Allen Gardy was well-entrenched at Doylestown High School some years before Michener started playing basketball.[11] Gardy promoted the essentials of a good basketball player. He stressed scholarship—the most important element. Next was good physical condition; he counseled his players to quit smoking, eat healthfully, and get plenty of sleep. In addition, he addressed eligibility; since the league had a new eligibility ruling that year, he admonished the players to take care not to affect amateur standing.[12] The coach impressed upon his squad that the use of brains when they played was the most important asset of a good basketball player. "Following this, in order of importance, he discussed speed, accuracy in shooting, fighting spirit and experience."[13] Gardy's early coaching brought a resounding first-game win.[14] Jim Michener played a forward position on Gardy's team and remembered the coach as a "big, bland, even-tempered stabilizing influence."[15] When he reflected on the great good his early instructors did him when they steered him away from destructive habits, Michener remembered Gardy's guidance.[16]

Junior Year: 1923–1924

In his junior year, Michener's activities expanded to include baseball, basketball, and writing. He was an associate editor of *The Torch*, the monthly (sometimes bimonthly) student publication; and he contributed to each issue. Although he would later counsel the Hill School students to write prose rather than poetry, most of his contributions to the Doylestown *Torch* were in verse form.

Writing

Michener wrote "The Night After Christmas," a parody of "The Night Before Christmas" and a prescription for Christmas excesses.[17] In response to punishment for passing a love note at school, he wrote "Silly Sentimentalities" and satirically questioned: "Why should the big red-blooded boys and girls of this school find amusement in making themselves conspicuous by casting their affections on one certain person?" He offered memberships in "The Society for the Abolishment of Silly Sentimentalists."[18] Also, Jim Michener liked all girls.

Michener's next literary contribution was "Mi Proprio Amo" (My Own Love)—a poetic comment on infatuated male students at Doylestown High School. The title came from a

The Night After Christmas
By JAMES A. MICHENER, '25

'Twas the night after Christmas, and all through the house
Not a creature was stirring, not even a mouse.
The kids were both sleeping in slumber profound
And nothing was making a bit of a sound.
I thought as I jumped in my warm waiting bed,
And pulled up the covers right over my head,
That since Christmas was over my troubles were past,
And I would have peace in the family at last;
When there suddenly fell on the crisp midnight air
A horrible shriek that was heard everywhere.
It came from the room of my eight-year-old son,
And there soon followed after a similar one.
I knew from the past that my sleeping was o'er
And I presently heard my dear wife at the door.
"Oh James," she cried, "Hurry, get up. Get those pills.
The darlings are sick. They've got headaches and chills."
But I, knowing better the cause of their pain,
(They'd eaten too much and were sick, it was plain).
I'd not make a fuss, but went quickly down stairs
And proceeded to ruin myself on some chairs.
After spraining my ankle and skinning my knee,
I found where the medicine chest ought to be.
I did not take pills, for I knew what was best,
I took one big bottle and left all the rest.
I grabbed a big spoon and then hastened away
To the bedroom upstairs where the sick darlings lay.
Nuts, candy and fruit had wreaked havoc, I knew,
But I was quite sure of the right thing to do.
"They'll not live 'til morning." I heard my wife cry,
"Oh James, get a doctor. Do you want them to die?"
I said not a word, but went straight to the bed
And firmly took hold of my son by his head.
I opened his mouth, and proceeded with toil,
To give him a dose of good old castor oil.
His sister was next and she got the same,
And to hear those kids shriek, you'd have thought it a shame.
But I had no pity. I knew 'twas all bluff.
When I was a kid, I too, "pulled that stuff."
I knew that they'd hate it, I knew that they'd yell.
But I also knew that it would make them both well.
So I made them take it; then jumped back into bed.
And again pulled the covers up over my head.
I was soon wrapped in slumber, for I was quite sure
That, though they were sick, they had had the right cure.
I arose the next morning and found them all right,
And none the worse off for their illness that night.
And now hear the moral, dear friends, of this tale:
"Castor oil is the one cure that cures without fail."

The Torch, December 1923

THE TORCH

"Silly Sentimentalities"

By JAMES MICHENER, '25

At last the authorities of our high school have hit upon a most distressing evil that is abounding in our school. I refer to the "silly sentimentalities" that are so prominent of late.

I entertain the same opinions as do the faculty. Why should there be so much valuable time wasted on the absolutely foolish attachments, which invariably end in nothingness, at the most, and not infrequently in quarrels? Why should the big red-blooded boys and girls of this school find amusement in making themselves conspicuous by casting their affections on one certain person?

It annoys me, and many others also, to see some lovesick swain cast languishing glances upon some flower of his heart, and become insensible with ecstasy if she even so much as deigns to smile at him.

It may be as some of the advocates of these "sentimentalities" claim, that they are not silly, but natural. However, the thinkers, and well wishers of the school will not pay much attention to these thrusts by those who are foolish enough to think that they are capable of true affections at the tender age of fifteen or sixteen.

One of the boys who is proud to be classed as a "sentimentalist," has the open effrontery to inquire whether or not the people who are continually knocking him, and his associates, would have different opinions, if they had had the opportunities to be "silly sentimentalists" in their high school days. Such deliberate insults as these will not be tolerated much longer, and if that inquisitive boy must know, it is said, on good authority, that not a few of the people who are opposing this ultra-modern movement in our high school, had to fight off their admirers of the opposite sex in their younger days.

So I may as well add, now that I am assured that my readers understand my ideas on this subject, that it is not a case of sour grapes with me, although I wouldn't exactly be against a mild sort of friendship were my face to warrant it, but that I honestly believe that it should be abolished in this school. All those having the same trend of thought can join our society, "The Society for the Abolishment of Silly Sentimentalists," by paying the yearly dues, $1.00, to me.

The Torch, January 1924

Latin phrase frequently used by a fellow classmate, Lindsay Johnson; Michener gave him repeated credit for these three words in the poem.[19]

Michener called Lindsay Johnson a "treasured friend."[20] They collaborated on a poem, "The Castle of My Dreams," a fantasy refuge in times of oppression and finally in death.[21]

Seventy years after they appeared, we asked Michener if he could explain a few silly items written about him in his high school paper. In the "What Would Happen If?" column, one query was: What if "James Michener would get a haircut instead of having his head shaved?" Michener said he "favored real short haircuts."[22] Another question was what if James Michener and two of his colleagues "came to school on time every day?"—a comment about tardiness that dated to a young age. Michener said he stopped on the way to school "to do a lot of different things."[23] Also printed was a fictitious radio program for which Michener had no explanation: "Michener. Bass Solo. 'My! How I Love Freshmen!'"[24]

A *Torch* "Humor" section cited "Favorite Sayings of Famous People." James Michener—"Everything is Jacob in the house of Denmark."[25] When questioned about the meaning, Michener said, "It is a quote I still use; it bespeaks my early love of *Hamlet*."[26]

Sports

The 1924 Basketball season lasted two months—January and February. The editors of *The Torch* recapped the season, game by game. When he played, Michener was a forward. In the first game of the season, "'Jimmy' Michener starred for the locals with seven field goals, from all angles of the floor. The rest of the team played a good game." After this noteworthy start, his performance declined over the next five games. In the final game of the season, his name did not appear on the team roster; and *The Torch* reported, "Bigley and McNealy, who are filling Michener's place very creditably, starred for D.H.S."[27] Principal Ross had suspended Michener for insubordination.[28] This was the situation that prompted him to write the poem "Player's Soliloquy." In it he ruminates, "But you must not play. The faculty says no; and no it is."[29] The team won the 1923–1924 Bux-Mont—Bucks County-Montgomery County—League championship.

Editors of *The Torch* also recounted baseball statistics. Michener was the lead-off batter for each of the four spring season games but received no special recognition. The Doylestown High School season ended with two wins, two loses.[30]

THE TORCH

Mi Propio Amo

By JAMES MICHENER, '25

I stood out in the hall one day
    Awaiting for a fellow,
When Swartley stuck his face in mine
    And started in to bellow.
"Oh Jim, she's all the world to me
    She's lovely, sweet and fair,
Her eyes are wonderful to see;
    Likewise her face and hair."

I shoved him off, I'd heard that tale
    A thousand times that day,
I hate to see a fellow who
    Is hit by girls that way.
I thought I'd cure him once for all,
    'Twould do him good, and so,
I said as Lindsay Johnson says,
    "Mi proprio amo."

Then who should come but "Eggs" Hayman
    And shout, "There's no one like her—
Her face sublime, her eyes so blue,
    She really is no piker."
I'd like to take him at his word.
    I don't doubt that it's so,
But then, as Lindsay Johnson says,
    "Mi propio amo."

And then up strode Claude Wetherill
    Who said, "I do not care
What others think of their dear friends,
    For mine is the most fair."
I'd like to take him at his word.
    I don't doubt that it's so,
But then as Lindsay Johnson says,
    "Mi propio amo."

Friend Harry Bigley's views were next,
    "I don't care what you say,
They may be pretty, sweet and cute,
    But mine wins any day."
I'd like to take him at his word.
    I don't doubt that it's so,
But then as Lindsay Johnson says,
    "My propio amo."

And who came next but Philip Kratz
    And grabbed me by the neck.
"I'll have you understand," said he,
    "That she's the best, by heck."
Oh patience suff'reth and is kind,
    But it has bounds you know,
I kicked him in the jaw, and cried,
    "Mi propio amo."

And so it is with "Ken" and Groff,
    And "Ed" and "Oll" and "Twing."
They shout about their ladies fair
    And loud their praised ones sing.
But I sit tight and take it in
    For theirs may come and go.
I tell no man, but as "Lin" says,
    "Mi propio amo."

I am a friend to every man.
    My friendship knows no bound,
But a true friend, the kind I mean,
    Has never yet been found.
All of my friends rave 'bout their girls,
    Gosh! that is all they know,
I never say a word, but still,
    "Mi propio amo."

And now my friends, I want to say,
    If you are smitten, too,
And struck by some fair damsel's charms
    Who seems the world to you,
Go sing your songs to someone else,
    For I have cares also,
And I must say, as Lindsay says,
    "Mi propio amo."

The Torch, February-March 1924

The Castle of My Dreams

JAMES MICHENER, '25 and LINDSAY JOHNSON, '25

In lands that lie across the sea,
Close to 'a lovely bay,
Where I used to sit and dream, and dream,
And while the hours away,
A castle stands high in the air,
The castle of my dreams.
With golden turrets flashing bright,
Among the sun's bright beams.
'Tis there my thots so often fly
When I am sore oppressed.
'Tis there I always find repose,
And have my wrongs redressed.
'Tis there that all the good I've done,
Is safely stored away.
'Tis there that sadness has no claim
And everything is gay.
'Tis there I'd love to live and die,
And so, to me it seems,
When I am gone, I'd like to rest
In the castle of my Dreams.

The Torch, May–June 1924

"The Player's Soliloquy"

By J. MICHENER, '25.

To play, or not to play; that is the question
Whether your conduct warrants a D. D.,
Or a V. G. Whether the drag you boast of
With your dearest enemy, the faculty,
Is man upward course, or down. To work,
To toil, to sweat under the weary load
Of lessons heaped upon your weary back,
But not to play. Oh! no. To work, to toil,
But not to go upon the floor and bask,
In glory, in the eyes of some fair lass,
And listen to the cheers of friends who yell
Upon the slightest show of your great power,
To work. To ponder o'er some musty book
And gain great wisdom, but you must not play.
The faculty says no; and no it is.

The Torch, January 1924

Junior Year
The 1923–24 *Torch* Staff. Associate Editor, Michener, is pictured at the lower right.

Junior Year
1923–24 Doylestown High School Basketball Team. Michener is pictured at the lower left.

Senior Year: 1924–1925

By all accounts, Michener's final year of high school was sterling. He was president of his senior class, he was editor-in-chief of *The Torch*, he excelled in basketball, he spoke publicly, he graduated with honors, and he received an award of a fine college scholarship.

We, the members of the Editorial Board, here wish to express

Our Appreciation

of the untiring work of the outgoing editor

James A. Michener

As his final year of high school got underway, the local newspaper listed the 60 members of the senior class in alphabetical order—first 26 boys, then 34 girls.[31] The following spring 56 of these students graduated, comprising the largest class ever graduated from a Bucks County high school.[32] Michener was among them.

In recognition of his year as editor-in-chief of *The Torch*, the appreciation page of the *Commencement Number of The Class of 1925 : Doylestown High School : June, 1925* prominently displayed his graduation picture and a note of gratitude.

Writing

As editor-in-chief, Michener's contributions appeared on the editorial page. In May 1925, at the age

Editor-in-Chief
***The Torch*, June 1925**

JAMES MICHENER '25

AN OLD, OLD THEME

If all the editorials on school spirit which have been handed to me within the last four years were put into one issue of the "Torch," they would fill it. Every call for material brings forth one more such editorial. These editorials, however, are always in an abstract form.

"We should have school spirit. It is something grand, noble, exalted. It is something that keeps the school moving. It is the force that prompts students to be good." Those are excerpts from the overwhelming flow of editorials on the subject. I am not criticizing. I could not give as good a definition of school spirit as some of the papers contain and I shall not attempt it.

However, what I can do, is to give an example of the finest show of school spirit I have ever witnessed. The members of the boys' basketball team had been invited to a banquet by a group of Doylestown business men. It was a sumptuous affair; chicken, potatoes, gravy, cranberry sauce, vegetables, pie, even ice cream to the more ravenous.

The boys had no thought of school. It was a relaxation from the routine. No one had even mentioned the fact that they were there as representatives of the school. They were just a gang of boys.

Toward the end of the festivities the boys were asked to sing. Obligingly, and at the same time embarrassed slightly, they grouped themselves about the pianist.

They were handed slips of paper with twenty four popular songs printed upon them. The pianist had the music right there for every song on the list. The boys were looking at their slips, endeavoring to choose a song which would sound least terrible.

The pianist was ready to start and she asked them which song they were going to sing.

Instantaneously, and almost simultaneously, over half the boys replied, "For we are jolly students." The pianist did not have the music for it, and was not sure that she knew the piece by heart, so the boys started off without any accompaniment and sang their song with as much spirit as I have ever heard it sung.

There is no moral to this story. It was a very ordinary occurrence, and yet, to several persons there, it was the outstanding happening of the whole banquet. It brought home to me the fact that school is probably the biggest thing in life right now. But, of course, school may be made very matter-of-fact, and often it is the little things that make it interesting. The more interesting it can be made, the better we like it, and the better we like it, the more we get out of attending it.

A song is not much. The rendition of it by a group of boys whose voices are changing is much less, and yet a song showed me what school spirit really is. It is respect and love combined.

Michener's Editorial in *The Torch,* **May 1925**

of 18, he wrote "An Old, Old Theme." He explained the difficulties of defining "school spirit" and recounted with warmth an incident he had observed which characterized "school spirit" for him.[33]

Sports

The Doylestown High School league schedule of 21 basketball games ran from December 1924 to March 1925; there were also non-league games. It was a long season.

DOYLESTOWN HIGH SCHOOL BASKETBALL RECORDS

Doylestown High led the rest of Bux-Mont League in point scoring with a total of 580 points. Hatboro High was second and Perkasie High, the champions took third place. Leading the D. H. S. players was "Jimmy" Michener. the fast-moving forward. Michener rolled up 153 points, the same total that was registered by Harry Bigley last year. Thirty-seven of these points were the results of foul goals, the other 116 coming from 58 field goals. Second to Michener was Captain "Ed" Twining, with 150 points. He netted two more field goals than Jimmy, but did not equal him in fouls. "Irish" McNealy was third with 50 field goals and 29 fouls and "Big Bill" Polk fourth with 68 points. "Jack" Waddington rounded out the quintet with 59 markers.

In foul shooting McNealy led the league. He caged 29 out of 45 tries for an average of .644. McNealy also led the team in foul shooting for the whole season, with 80 out of 188 tries safely made for a mark of .850.

1924-1925

Player	Field Goals	Foul Goals	Foul Tries	Points	Foul Av.
Michener	110	58	108	278	.537
Twining	94	44	83	232	.530
McNealy	68	52	80	188	.650
Waddington	53	22	44	128	.500
Polk	41	15	36	97	.416
Hellerman	9	10	25	28	.400
Carter	1	2	5	4	.400
Tucker	2	0	0	4	.000
Horner	1	0	0	2	.000
Jones	0	1	2	1	.500
Totals	379	204	383	962	.533

BUX-MONT LEAGUE RECORDS

Player	Field Goals	Foul Goals	Foul Tries	Points	Foul Av.
Michener	58	37	66	153	.561
Twining	60	30	54	150	.556
McNealy	50	29	45	129	.644
Polk	28	12	25	68	.480
Waddington	26	7	20	59	.450
Hellerman	5	5	10	15	.500
Carter	1	2	5	4	.400
Tucker	1	0	0	2	.000
Totals	229	122	225	580	.542

The 1924–25 Doylestown High School Basketball Record

Again, Michener played one of the important forward positions. McNealy, the other forward, "was all over the floor and when he was not ringing up baskets he was feeding the ball to 'Jimmy' Michener, his running mate at forward. Michener dropped six field goals through the net and succeeded in three of his six foul tries." The season opened with a walkover win of 64 to 2.[34]

In February 1925, the local paper reported a 24 to 17 Doylestown win: "'Jimmy' Michener, who at all times desires to be an unsung hero, was the 'works' as well as the salvation for the champs again last night. Michener, playing his great game at forward, not on the sides or down under the basket, but in the middle of the defensive fracas, registered three field goals and shot seven fouls without a miss, thus accounting for 13 points for Doylestown."[35]

A few weeks later, even though they had won, the report was lackluster: "To have selected stars last night on the Doylestown team one would have had to look up to the sky." But, just before half time, "'Jimmy' Michener took his team into the lead with two fouls that registered properly, ..."[36]

Late in March, after Doylestown had lost the 1925 league championship, the *Intelligencer* sports writer opined that the season was at least one month too long. The team "was absolutely 'burned out' from too much basketball."[37] Although they were not the 1925 Bux-Mont League champions, the Doylestown players led the league in point scoring. "Leading the D.H.S. players was 'Jimmy' Michener, the fast moving forward."[38]

Extracurricular Activities

In April 1925, the Doylestown Legionnaires and Rotarians sponsored Boys' Week. Three students were invited to talk; James Michener was one of the three. He titled his speech "The Heart of the Boy," and said, "The heart of a boy is the puzzle, and can only be solved by reaching it through some trait or hobby that interests the boy. By minimizing his defects, by being kind to him and by bringing out his fine characteristics and desires, this can be accomplished."[39] He spoke from experience.

Forty-seven students and friends traveled to Washington, D.C., for a three-day 1925 senior class trip. Michener was among the travelers from Doylestown who stayed at the Hotel Potomac. It was "the largest group of seniors that had ever gone to the Capital to 'see how things are run' and shake hands with President Coolidge."[40] An article, "The Grand Army of the Class of 1925," chronicled the progress of Michener's high school class from raw recruit freshmen to polished senior captains. But of the senior trip the class wrote: "One would hardly suspect us of being well-trained captains if he had seen us in Washington, the first night."[41] Michener's memories of the trip were that he met President Coolidge, saw museums, dined in restaurants, and had a good time.[42] Michener had progressed to polished captain status.

Scholarship

At Swarthmore College commencement exercises on June 15, 1925, President Aydelotte awarded James Michener a $2000 scholarship. Michener was working and did not attend the Swarthmore commencement to accept his award.[43] The Doylestown newspaper reported:

> James Michener, a member of the graduating class of Doylestown High School and one of its outstanding students and athletes for several years, has been awarded by Swarthmore College one of the most coveted scholastic honors of the year.
>
> Michener, in competition with 155 candidates from twenty-seven states, has won one of the five open scholarships awarded by Swarthmore College—a four years' colrse [sic] valued at $2000.
>
> As a member of the local high school Michener ranked highest in the psychological tests, was a scholastic leader, editor of the school paper and won his "D" [letter] in basketball and baseball.[44]

Miss Garner, a Swarthmore graduate, who Michener says was his high school Spanish teacher, nominated him for this award. She placed his name before the selection committee because he was an "A" student in her class and showed special abilities.[45] Other biographers describe her as a Latin or as an English teacher. Unfortunately, Doylestown High School does not have faculty records back to the 1920s, but Miss Garner was pictured with the faculty in the 1925 Commencement Number of the *Torch*. There was a Catherine Roth Garner, French language major and head of the French Club, in the Swarthmore graduating class of 1924.

Graduation

Michener graduated from Doylestown High School on June 23, 1925. The local newspaper carried his story and photograph on the front page. Although he did not receive the award for "Best All Around Student," he was one of six graduates designated "Honor Rank"—and the only boy.[46]

Doylestown High School had abolished valedictory and salutatory orations eight years previously. At graduation exercises, as class president, James Albert Michener presented the class gift and gave the class president's address—"Diversions in the Student's Life."[47] The class recognized that students received many honors for extra-curricular activities but no awards to induce interest in scholastic work. They set up a $500 endowment with instructions for investment and awarding the interest annually to the member of the senior class with the highest scholastic average. They named this perpetual award "The Class of 1925 Scholarship Award."[48]

DOYLESTOWN, PA., THURSDAY, JUNE 25, 1925

HONOR STUDENTS AT DOYLESTOWN HIGH

FIFTY-SIX GRADUATED FROM THE HIGH SCHOOL

Believed to Be the Largest Class in the County

ADDRESS BY DR. PRINCE

Three Interesting Papers on "Tardiness, Absence and Excuses"—Thirty-three Girls and Twenty-three Boys in the Class This Year

DOYLESTOWN, June 24.—Over 500 persons crowded the school auditorium last night to capacity when the largest class in the history of Doylestown High School received diplomas from William H. Satterthwaite, Jr., president of the school board.

It was the thirty third annual commencement and so far as is known the fifty-six graduates composed the largest class ever graduated from a high school in Bucks county. Last year graduates, including eighteen

The picture shows, in top row, left to right: Miss Marie L. Barton, a leader in academic course; Miss Mary Martin Armstrong, also a leader in the academic course; Miss Esther Mae Gehman, honor student in the homecraft course; Miss Alice Hennessy, honor student in the commercial course; and Miss Jane Marie Kohler, a leader in the academic course; and below, James Albert Michener, honor student and president of the graduating class of Doylestown High, who received diplomas last evening. Michener was awarded one of the five scholarships offered by Swarthmore College in competition with students from many States. The scholarship of four years is worth $2000.

DETERMINATION MAKES LIFE'S BIG SUCCESSES

Dr. Prince Tells Graduating Class at Commencement

CHARACTER IMPORTANT

Too Many Young People Seeking Success in Life Are Attracted By the Clamor of Title and Social Leadership—100 Per Cent Service Is Greatest Accomplishment

Left: Michener's High School Graduation and Scholarship Announced in the *Bucks County Intelligencer*. June 25, 1925

Below: Michener's Graduation Speech Printed in the Doylestown High School Commencement Bulletin. June 23, 1925

DIVERSIONS IN THE STUDENT'S LIFE.
By James Michener, Doylestown High
(Address made by President of Graduating Class in Presenting Gift)

The student, who today attends a modern high school, finds conditions which surround him much different from the environment which school life offered twenty years ago, when studies were the one and only interest. He enters upon an aura of diversion. There are innumerable activities that are constantly taking place in the school. The principal ones are athletics. Then come the "Torch," the student council; the literary societies; the work with the library; dramatics; school lectures and concerts. These are only the activities in the school. There are also those social functions outside the school which are so abundant and which interfere with the student's studies.

Since each student is necessarily ambitious, it is natural that he aspire to as many honors as possible. He makes an effort to participate in everything. Caught in the whirl, and inspired with the thrill of it all, he continues, taxing himself physically and mentally.

Late hours are kept. This state of affairs continues for several weeks, maybe months, and then something snaps. It is generally the scholastic standing which suffers.

Study is often eliminated from the program of study. Finally, when the Springtime comes, and the final spurt for a high scholastic average is made, the student realizes how far below the standard he has allowed himself to fall. Then comes the unpleasant awakening. It is absolutely impossible to learn a year's work in May and June. A great many students have learned the truth of that statement this year.

This lack of concentration is due to the fact that outside influence counterbalances the desire to study. The reason that there is such an interest in these activities is because they are exploited so highly—there is so much

personal honor to be obtained; so many flattering write ups of athletic achievements; so much gratification in being the head of some-one-thing-or-other. Every high school student, especially a junior or senior, has an abundance of conceit. This conceit is easily appeased by participation in athletics or by being a member of one of the various boards. And, of course, extra-curricular activities do have their values.

The school offers "D's" as awards to the student who shows athletic prowess. Members of the various teams are cheered, following a victory. The school paper prints the pictures of the different governing bodies of the extra-curricular activities. The keynote to the success of these activities is the fact that, by awarding a small prize, a desire is created to participate and to achieve honor, but there is no inducement which stimulates interest in scholastic achievement.

Realizing all this, the Class of 1925 feels that it is justified in creating that which we hope will be an incentive to greater effort and to greater interest in scholastic work.

We have no desire to donate a gift which makes for external show. We do desire that this gift have lasting qualities. It is with great pleasure that we present to the school the sum of five hundred (500) dollars, representing the class savings and earnings of four years. This money is to be invested and held in trust and the annual proceeds, which will approximate twenty-five (25) dollars, are to be awarded at commencement time to that member of the senior class whose average in general scholarship for the four year course is the highest.

Let this gift be known as "The Class of 1925 Scholarship Award."

Below: Senior Bio

JAMES MICHENER
"Jimmy"
Doylestown, Pa.

February 3, 1908

Baseball 2-3-4
Basketball 2-3-4
President Class 4
Editor Torch 4

"I'll speak in a monstrous little voice."

Has anybody here seen "Jimmy"? Well, listen awhile and you will. Or if you happen to be deaf, just keep your eyes open for a jail-bird haircut and the biggest feet in the Class of '25. Then you will recognize the proud possessor of the same.

Jimmy is our big boy this year.

To tell the truth, we're not sure that D. H. S. can survive after Jimmy graduates. At least it will be a dreadful shock.

One thing we can never doubt is Jimmy's school spirit. Any of his speeches before the school will prove that. For this reason he has made a faithful class president.

Jimmy has quite a way of his own with the girls, for he truly thinks that "the boy that's 'fraid of women 'll never hev whiskers." We're not quite sure what the girls think.

Jimmy aspires to be a teacher of mathematics and we don't doubt that he could impress his pupils. No matter what he becomes, we wish him the best of good fortune and we know that he will come out on the top.

Summer 1925

On August 13, 1925, John Philip Sousa, more than 70 years old and lacking "none of his old time vision" brought his band back to Willow Grove Park. Over 20,000 people crowded into the big pavilion to hear the "March King."[49] Michener described Sousa and the park—by its fictional name, Paradise Park—in his book, *The Fires of Spring*. It was not fiction that, through his summers of work at Willow Grove Park, Michener "knew Sousa personally and heard his concerts four times each day."[50] Michener started working at Willow Grove when he was fourteen, worked there the summer after high school graduation, and continued into his college years. He also hitchhiked in the West the summer after high school graduation.

Doylestown Activity

Jim Michener delivered newspapers throughout his junior and senior high school years. His paper routes gave him insight into the complexity of life in a small town; he knew the occupants of every house in town and the problems of each family.

What events took place in Doylestown that may have shaped Michener as he attended school and worked there in the years 1921 to 1925? Headlines and snippets from the *Bucks County Intelligencer* chronicle births, deaths, accidents and sicknesses, hospital admission and progress reports, marriages and a large number of divorces, the results of "Better Baby" contests, and who was going in and out of business. The paper contained detailed coverage of family reunions including the Michener-Worthington reunions, which James Michener attended with his family.

Fires were a big item; in one four-month period, 39 Bucks County fires occurred. Firemen were often hurt. In 1922, Pennsylvania licensed a record number of passenger cars—700,000. Even though this was a small number of vehicles by today's standards, reports of auto—described as "machine"—accidents occupied columns in every paper: auto-auto, train-auto, auto-bicycle, auto-pedestrian, and auto-trolley. A few aircraft—also "machine"—crashes occurred.

Items of a legal nature appeared. Farmers asked the state to pay damages when deer destroyed their crops. Even domestic suits for small damages generated detailed reports.

Prohibition was in force, and infractions were numerous. Moonshine raids were plentiful. Some of the stills were elaborate and costly. The Prohibition Commission made rulings. It ruled that a person could not make dandelion wine for family use. Those desperate for alcohol drank commercial products like Lilac Vegetal after-shave with disastrous results. Domestic unrest related to alcohol consumption was a common news report: "abusing wife and continually drunk" and "assault and battery associated with intoxicating liquors." The Women's Christian Temperance Union held frequent meetings.

Raids took place on local gambling houses. Gaming with punch boards and slot machines also led to arrest. Selling cigarettes to boys resulted in a fine of $25. A 1925 bill introduced in the Pennsylvania legislature would have legalized pari-mutuel betting on horses; the predicted revenue was $3,000,000—95% to go to the State Highway Department.

Should a married senior girl graduate? Allowing it would be a first. High school students often did not go on to college, because they did not see the advantages of a higher education. The paper carried news of Chautauqua, the patriotic education association. Church news was common; church meetings, speakers, and receptions warranted press coverage.

Citizens criticized garbage collection services; the collector refused to continue without more pay. Doylestown instituted daylight savings time for the first time. A farmer found the body of a discarded baby in his field; suicides, deaths from pneumonia, murder by poisoning, deaths from diptheria were newsworthy. The editors described people in their seventies as "aged."

With the exception of a single column of excerpted news from the United Press, there was little national and international news in the local paper; and newspaper photographs were rare. Those readers interested in broader coverage had Philadelphia and other papers delivered.

THE SWARTHMORE COLLEGE YEARS: 1925–1929

Michener arrived at Swarthmore in the fall of 1925, having received honors at Doylestown High School and having won a prestigious college scholarship that granted him financial independence. A brief summary of the Swarthmore College history to 1925 sets the stage for Michener's arrival. His four Swarthmore years are then chronicled, followed by a Swarthmore College update that includes his generous financial gifts to his alma mater.

Swarthmore: Early History

The Hicksite Religious Society of Friends began documenting a need for a higher education school for its members in 1854.[1] The leaders for education, Martha Tyson and Benjamin Hallowell, socialized the idea with other members until, finally, it was brought to a Friends Yearly Meeting in Philadelphia in 1860. The Friends approved a school, and Edward Parrish, a Philadelphia pharmacist, led the campaign for funding. The school was incorporated in 1864—the official start of Swarthmore College. After the Civil War ended in 1865, the search for initial funds continued. The basic plan for the school provided for a coeducational institution far in advance of other school structures of the day, a location in a rural site distant from city corruption and distractions, and a board of managers made up of Quakers who would guide the intended guarded education of the students.

The organizers purchased land at West Dale about 11 miles southwest of Philadelphia. They named the school after Swarthmoor Hall in England, home of Margaret Fell and George Fox, founders of the Quaker Protestant religion in 1652.[2] Chosen first president of the school in 1865, Parrish needed to raise cash and was able to solicit funds only slowly by visiting members of the Society on horseback. Finally, Swarthmore opened in the fall of 1869 in a single large building called Main— renamed "Parrish" in 1902.[3] The architectural plan provided for a central building with porch flanked by symmetrical wings on either side. This approach was also used in 1893 at George School in Newtown where Michener later taught. Of the initial 199 students, all Quakers, about equal numbers were boys and girls.

Debate soon sprang up as to the mission of the fledgling school: Was its purpose to safeguard Quaker precepts or was its purpose to educate in a broad, liberal, and intellectual manner? The answer came in 1870, when the Quaker Board forced Parrish to resign for being too permissive and not properly "guarding" Quaker ideals.[4] Edward Magill was appointed president; he pleased the Board by issuing 100 strict rules of conduct, which were in effect for years.[5]

Parrish Hall in 1994. Michener Attended Classes Here. (Joy V. Bliss photo)

The school slowly expanded. There was no organized athletics program and little social life. Teaching was a common profession after graduation. The Quaker Meeting House, 1880, housed the official religion; all other religious services were discouraged.[6]

Disaster struck in 1881: fire gutted Main.[7] Generous assistance came quickly. A year after the fire, some classes had already moved back into partially reconstructed Main. The school newspaper, *Swarthmore Phoenix*, came into existence to herald the rebirth.

Magill retired in 1889,[8] and three presidents followed in quick succession. Finally, Joseph Swain became president in 1902 and helped set the course towards excellence.[9] Swain, the president of much larger Indiana University, accepted the position on the promise of much more presidential control and an endowment to supplement teachers' salaries and acquire badly needed equipment. Swain did a notable job of maintaining Quaker heritage and feeding its growing desire for excellence. He started student government and raised the board, room, and tuition to $450 per year to pay for improved faculty. The endowment was raised.[10] This allowed for installation of new infrastructure, acquisition of laboratory equipment, and hiring of distinguished teachers for the expanding curriculum. Sports expanded. Academics improved immensely; yet student fun was readily available since there were 62 clubs on a 400-student campus.

By 1912, the public speaking department at Swarthmore under the direction of Paul M. Pearson promoted Chautauqua—the patriotic traveling education, lecture, and stage show based in New York state. Chautauqua continued to use students, including James Michener, into the late twenties.[11]

For Quakers, World War I was a philosophical problem, since patriotic students and faculty were pacifists in principle.[12] The debate raged as students trained on campus. As the male student population decreased, the women's influence on campus life increased. After the war, many Swarthmoreans helped in the reconstruction of Europe.[13]

Swain retired after 19 years as president.[14] The school was stronger: 45 faculty members and a low student to faculty ratio of 11 to 1. Starting in 1921, the new president, Frank Aydelotte, a teacher from MIT, improved Swarthmore even more. He was considered the most influential leader in school history,[15] and he was the first non-Quaker president. One of his achievements was to encourage enrollment of students from all over the United States; he did this partly through founding Open Scholarships. A friend of the college established the scholarships in 1922.[16] One of these scholarships was awarded to Michener three years later.

Aydelotte had studied in England as a Rhodes Scholar and served on the national board as American secretary to the Rhodes Trustees. He was keen on introducing a Swarthmore Honors Program for independent study by exceptional students.[17] He convinced the college board of the soundness of the new idea; change was more acceptable now, and Aydelotte was adroit at personal relations. The Honors Program meant lifting the standards for student entry even higher. New faculty with excellent credentials were hired. The school de-emphasized competitive sports to help it concentrate on new scholastic activities.

Once approved, the Honors Program took shape rapidly. The plan was to have each honors student take independent seminar study in two or three departments. Only juniors and seniors could participate in the two-year program. Two or more teachers would sit with five to seven students and discuss the subject at hand. A unique feature of the Honors Program was, and still is, final examinations given by experts who are not Swarthmore teachers. The first Honors Program started in 1922–23 in two fields: English literature and social sciences.[18] It attracted national attention. Jim Michener was in this Honors Program throughout his junior and senior years.

Swarthmore: Michener The Student, 1925–1929

Based upon information in Swarthmore student publications, Michener's college years mirrored his progression through high school. That is, there were few news notes in his early college years; but, by his senior year, a veritable explosion of items detailed his varied campus activities. By use of these collegiate records, Michener's year-by-year rise to prominence at Swarthmore College is documented.

Freshman Year: 1925–26

James A. Michener entered Swarthmore College in the fall of 1925 financed by a $2000 Open Scholarship. The scholarship paid $500 a year for four years and followed "the general provisions of the Rhodes Scholarships as to qualities of leadership, scholarship, and physical vigor."[19]

Michener broke some of the many college rules, but he was not a lone scoundrel. Articles that addressed rules for, and problems relating to, freshmen peppered the school newspaper during his freshman year. Both the sophomore and senior classes laid down laws. A freshmen vigilance committee, which did not hesitate to reprimand classmates, aided sophomores in enforcement.[20] A committee of seniors, appointed to advise freshmen, worked on a plan to institute a new system that would treat the newcomers as men from the start; and only those who could not act as such would receive special attention. The Men's Student Government Association also met to discuss at length the best solution to the problem of handling freshmen and appointed a committee to draw up a set of governing rules.[21] Michener's biographers tell stories about his escapades on campus.[22] These include choosing to live an independent life-style rather than accepting dormitory quarters and breaking the Quaker rules concerning fraternizing with women.

The gentlemen of the college strictly adhered to dining room manners. The sophomore head of the Table Committee tutored freshmen in table manners: They were to stand until the coeds were seated, strictly observe the silence period, and conceal the true size of their appetites. They also were lectured on the method of picking mixed tables and the customary practice of the so-called rotation of the "eds" and "co-eds," so that they might become better acquainted.[23]

Although he later became an outspoken opponent of fraternities,[24] Michener joined the Phi Delta Theta fraternity his freshman year and dropped out at some point in his junior year.

Michener played tennis and basketball in his freshman year. Shortly after his arrival on campus, he entered the men's singles tournament, winning the first game by default but then suffering a resounding defeat.[25] He is not mentioned again in conjunction with tennis at Swarthmore. As a forward on the freshmen basketball team, in his first game, "Michener was the outstanding star of the game and … he proceeded to hang goals from all manner of positions on the floor."[26] Ending the game as the high point player with eight field goals and four foul goals, he scored more points than in any subsequent college game.

Convocations, called "collections," were held in Collection Hall each day of the school week. Students, faculty, and outsiders performed or gave talks on a wide variety of subjects. After Easter of his freshman year, Michener gave a review of his interesting travels during Easter vacation.[27]

Four times a year, the school newspaper printed grade point averages separately for men and women. The students were further subdivided into non-fraternity and fraternity. At the end of Michener's freshman year, his fraternity was highest in scholastic standing of all the male groups.[28] The practice of publicizing grades in this manner came under considerable criticism as being unfair; because honors students, who received no grades, were averaged in at an arbitrary value so high it was rarely attained by a student in the regular academic courses.[29]

Although he would later perform in several college productions, Michener was not in the annual freshmen benefit show[30] and did not write for the student literary quarterly, *The Portfolio*, as a freshman.

Sophomore Year: 1926–27

In his sophomore year, Michener played basketball for his fraternity, Phi Delta Theta, in the interfraternity basketball

---

PIRATE GOLD   *The Portfolio*

And now we too must bury pirate gold,
For stolen things cannot remain above
The ground. Too soon they wither and grow old.
Hand me a spade—for we must bury love.
Three hundred years ago, beneath this tree,
A band of pirates beached a little boat,
And carried from it with great secrecy,
Such wealth of golden doubloons as we see
In dreams. They poured it forth, then stopped to gloat
And gaze upon their stolen board. That star,
The same that shines so brightly through the tree,
Guided them to their hiding place. With spades
They dug a trench ,then every golden bar
Was buried fathoms deep,—the profits of their raids.

Then to protect their wealth from strangers' eyes—
A half-grown youth walked to the open pit,
Standing there with face turned to the skies,
And as he dreamed of home, his throat was slit.

His body toppled in upon the gold.
Long since his heart has stopped, his flesh is cold.
His bones grow whiter with each passing year.
He is a silent watchman, guarding here.

Tonight we stand above his aged bones
And dream of castles, kings and queens, and thrones,
For you have stormed the galleons of my heart
And stolen what was never meant for you.
Now you stand there and tear it all apart.
Smiling to see me as I rise and start
As if to take it from you. If you knew
How long I waited for this starlight night
In which to give you love, you would not smile
Because you have it now, Your gay delight
In playing with a toy will last a-while,
Then turn to bitterness. It is not right
That happiness should ever spring from might.

James H. Michener.

The Portfolio, March 1927 (Sophomore Year)

DOS SABIOS

From the Spanish of Calderon

A wise man of whom oft they tell, one day
Became so poor and needy in his state,
That he could scarce sustain himself with what he ate
Of herbs, that grew along the way.
"Is there another wretch," he paused to say,
"Upon this earth more poor, more sad than I?"
And when his head he lowered with a sigh,
A sudden answer found he, for there kneeled
Another wise man, eating from the field
Even the refuse he had thrown away.

JAMES MICHENER

The Portfolio, November 1926. (Sophomore Year)

tournament. His team won the cup in an exciting final game, and his play was described as outstanding.[31]

Michener was never a member of the literary publication staff, but he made several contributions of poetry to the student quarterly, *The Portfolio*. Two of these contributions appear during his sophomore year: "Dos Sabios"[32] and "Pirate Gold."[33]

Junior Year: 1927–28

For his junior year, Michener was selected to the Honors Program. In the program, he took seminars in English literature, history, and philosophy.[34] These seminars, which required completion of in-depth studies on specific topics in a short time, were a mirror for his future career. He learned how to study and absorb information, and he also learned the value of independence. He told us of the times: "When I took the tests later, I didn't get high grades, they were off the chart—there was no way of comparing them. And that's true in all those fields. I was a guy who was almost ordained to do well in the Germanic type of higher education. I got "A" in everything. It took me about two days to figure out the professor—what his bite was and what he wanted me to do and then I did it. I'm not sure it was an education, but it certainly was [for me] at that time."[35]

Michener again played the forward position for his fraternity basketball team. At the interfraternity tournament held in December, the Phi Delta Thetas were not able to retain the cup they won the previous year.[36] It was some time later in his junior year that he dropped his fraternity.

Michener wrote two poetic contributions for *The Portfolio* in his junior year: "The Wizardry of Dis"[37] and "Spring Virtue."[38]

THE WIZARDRY OF DIS
by
JAMES MICHENER

Do not turn on the gas, my son, it costs
A great deal to burn a light six hours,
And too, it won't be dark yet for an hour
Longer—my eyes can see to read this page,
And even if they should not take the meaning
Of some word that has ink upon its letters
I think that I can quote the passage here
And never need the words that are black stained.
I haven't read this poem for six years
And yet it all comes back to me tonight:
The poem that I wanted to forget.
The first one in the first book that I wrote.
How long ago was that? You would not know,
Would you? It must have been ten, twenty even
More than that—How old are you my son?
You cannot be much more than seventeen.
Eighteen, you say? Well you have grown, my boy.
I saw you first when you were only seven
And laughed and hugged me when I read to you
The story of the funny gingham dog.
But I am wandering. Yes that I am—
What's that to you? You blush to think that I
Should recollect that time so long ago
When you were but a little laughing boy.
Tonight I am that little laughing boy;
Perhaps the little crying boy, whose heart,
Set upon something, sees plainly now, at last,
He cannot have it. Tonight you are the man—
I think that I can see in you all that I was
When I was seventeen—oh son, the dreams
Youth cannot if he will, confide to age.
Perhaps you see yourself a king of Rome,
To whom the vassals of a thousand states
Incline the head and bend the servient knee.
Or is it as possessor of a love
More fair than that which Helen owned?
That is the dream of youth: a fond caress,
Offered by lips half hesitant to give
That which they cannot longer hold
Within themselves. My boy of seventeen

Is blushing when I speak of love—But you
Forget that kisses are etheral gifts,
And evanescent as the cobwebs mist
On new mown hay before the sun is high.

Or have you, as I fear you have, the dream
Of Immortality gleaned from a book
That is the product of a frenzied mind?
A little ill-clad book of first sung poems!
How many hopes and dreams lie shattered here
Between the covers of this wayward book.
They are the dreams that eat the dreaming heart,
And cruelly stifle all that might have been.

But as I said before, you do not look
As old as seventeen and yet you say
You're more. I was as old as you the night
I wrote this poem. That night I did not sleep,
But lay awake and tosed, a restless boy
Dreaming of Immortality that lived
Upon a scrap of paper.

Next morning
When I leapt up from my bed to read it
Once again (although I knew each word by rote),
I could not find the paper anywhere:
Under the bed, the bureau, everywhere
I looked, not doubting I should find it soon,
Hiding behind some object in the hall
Where it had fallen from my unclosed desk.
I never thought to write it down again
While I was certain of the metered lines
And verses. No, I would find it soon, perhaps,
Where I myself had laid it. But the day
Passed peevishly into a tiresome night
And not once did the paper come in sight,
And it occurred to me that evening, as I sat
Before my desk again, that I had best
Write down those lines once more while I remembered
Still fresh within my mind. But when the task
Was fairly started I could not recall
Some certain lines I knew that I had used.
"The Wizardry of Dis" began the first—
(Dante, you know, used Dis instead of Hell
In places, and I had been reading Dante

When I wrote those lines.) But what came after that
I could not quite remember, 'though the night
That was the cause of losing the original
Was full of "Wizardry of Dis" and all
The rest. Now when I wanted to recall
Those vagrant lines that would not let me sleep
Twelve hours before, I could not, and my pen
Scratched idly on the pages white before me.

Well, when the book appeared, this poem, was first
Among them all. I would not have it placed
Anywhere but at the first. I think the man
Who printed it knew that of all the twenty-three
It was the one worth printing. And it was,
But no one ever told me so and I
Do not believe that any reader of my poems
Has ever known that it was best. Perhaps
The readers were not those who could discern
The beautiful were it upon the page
Of any book. I fear that that is true:
Great thinkers turn their minds upon great books,
And mine was never great.

But now it all
Seems clear to me. I see that I am not
The man I thought I was. And yet, who knows:
Perhaps if I had found that line, that line
That started "And the wizardry of Dis—"
And if I had but placed it in the poem
The critics who now scorn would praise my works—
For it was great, it was—it was—I swear
It was as great as Shakespeare, Keats or Byron—
I know it was, and I was great, but for
A slip of paper that I could not find.
But what is that to you. Tell me, my son,
You are not smiling, are you. I cannot
See you for the night has crept upon us
While we talked.

The Portfolio, October 1927 (Junior Year)

SPRING VIRTUE

by

JAMES MICHENER

In a nest high in the branches reaching to the sky sat a woodbird singing sadly, to the night that would not answer.

"For the emptiness of loving
Is the fullness of a death."

and the breath of an air that passed moaningly through the leaves echoed the lamentations.

For the nest, formed with care, for the eggs that once were there, now swung unused. Storms had come and the trees had bowed their heads to the lashings of the winds, and the clashing of the branches bent the nest until the four eggs fell to the earth and Death smiled upon them instead of Birth.

And the trees in the breezes that now scarcely bent or lowered heard the threnody of slumber:

"Lullaby, my unborn children,
Lullaby.
Sleep serenely, oh my children,
Sleep and rest.
For I wait here on the nest,
Wait and weep,
With an ever watchful eye
To guard your sleep.
And I sigh,
A lullaby, a lullaby."

Underneath an open window sang a lover——he had come tonight to wake her from her slumbers and in hesitating numbers to tell her that he loved her.

A Summer and an Autumn and a Winter he had loved her, but the coldness of her glances and the harshness of her actions told him that his thoughts were foolish—warned him that his hopes were idle.

Now the Springtime burst upon them and the warmth of April's sunlight coupled with the birth of Maytime when all nature mates, gives and receives embraces, when flushed faces lower, blushing, having read a question, made her give an answer.

They were helpless, drunk with Springtime. Often when he passed he touched her, or her hair brushed past his face and the blood would race to his temples and to hers.

Or a shoulder strap would slide toward an elbow half revealing shoulders of a pearly whiteness, half concealing breasts of ivory.

Springtime caused these things to happen; Springtime brought him to her window with his mind filled with the visions and his aching heart articulate with song.

The Portfolio, **March 1928 (Junior Year)**

With a voice that faltered badly and a tune that sadly told the story he began:

"Love, come out into the moonlight,
For the entire world is mating;
And I stand here in the starlight,
Waiting, waiting.

Sleep has come to all but lovers
And the night is waiting for you—
One sad message near you hovers:
'I adore you.'

Come, for Springtime knows no virtue,
Spring is an eternity—
Love, I could not harm or hurt you.
Do not fear me.

Love, come out into the moonlight
Where a lover waits for you,
Swearing, in a flood of starlight:
'I adore you.' "

When he finished she was standing in her window, with her hair about her shoulders and a low dress banding all her loveliness.

There she stood a single moment and he caught the glimpse of beauty fraught and laden with delight——oh, the night could offer little for the Spring had brought the maiden.

But the woodbird, mourning ever for the never answered pleading sang again her song of sorrow and the trees receding in the breezes cooled the forehead of the lover as he waited for an answer.

"Softly, gently, in the branches,
Like a cradle swings my nest
Empty of the eggs I gave it,
Empty of the gifts of love.
Oh my lullaby is ended
Ere I sang three notes of love.
Empty nest, like cradle rocking,
Be my sepulchre, my tomb.
For the emptiness of loving
Is the fullness of a Death."

But the song of tribulation fell on ears that would not hear it, for he thought of naught but loving, and the fears and tears of nature were to him as whisperings of a question that was answered.

She was coming. Spring had called her, and the virtue of a winter faded from her as the snows melt and fade before the sun that brings the rose.

As she came he heard her singing and his answer was completed:

"Love is like a swallow
As it flies
Through the skies,
Daring me to follow
Toward a sun that blinds the eyes

I have heard it singing
In the night.
And its flight
Is an endless winging
To an ether of delight.

Onward I must follow
Until day
Streaks the gray
And the tired sleepy swallow
Drops once more and flies away.

For my love is calling
And the moon
All too soon
From the heavens falling,
Ends the loveliness of June."

As the last words came from lips closely covered with a kiss and the freshness of her dress was crushed and crumpled in a long embrace, there came an answer from the woodbird who had seen the lovers:

"Love is not a winging swallow
But a snake coiled round a stone.
And it lays there, cruel, hollow,
With its gay song but a moan.
Love is Death
And its breath
Chills the heart of one alone.
For my nest will hold no fledglings
And the emptiness of loving
Is the fullness of a Death."

"Jim Michener and Co." was responsible for the comedy sketch "Frankie and Johnnie," one act of the twenty-act student annual variety Hamburg Show. "Besides reading the story in the form of a poem, taking the parts of both the Sheriff and the Warden, and acting as a bar, 'Jim' further displayed his versatility by holding up a sign marked 'Silence' at times when the crowd seemed to be becoming unmanageable."[39]

As a member of The Little Theater Club, Michener made his debut as "Henry" in the club's spring play, *Outward Bound.* The lovers, Ann and Henry, were difficult roles, and "the parts of these two, rather than their acting, at times, became somewhat boring."[40] The atmospheric play with a strange theme differed from anything previously produced at the college, and the audience greeted it with appreciation.

Senior Year: 1928–29

During his final undergraduate year, Michener was again in the Honors Program. Besides academics, which absorbed much of his time, he was active in sports, drama, public speaking, and contributed to the *Swarthmore Phoenix* and *The Portfolio.* It was a busy year.

Sports

Michener promoted school spirit in a speech at an outdoor mass meeting prior to an October game. He perceived a tendency among the student body to underestimate the game. He spoke about the contest and gave its probable results.[41] Students rallied around him.

After three years of jayvee basketball, Michener broke into the Garnet's varsity ranks his senior year. He was not a letter winner, but he played in five of twelve games and had both failures and moderate successes.[42] At one point, it was reported that eye trouble handicapped him and caused missed foul shots.[43] Now a non-fraternity man, he played basketball for the Wharton Club in the interfraternity basketball tournament. They lost, but Michener and a teammate fought for individual honors. Michener finally led in the scoring column by one field goal.[44]

In a letter to the editor of the school newspaper, Michener wrote that he had found a basketball game between freshmen and the Cocoa family such an interesting contest for both players and spectators that he asked: "Why not more athletic contests of that type?" Even though he was playing varsity, he felt that the majority of sports should be styled after intramural play, not varsity.[45]

Drama

For the school's annual Hamburg Show, he played one part of a two-person pantomime, "The Hero." The school newspaper headline proclaimed: "Michener Stars in Silent Drama." The play, which was touted as the thrilling life story of a World War I soldier (Michener), traced events after college graduation in 1916. "It shows him leaving college; then happily married; soon snatched by the war; sailing over the sea; visiting the dens of Paris; marching into death; proving himself a hero; and finally tells of his triumphal return to America. It is climaxed by his reunion with his bride, who presents him with a pleasant surprise."[46] Judged the best performance in a Hamburg Show in years, it was a highlight of the evening's entertainment. Michener's acting was "superb," and the duo "brought down the house."[47]

During his commencement week, Michener, cast as Orsino, Duke of Illyria, performed in *Twelfth-Night*, the senior-junior play. Justifying the selection of Michener, the school newspaper editors reviewed his past performances: he had displayed excellent talent as Henry in the previous year's production of *Outward Bound* and proved himself worthy in a rather difficult pantomime, "The Hero."[48]

From a large number of original plays submitted in a student competition, the faculty selected five for presentation; Michener's "Gold" was one of the five.[49] Awards were made by a vote of the audience, and Michener's play came in second. The report read that it was a "tremendous undertaking but nevertheless it was most successfully presented. The scene of a forest in medieval England was well reproduced. The individual lines left more impression than in the other plays and included some fine poetry."[50] Michener neither acted in nor directed the play.

Writing

Although he never served on the staff of the student newspaper, the *Swarthmore Phoenix*, at a Men's Student Government meeting in his senior year, Michener and the class president, Thomas Hallowell, spoke up to deplore the publishing of unsigned letters in the paper and asked that the practice be discontinued. Following some discussion both in favor and against the suggestion, no action was taken.[51] Shortly thereafter, Michener submitted a signed letter to the editor concerning basketball; the editor printed the letter and appended Michener's name.

In another item written for the *Phoenix*, Michener reviewed five one-act plays presented by students of a play production course. The review demonstrated his attention to detail and his diplomacy, even at

---

PERSONAL OPINION

To the Editor,
Swart~~~re Phoenix.
Sir:
Since the basketball game between the Freshman and the Cocoa family resulted in such an interesting contest; and since the spectators enjoyed it more than the players, if possible; and since the tenor of the game was clean, even when the game was fastest; and since it is probable that the conditions which so resulted might be reproduced at will, the natural question to ask is this:
Why not more athletic contests of that type? The question should have been asked a long time ago, but it seems especially applicable now. It may be termed a heresy to say that the silly little game played that afternoon was of any real value, but I will say that and I will add that it was of more value, to spectators and to players than the P. M. C., Delaware, Ursinus, St. Johns, Carlisle, Selinsgrove, Drexel, and Pharmacy games.
I think that most interested persons will agree that a game like that, or like the fraternity series, played with good humor and a fair degree of proficiency, is of some real value. For myself, I should say that it was of the greatest value.
It is inconceivable to believe that any game other than an intra-mural one would have ended pleasantly after a dispute such as the half-row over the time at the end of the cocoa contest.
Therefore, why not a schedule, or attempted schedule, of athletics for the students here at school who cannot make the varsity teams? I think that sport, as such, would take on a more positive aspect.
For the victory craving students and alumni there could always be the varsity, playing in the orthodox way, with other colleges. But the majority of the sport should be played at home, among teams composed of students from home.
And to all who laugh at such proposals, I will ask but one rhetorical question: Wasn't that game, foolish as it was, a better game in many respects than the more deadly serious ones; and was not it a great deal more enjoyable, more conducive to what we term sportsmanship, more physically clean and interesting than many inter-collegiate battles?
Sincerely,
James Michener, '29.

Phoenix, March 12, 1929

this young age, in addressing defects and giving constructive criticism while, at the same time, praising the overall production.[52]

Michener's other writings during his senior year included "The Dramatists—In Three Acts," a three-page poetic contribution to the fall literary quarterly in which he described three facets of youthful love: comedy, romance, and tragedy.[53]

Endowment Support

In the spring of 1929, the students launched a campaign to aid the school's endowment drive. Twice at collection, after the students had dismissed the faculty, Michener humorously presided from President Aydelotte's chair and encouraged 100% student participation in this alumni project.[54] All four classes of undergraduates met this goal.[55] Thus, Michener was an early supporter of Swarthmore endowment campaigns, support which would continue throughout his life.

Graduation

Each year, seniors elected a member of their class to deliver the prestigious "Ivy Oration," a speech given at the traditional planting of the ivy on Baccalaureate Sunday. James Michener was their choice.[56] In his oration, he urged his fellow students to value the carefree interlude college provided between high school and responsibility, and he addressed a problem he perceived: two polar college groups—students and athletes. The *Phoenix* reprinted his speech:

Ivy Oration

There is a persistent and pernicious delusion to which the governing bodies and faculties of the higher educational institutions still subscribe. It is generally best expressed in the orientation day addresses which are annually thrust at freshmen, as they begin their four years of college. The speaker narrates the story of some great man who has risen to lofty heights because of a college education. An analogy is drawn between this case and the potential similar ones, and the weight of the argument is that all incoming students have been drawn to college for the specific reason of learning ways in which to earn a better living than would otherwise be possible.

But if the orientation day speaker were to tell the truth, as he must see it, if he has been connected with college life for any length of time, he would tell the incoming men and women that they were representatives of a very fortunate class; the class which has been offered a four years' interlude between the preparation necessary for earning a subsistance [sic] wage and the putting into practice of that knowledge. He would add that they were the ones who had been financed by parents, friends or philanthropists who were willing to incur the expenses of this vacation. He would say that the group before him was neither brighter nor duller than those who had not joined it after high school, and finally, if he were wise, he would make a few suggestions as to the best way to spend the four years.

Unfortunately, there have been few such speakers. Men may have thought these things, and they may have seen how true each time was, but no one has dared to offer the advice to young students, for there is the old tradition that men and women come to college to work, and that is the educational delusion.

For young people are not sent to colleges and universities to work; they are sent to discover ways in which to use to the fullest extent the products of work.

Each student coming into college is very nearly as able a wage earner as the corresponding student who is leaving. Twelve healthy years of preliminary education prepares a man for work. He is physically mature, mentally capable and morally responsible at the age of eighteen. Why, then, four more years of education? The present day answer is, "To develop these potentialities." The correct answer is, "To postpone their application."

During this period of rest before application, the student has many [p]roblems facing him. He has come to college to discover the various ways of spending money rather than the many ways of earning it, and in many of the results of college, the ultimate effect is to unfit men for earning higher wages rather than to prepare them all the better. Not infrequently one acquires tastes, or forms costly habits and almost invariably—here is the benefit of college—accepts ideals which are later to prove a detriment upon his earning capacities, rather than an aid. To offset these negative results it is necessary that a large degree of positive virtues be present, and for these we must look to the individuals who have availed themselves of the pleasant opportunity of education.

In theory each freshman enters college on an equal basis with each other freshman. Some are to seemingly advance in four years while others seem surely to retrogress, but at the start, it is democratic to suppose that all are equal. The aim of each is to acquire some degree of happiness, some degree of personal achievement, some degre [sic] of collgiate [sic] success. The way these aims are pursued is interesting. Upon the choice of action, which each student makes, depends to a large degree his college happiness.

There seem to be but two ways: the student and the big-man-on-the-campus. All other possible ways of going through college are variations of these two fundamental differences in the educational system. This is true for many reasons, but chiefly because the college itself makes the division. For the faculty only the student exists; for the student body only the big-man-on-the-campus. So far the main failing of college has been the impossibility of reconciling these two differing classes.

For if college is to teach us how to spend our money and our time in beter [sic] ways, if it is to be an adventure in beautiful life, if it is to be an interlude of pleasant rest before a future struggle, the institution which prepares it should certainly understand and accept the various means to this end. It is important that the student choose wisely, according to his abilities; it is also important that he be recognized as having done so. The two classes, the student and the big-man are very nearly incompatible, and their nature directs the choosing of the students. And if one chooses either, the other is necessarily foregone.

It is upon the expediency of this plan of education which we should comment as we graduate from it. And as we look in retrospect at what had happened to us, we find our own class clearly cut into the two groups, and we likewise find the interest of the faculty allied with one group; the interest of the alumni and student body allied with the other. It would be pleasant if we could give as our gift to the college, the start toward a reconciliation. For each of the plans has value, and it would be much better if the entire college, faculty and all, accepted and acclaimed the man who has done fine things on the football field or in politics of the school or in the many offices of honor. And likewise it would be well if the entire college accepted the student.

As to the necessity of a definite choice, one might advise a middle course, but to an observer of college life, it becomes apparent that the middle course is not as productive as either of the two extremes. It lacks the quality of providing a firm foundation for the student's life, and while much can be said for the ideal of a well rounded man, such a man, like the well rounded stone, has too great a tendency to roll. The end of education is certainly not the production of a super athlete who can do the hundred in ten flat and a math problem in ten days, nor is it the turning out of scholars whose interests are equally one sided. Instead, there should be the modifying tendency of life with men and women of all kinds, but this does not mean "the well rounded man." It means "the man with an interest, and with many interests."

Since we assumed, at the beginning of the discussion, that all entered the college as equals, it is not an error to conclude by assuming that we all leave it as equals. The man or woman who has run the offices of the college while here, who has swaggered over the campus with many medals and watch fobs is no better prepared than the student who received a straight A. But he is as well prepared. That is why college meets in a community system, to make the very preparations which some have ridiculed, and it is to be lamented that the students and the authorities do not realize this.

And so we leave, some with watch chains weighty with gold, some with books well marked for future reference. We are almost equal in our potentialities, now. We have lived the four years of rest here in the most beautiful of all surroundings, with great books, great friends and great thoughts. We have been well prepared for what is to follow, and if we are no more capable of earning than we were when we entered, we are at least better qualified to spend what we do earn, and in that lies the secret of happiness.

The memories return, and we can recall that first day of addresses in the Orientation program, and we can smile at what was told us, for we know—now. As we depart, each has in his heart the knowledge that it was very pleasant; very unproductive in material things; certainly an adventure in the beauty of living. And then, perhaps there comes the resolve to repay the society which supported us for four years, and we look for the last time across the campus where we have enjoyed ourselves, and we dedicate ourselves, silently, to the task before us, saying, with a happy smile, "On, and ever on!"[57]

Michener learned that his mind was his future. The scholastic Phi Beta Kappa organization inducted him,[58] and he graduated with Highest Honors,[59] the Swarthmore equivalent of *summa cum laude*.

In the school yearbook, *Halcyon*, Michener's photograph appears only once during his Swarthmore College years. He is pictured with the varsity basketball team of 1929.[60] None of the four yearbooks contain his student portrait and biographical data. He refused to have his senior picture in the *Halcyon*.[61] However, his home address is listed as "81 N. Clinton St., Doylestown, Pa."[62] This was one of eight homes in which he lived during his childhood; photographs on the next page show the home today.

Michener Comments on His College Years

Numbering among Michener's writings about his college years, his semi-autobiographical second novel, *The Fires of Spring*, fictionally deals in part with his youth, including college.[63] Biographers and others have scrutinized the book in an effort to find the private side of James A. Michener.[64]

We asked Michener what he had prepared himself for at Swarthmore. He replied: "Nothing! Absolutely nothing. I never in my education up to now, ever had one hour of guidance—from *anybody*! Our system in those days—they were just beginning the system—looked for bright young people. And when they found one, they took care of him. I got the scholarship to Swarthmore because a teacher who had gone there said, 'You're the ideal type of kid who ought to go to Swarthmore,' and she arranged it."[65]

Writing to George A. Walton, head of George School, four years after he graduated from Swarthmore, Michener addressed his concern for the lack of career planning for students in the 1920s. He was applying for a teaching position and wrote: "One master alone can bring an able student up to a standard of proficiency representing that student's ability, but such work loses its effect unless student, and teacher, are aware of direction in their work. This direction—and not the individual classes—is the important thing. It can be kept before the two people concerned, student and teacher, only if the whole curriculum is attended to."[66] Fortunately, throughout his life Michener has shown adaptability for new experiences. The breadth of his undirected formative experiences was broad enough to serve as a career plan.

Michener commented on whether college prepared him for the Depression: "I would say that I was able to graduate from Swarthmore in 1929 without having had a *clue* that the whole thing might fall apart—which it did—the year I went to Hill School. We didn't study that sort of thing. We didn't talk about it. And here the whole world was going to collapse. We didn't know it. I didn't know it. But when I got to Europe and it was forced upon me, I was a very rapid study."[67]

Michener at 81 North Clinton in Doylestown in 1993
(John Hoenstine photo)

Michener on the steps of 81 North Clinton in 1993
(John Hoenstine photo)

Summer 1929

In the Spring of 1929, Michener's Swarthmore College graduation and Hill School teaching position for the fall were announced in the *Bucks County Intelligencer*.[68] Also mentioned was his upcoming employment with the 1929 Chautauqua summer road tour.

During the summer, Michener performed with the well-funded[69] Swarthmore Chautauqua, the largest unit of Chautauqua in the East,[70] and traveled with it throughout western Pennsylvania. He was one of the male leads in a play, *Skidding,* and a "professional puppeteer of moderate skill."[71] *Skidding,* which ran in a Philadelphia theater that year, was a popular play of the time.[72] Michener wrote part of the Chautauqua marionette show script and performed the afternoon show. When he later applied for a position at George School, he included in his "certain special equipment" for teaching, a list of hobbies including "training on Chautauqua with marionettes and stage plays."[73]

Swarthmore: 1930 to the Present

By 1930, nearly one-third of the student body was in the Honors Program. Because of its success, the school continually improves the Honors Program to aid the process of advanced study. The early success was due to Aydelotte's fund raising prowess.[74] Increasingly, Quaker students were turned down at admissions as scholastic talent from the nation applied. The current Quaker enrollment is about seven percent.

Aydelotte left Swarthmore in 1940 to head the Institute for Advanced Study at Princeton, New Jersey. He left a campus with vastly improved standards, enhanced image, stabilized finances, and increased landscape beauty. The first non-Friends became members of a less provincial Board of Managers during his tenure.[75]

John Nason, an Aydelotte supporter, became president in 1940.[76] By 1942, uniforms were back on campus.[77] The Navy sent students to Swarthmore, including the first blacks; and this kept enrollment up and finances steady. After the war was over, Swarthmore students helped reconstruct Europe as they had done 25 years before.[78] Board, room and tuition rose to $675 per year, considered high in its day. The ethnic atrocities of World War II brought attention to racism; the college debated and examined quotas and admissions rules. Nason resigned in 1953 after 21 years on campus.[79]

Courtney Smith, another Rhodes Scholar, became the ninth president in 1953.[80] Swarthmore's Centennial year was 1963–64. It was celebrated to the fullest; President Lyndon Johnson and other dignitaries attended commencement.[81] In 1969, Smith died suddenly while working in his office on campus.[82] Student power and black power protests strongly affected Swarthmore in the 1960s—as they did many other colleges and universities. It took a number of years for the Friends to encourage admission of Blacks. The Afro-American population was about nine percent of the student body in 1985. The new president, Robert Cross, entered at a time when there was student unrest on several issues.[83] Michener gave $100,000 to Swarthmore in 1970 to establish a black studies program and the Black Cultural Center located in Robinson House.[84] Stress and the lack of Board support led to Cross's resignation in 1971.

Robinson House, The Black Cultural Center Endowed by Michener in 1970
(Swarthmore College photo)

After an extended search for a successor, Theodore Friend III became president in 1973.[85] He clearly realized that broad equality and individual excellence needed balance in a modern institution. The endowment drive of 1979 ended early due to generous gifts; the fund assured economic stability in changing times.[86] After succeeding in improving the balance on campus and reestablishing a positive school image, President Friend resigned in 1982.

The Board then chose David Fraser, a well-known medical doctor, for the presidency.[87] His professional background added to the Swarthmore optimism of the 1980s. Tarble Social Center, formerly the Carnegie Library where Michener had studied, burned to the ground in 1983.[88] A new fund drive was launched. James A. Michener announced a two million dollar gift to Swarthmore in 1984 as a tribute to the quality education he had received there from 1925 to 1929.[89] In 1986, an innovative Writing Associates Program was introduced;[90] some of Michener's unrestricted gift established this program and enhanced the Honors Program.[91] He gave an additional unrestricted five million dollar gift in October 1991. The new gift went to fund scholarships, assistant professorships, and seminar courses.[92]

SWARTHMORE PHOENIX

SWARTHMORE COLLEGE, MARCH 19, 1929

JAMES MICHENER CHOSEN
TO DELIVER IVY ORATION
BACCALAUREATE SUNDAY

Officers Elected to Take Part
in Activities of Class
Day, May 31

The Portfolio

A LITERARY QUARTERLY PUBLISHED BY THE STUDENTS OF SWARTHMORE COLLEGE

THE HILL SCHOOL TEACHING YEARS: 1929–1931

Securing A Teaching Position

Early in 1929, John A. Lester, Head of The Hill's English Department, traveled to Swarthmore College to recruit a graduating student to teach in that department. According to Michener, "The Hill, which was its proper name—capital 'T' capital 'H' (they never used the word 'school')—usually had Ivy League teachers from within that second tier of Amherst, Williams, and Wesleyan. They had gone out of their way to take a Quaker from Haverford, kind of a brother-sister school to Swarthmore. Having had good luck with one Haverford man, they decided they could risk a Swarthmore man, and they sent John down to find some Swarthmore eligible."[1] With little hesitation Michener continued, "And so Lester found me out. Now, I would think that in the field of English there would have been only one person to recommend. The other male students, although there were several good ones, were just not academic. So the choice was made at The Hill. When they decided to come to Swarthmore, it was almost automatic that they would turn me up. They wouldn't take any women."[2]

Following Lester's visit at Swarthmore College, a February 27, 1929, note from The Hill's Headmaster, James I. Wendell, invited Michener for a March 3 interview to discuss the opening in the English Department.

As a native Pennsylvanian who grew up within 30 miles of the school in Pottstown, what did Michener know of The Hill before this job opportunity arose?

February 27th, 1929
My dear Mr. Michener:
I shall be very glad to have you come to The Hill next Sunday, March 3rd, at which time I shall be able to discuss with you the opening in our English Department.
Kindly advise me of the time of your arrival so that I may be on hand to welcome you.
Very sincerely yours,
James A. Michener, Esq., Swarthmore College, Swarthmore, Pa.
F:L

Wendell's Invitation for a Job Interview

"We knew about it and Lawrenceville [Princeton, New Jersey] as very, very expensive social schools. Our paths never crossed. We were very proud of them; we knew they were top-flight schools but they were way beyond us financially—I think in education also."[3]

Michener replied to the invitation with a telegram that supplied his train's arrival time.[4]

The day following Michener's interview at The Hill, Dr. Lester wrote Headmaster Wendell strongly recommending the English Department teaching position be offered to Michener.[5]

On March 8, 1929, Dr. Wendell offered Michener an English Department appointment at an annual salary of $1500 and all living expenses. This was the new salary scale minimum for that year,[6] and it was Michener's starting salary.[7]

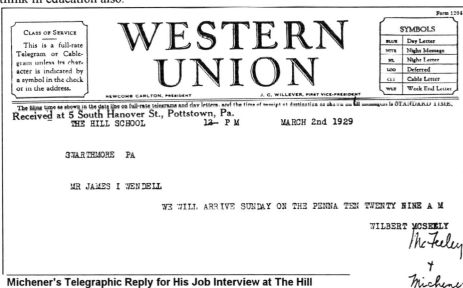

Michener's Telegraphic Reply for His Job Interview at The Hill

Two days later Michener accepted. Only twelve days had elapsed between the time Wendell wrote the invitation to interview and Michener wrote an acceptance of his appointment. In those twelve days, three letters were transmitted through the United States Postal Service, a personal interview was arranged and conducted, and the job was secured.

Headmaster Wendell responded to Michener's acceptance with an enthusiastic note. He expressed delight that Michener had decided to "throw in your lot with us next autumn… ."[8]

THE HILL SCHOOL
REPORT

March 4, 1929.

Dear Mr. Wendell:

I think it would be well if you were to offer a position in the Department of English to James A. Michener, of Swarthmore College, Swarthmore, Pa., whom you met last Sunday. My favorable impression of this man's character and personality was corroborated by others who talked with him on that occasion. I hope we shall have him in the department for next year.

I am returning with this, papers relating to other candidates, and a letter from Mr. Test of Haverford College, which will naturally attended to together with the applications of other candidates whom we have interviewed.

Yours very truly,

John A. Lester

Dr. John Lester Recommends Michener

March 8th, 1929.

My dear Mr. Michener:

I am happy to offer you an appointment at The Hill next autumn at a salary of $1500 and all living expenses, including room, board and washing. Mr. Lester is very favorably impressed with your candidacy and I am hoping you will feel impelled to join forces with us in our work for the coming year. I shall greatly appreciate a prompt reply from you as to whether or not you can accept this offer.

Very sincerely yours,

Mr. James A. Michener,
Swarthmore College,
Swarthmore, Pa.

Hill School Job Offer

With The Hill position secured so early in 1929, Michener escaped the unemployment problem created by the October 1929 stock market crash. Many of his classmates were unable to find jobs and remained unemployed—some even for years.[9]

In his memoirs, Michener detailed his early pre-teaching jobs but disposed of his years at The Hill and George School in one paragraph each.[10] Of The Hill, he wrote, "I had landed a fine teaching job at The Hill, in Pottstown, Pennsylvania, a private school for the sons of well-to-do parents where, as is so often the case with energetic beginning teachers, I learned far more than I taught."[11] Asked if he had prepared himself for a teaching position, he said, "No, but it worked; it worked itself out. Hill School wanted somebody like me. I filled the bill."[12]

Swarthmore College
Swarthmore, Pa.
March 10, 1929

Dr. James Wendell
Headmaster
The Hill School
Pottstown

My dear Dr. Wendell,

I am glad to say that I accept the position offered me in your recent letter. The terms therein stipulated are satisfactory.

Will you kindly forward me, if possible the catalogue of the school?

Sincerely,
James A. Michener

Michener Accepts

On October 11, 1929, *The Hill School News*, a student publication, reported the four new faculty members for the year. Mr. James A. Michener was among the new masters.[13]

The Hill: History to 1929

Michener assumed his teaching position at The Hill in the fall of 1929. To illuminate the climate and conditions that were present when he arrived, it is helpful to look back to the beginnings of the school for an understanding of The Hill. What was the philosophy that had developed and subsequently existed on Michener's arrival? And what effect did it have on him during this first teaching experience and in the ensuing years?

Like other similar schools, the attitudes, spirit, and philosophy at The Hill were dependent upon the leadership of the then current headmaster. Who were these men, and how did they shape the school into the institution Michener joined as faculty in 1929?

Matthew Meigs: Principal 1851–1876

For 70 years—from its inception in 1851, until it was sold to the alumni in 1920—The Hill was a proprietary school owned by the Meigs family.

On May 1, 1851, in Pottstown, Pennsylvania, Rev. Matthew Meigs (1812–1889), opened his Family "Boarding School, of a high order, for Boys and Young Men"[14] on "the hill," as Pottstonians referred to it. Meigs stressed that he was not founding yet another private school, so common at the time, but rather "a type of school quite new and rare in America."[15] A home, begun by David Potts in 1793, was the lone building on the site.[16] The first year enrollment was twenty-five boys.[17] Students boarded and lived under surrogate family rule where instructors and students resided together as one patriarchal family. Meigs desired to enroll boys who readily obeyed authority and who were accustomed to restraint of moral principal.[18] Character development was the school's paramount aim. In 1874, the school's name was changed to "The Hill."

Meigs had had a rather stormy career as a teacher, administrator, and Presbyterian minister; in these positions, his educative ideology often had involved him in controversy. Although his formal ministry had been brief, during his tenure as Hill School principal, a deep sense of Christian values and purpose underlay all of his educational ideas.[19]

Matthew Meigs' lifelong interests were literature and linguistics, including the classical languages.[20] The school circular of 1851 described Meig's academic program: "The Course of Instruction is extensive, thorough and practical; including the usual preparation for College and the various branches of a substantial English education; and will be conformed to the future business of the pupil, so far as it may be reasonably anticipated." Meigs' reference to "future business of the pupil" is important; the phrase was used for years, and as the times dictated, it did not necessarily imply preparation for college. The school routine was vigorous schoolwork, family meals at which the principal and Mrs. Meigs presided, sports and play, and mandatory Sunday service at the Presbyterian church.[21] Matthew Meigs provided a comprehensive curriculum and stayed with "English education" when other schools abolished it.[22] In the early years, diplomas were not awarded; a boy stayed as long as he wanted and needed.[23]

Descriptions of Meigs by two early students "conjure up a regime of almost military strictness, administered by a disciplinarian who inspired awe and respect … ."[24] Many think that he did not have the qualities needed for a headmaster building a school and that Mary, his wife, held the school together.[25]

John Meigs: Principal 1876–1911

John Meigs (1852–1911), son of Matthew, took over in 1876 when The Hill was faltering. His older brother George, who had been acting as surrogate principal at The Hill, suffered an incapacitating heart attack. John was called home by his mother to assume a duty he never wanted.[26] He dedicated the remaining 35 years of his life to The Hill, was recognized as one of the greatest headmasters of his age, and is called the school's "Master Builder." He built a struggling private school into one of nationally recognized eminence. "The final result was really the fruit of his indomitable will, the high standards he

FOUR NEW MEMBERS ADDED TO THE SCHOOL FACULTY

Messrs. Abernethy, Elicker Michener, and Butcher Come To The Hill This Year

Among the new masters coming to The Hill for this year are: Mr. James A. Michener, Dr. Charles R. Elicker, Mr. Robert W. Abernethy, and Mr. Frank Butcher.

Mr. James A. Michener, who is in the English Department, graduated from Swarthmore in 1929, with a degree of Bachelor of Arts and highest honors in English and two minor subjects. He acted in Chautauqua last summer, and also was on the Dramatic Club in college. Mr. Michener was also on the basketball team.

Dr. Charles R. Elicker attended [?] University for two years. He [?] the Jefferson Medical [?] degree of

Hill School News, October 11, 1929

uncompromisingly expected, his genuine love and understanding of boys, and the help of his wife, Marion Butler Meigs."[27]

Designation of classes as "forms" began in 1880. Assignment to a form was based upon the result of English proficiency examinations. Sixth formers were seniors, fifth formers, juniors, and so on. By the mid-1880s, three areas of study were offered: "classical," "scientific," and "business"; and college preparation continued to be emphasized. By 1901, preparation for college was exclusively the "future business" of Hill boys. However, a 1901 graduate commented that he had a surplus of work in languages with a minimum in science.[28]

In 1888, *The Hill Record*, The Hill's first student publication, was established to stimulate literary interests. The *Record* continued as the omnibus outlet for student writers, until the appearance of the first yearbook, *The Dial*, in 1898. "Interest in writing and editing was given a new opportunity when *The Hill School News* was founded in 1902. With the establishment of this newspaper, the older *Record* became exclusively a literary magazine and served as the writing cradle for a number of writers who later achieved distinction."[29] The *Record* was the publication Michener (and others) reviewed when he taught at The Hill.

Mike Sweeney, for years the important athletic director, began his career at The Hill in 1896 and remained a formidable presence on campus during the Michener years. Sweeney believed in character development through athletics,[30] and even at the turn of the century, his program was extensive.[31]

Lawrence Rhodes, class of 1901, said, "No one who attended The Hill during those early days will ever forget the Headmaster, John Meigs. ... He was one of the men who has made a lasting impression on my life. His imposing personality commanded attention and respect. With him, rules were made to be obeyed. . . . Yet he was tender-hearted and sympathetic."[32]

In later years, the alumni became heavily involved in their school; but during the years the Meigs family owned the school, alumni were hesitant to support it with donations. The earliest tangible evidence of alumni interest in the school was the Romanesque-Gothic chapel built with money raised by the alumni association. It was dedicated in 1904.[33] Alumni largely withheld contributions until after 1920.

John Meigs died of a cardiac ailment in 1911 and is buried under the chapel cloister. Marion Meigs lived on campus until she died in 1946. Her ashes are buried at the head of her husband's grave.[34]

Alfred G. Rolfe: Acting Principal and Headmaster (1911–1914)

When John Meigs died, his son and heir apparent, Dwight Meigs, was not ready to take over as principal. The interim choice was Alfred G. Rolfe (1860–1942), teacher at The Hill since 1890. "The choice was clear: no one could match Alfred G. Rolfe in experience, wisdom, personality, and prestige among both faculty and alumni."[35] Rolfe was acting principal, 1911–13, and headmaster, 1913–14. Rolfe's years as headmaster were not of his own choice, "but had they been he could scarcely have picked years more mellow and less troubled."[36]

Although he made no fundamental changes in the school's program during his regime, Rolfe further strengthened the family concept of the school by encouraging the residence of more married masters as form advisors in the dormitories.[37] Formation of the English Club, for reading and discussing literature, enhanced literary interests. Rolfe was its founder and inspiration for over thirty years.[38] Michener had no involvement in the English Club; he said, "It was strictly sixth form in students and faculty."[39]

Rolfe had come to The Hill as a Greek language teacher; he taught Greek for four decades, until it disappeared from the curriculum. After his term as headmaster, Rolfe continued to teach until 1942—two years after his official retirement[40]—for a total of 52 years of service to The Hill. He was an established presence when Jim Michener arrived in 1929.

Two of Rolfe's colleagues compiled and edited a book of Rolfe's prose and poetry, *Mr. Rolfe of The Hill*. In the foreword, Headmaster Boyd Edwards showered Rolfe with accolades: "You might almost call him the manufacturer of the social and spiritual climate of the Hill."[41]

There are many similarities between Mr. Rolfe of The Hill and Mr. Chipping of Brookfield—James Hilton's fictional professor and prep school in *Good-bye Mr. Chips*. They were witty and beloved doyens with longevity that continued past retirement, and both taught at schools that "went up and down, dwindling almost to non-existence at one time, becoming almost illustrious at another."[42]

Dwight Raymond Meigs: Principal 1914–1922

Dwight Raymond Meigs (1884–1930) had been carefully groomed to succeed his father. From the time of John Meigs' death, until he became headmaster, Dwight Meigs was assistant to Rolfe. Dwight's tenure as proprietor and headmaster proved to be a low point for The Hill and the sunset years for the Meigs family. The alumni purchased the school from the Meigs family stockholders in 1920 and began operating it as a non-profit corporation governed by a board of trustees.

During Dwight Meigs' tenure, the "academic program was restricted almost entirely to college credit subjects, and college preparation became even more standardized."[43] There was a decline in the study of Latin and Greek and greater election of modern languages. The library was small—about 5000 volumes. The scope of extra-curricular activities also remained narrow: debating, the publications—*Dial, Record*, and *News*, musical organizations, and mandatory musical programs. Men of note in political and civic affairs came to The Hill to speak.[44] To ease the transition from The Hill to college life and to give students more responsibility for their own conduct, Dwight Meigs and influential alumni supported liberalization of rules for the older boys.[45]

After the alumni purchased The Hill, Dwight Meigs reluctantly stayed on as headmaster for one and a half years; Rolfe stepped in to finish the last half year. Dwight Meigs died from a self-inflicted bullet wound in 1930.

Boyd Edwards: Headmaster 1922–1928

In 1922, the board of trustees unanimously appointed Rev. Boyd Edwards to the headmastership, a position he held until his dismissal in 1928. His early goals were to encourage warm personal relations among members of the school community and to increase the pleasantness of campus social life.

The faculty became more influential in school affairs. In the 1920s, the Progressive Education movement was reaching the peak of its influence, and almost all the faculty expressed at least a vague dissatisfaction with the narrowness of the curriculum and cram-type examinations.[46]

As an executive, Edwards was criticized. During his tenure as headmaster, The Hill suffered from financial difficulties as well as lack of leadership; enrollment increased, but entrance requirements were less stringent.[47] The trustees requested progress reports from Harvard, Yale, and Princeton on the accomplishments of Hill students; Princeton reported that the Hill boys were at the top in extracurricular activities and at the bottom in scholastic standing.[48] Boyd Edwards departed after six years; the trustees' first selection of a headmaster had proved disappointing.

James I. Wendell: Headmaster 1928–1952

James I. Wendell replaced Edwards as headmaster. He had arrived in 1913 to assume the duties of instructor in English and assistant track coach. In total, Wendell was with The Hill for 39 years. In 1928, at a time when the school was experiencing grave difficulties, he was appointed headmaster—a position he held for 24 years. It was during Wendell's first year as headmaster that he hired Michener to teach in the English Department.

We asked an alumnus who was a student under both Edwards and Wendell whether he had memories of the change in administration. He said that he was not aware of any turmoil and added, "Boyd Edwards was a great person, but he was not a strict administrator, and I think the finances of the institution had suffered. Dr. Wendell was a financial administrator, and he put the school back on a more sound fiscal ground. But he was not the human being that Boyd Edwards was. I mean, you'd think twice before you'd go to Wendell and tell him any of your troubles, while with Boyd Edwards, you surely would go."[49] Most students found Wendell to be a strict disciplinarian. One alumnus described him as being "very impressed with himself."[50]

In his book, *The History of The Hill School : 1851–1976*, Paul Chancellor, Latin instructor and a Michener colleague, assessed James I. Wendell: Wendell shared Michael Sweeney's belief in character development through athletics and Dwight Meigs' feelings for rather rigid social conventions. Relations with faculty and students were impersonal. His tenets for education were first, "the finer things in life," then character development, and lastly, scholarship.[51] Reflecting his stubborn belief in the primacy of character qualities over scholastic achievement, Wendell remarked, "We are not going to cut our cloth to the measure of IQ's."[52]

We asked Michener to comment on Wendell and on Chancellor's assessment of Wendell. Michener said: "He was a big, handsome athlete who graduated from Wesleyan as a champion hurdler. Chancellor's quote epitomizes him precisely. He was afraid of men who were too academic or exploratory, hence his not-voiced suspicion of John Lester and, I would suppose, of me. I liked him. He was a teddy bear of a man; what you saw was what you got and he treated me fairly, even though I suspect that in the darker years of the depression, when Hill hurt, he might well have off-loaded me, the cause being that I wasn't the ideal Hill type."[53]

Wendell married Marjorie Potts, descendant of the founder of Pottstown. Marjorie impressed her cultural interests and high standards on The Hill; and she improved relations, which were at a low ebb, between the school and the citizenry of Pottstown.[54] One alumnus commented that Mrs. Wendell more than made up for her husband's austerity and lack of human understanding: "She was a fine woman who looked after the students—many of us homesick. She was a very gracious woman, and I'll always remember her. I think she was really more responsible than her husband for improving relations with the town."[55]

Asked his impression of Pottstown-Hill School interaction at the time he taught at The Hill, Michener said, "I would think each faculty member developed one or two relationships in the town, but I doubt they would ever bring them on campus. I believe it would just be us going out." He confirmed poor relations with the city: "Not close—almost animosity."[56]

The students also had some problems with the Pottstown residents. The town boys—"townies," as they would call them—would taunt The Hill boys. One alumnus remembers that when they had enough taunting, four or five Hill boys would go down there and take them on. "Of course in those days, you used your fists—there were no knives or guns or anything—it was just who was the better man after you squared off. We just wanted them to know that up on the hill we weren't sissies. We did gain some respect in that manner."[57]

In 1928, money donations, reportedly held back through lack of confidence in Boyd Edwards, came in abundantly. Endowment of scholarships increased; faculty benefits improved to include new residences, a pension plan, and a new salary scale—minimum of $1500 and maximum of $3500.[58]

John A. Lester: Head of the English Department

Although he never held one of the hierarchical offices at The Hill, Dr. John A. Lester of the English Department, who recruited Michener at Swarthmore College, led the Progressive Education movement that was running at full tide in the 1920s and 1930s. He headed the nebulous personnel department concerned with "capacities, achievements, interests, and needs of boys."[59] His influence led to the implementation of educational testing and measurement, remedial reading, and greater detail in student records.[60] Michener referred to Lester as "an admirable man."

Lester became controversial when "he explored more deeply than any of his colleagues the philosophy and methodology of education."[61] Disagreement with Headmaster Wendell over the extent of desirable change led to Lester's early retirement in 1933 after 27 years at The Hill. "Although many of the older faculty members dissented from Lester's ideas, many of the younger men found in him an inspiration and a champion of new, fresh thinking."[62] Michener said, "I was one of Lester's strong supporters and suffered thereby, as most other members of our department opposed him."[63]

Based upon a study of the 775 words most frequently misspelled in college entrance examinations, Lester wrote and published *A Spelling Review : For Preparatory Schools and High Schools*.[64] This book, used by Michener when he taught English at The Hill, brought back memories. He said, "It was my bible, used by all lower form students and by the young instructors. A fine, helpful idiosyncratic book."[65]

The Hill During the Michener Years: 1929–1931

The years between 1928 and 1933 comprised one of the greatest periods of construction in Hill School history; faculty residences, the science building, Sweeney Gymnasium, basketball courts, and the arts building were erected. On other fronts, the school did not abandon the basic concepts of John Meigs and retained the tradition of conservative education. Chancellor wrote, "The years 1928–1933 were a strange and ironic mixture of progress and near-collapse, of a light that brightened while the mechanism almost fell apart."[66] Into this arena came Michener on his first teaching job.

In 1929, the school property comprised about 150 acres on a Pottstown eminence overlooking the scenic Schuylkill River valley and surrounding green, rolling countryside. The layout of buildings and recreational facilities are identifiable in the accompanying reproduction[67] of a late 1920s aerial photograph of the tree-lined campus.

1 THE DINING HALL AND MAIN BUILDING
2 THE HEADMASTER'S HOUSE
3 THE SCHOOL AND COMMON ROOM
4 THE POWER HOUSE AND LAUNDRY
5 THE EAST WING
6 THE WEST WING AND ADMINISTRATIVE OFFICES
7 MEMORIAL HALL, LIBRARY, ASSEMBLY ROOM AND MASTERS' CLUB
8 THE UPPER SCHOOL
9 ALUMNI CHAPEL
10 MUSIC ROOMS
11 BOYS' COTTAGE
12 HILLSIDE
13 THE INFIRMARY
14 MASTER'S HOUSE
15 BASEBALL FIELD AND RUNNING TRACK
16 THE DELL FOOTBALL FIELD
17, 21, 22 TENNIS COURTS
18 THE FAR FIELDS
19 THE GOLF COURSE
20 THE DELL
23 SCHOOL GARDEN
24, 25 EMPLOYEES' DORMITORIES

Hill School Catalog 1929–1930

Aeroplane view of the School

During Michener's tenure, students applied to the headmaster for admission one year before planned matriculation. Every applicant submitted two letters of endorsement from the parents of a present or former Hill student.[68] An entrance exam was required unless the student transferred from a school recognized by The Hill: for example, Pleasanton School[69] or Shadyside Academy.[70] The exam classified a new student; failure rarely disqualified a boy.[71] With the exception of five outstanding students admitted to the fifth form annually, new pupils were admitted only to the second, third, and fourth forms.[72]

In 1929, the student roster totaled 427.[73] When Michener arrived, there were second through sixth forms in ascending academic order. English proficiency determined the student's form.[74] Michener taught second and third formers.[75] The 1929 course outline illustrates the required classes for these boys.

Consisting of three terms, the 1929–30 school year ran from late September through late June.[76] From its inception to the present time, The Hill has enrolled two types of students: "Day Students" and "Boarders." Day students return to their homes in the evening; boarders live on campus as part of the surrogate school family. In

OUTLINE OF COURSES OF STUDY

The curriculum is undergoing changes which will probably be effective in September, 1931.

(The number following the name of each study indicates the number of recitations per week in that subject.)

SECOND FORM		THIRD FORM	
2F. English	5	3F. English	5
2F. Latin	5	3F. Latin	4
2F. Algebra	5	3F. French	5
2F. Elementary Science	3	3F. Algebra	4
2F. Manual Training	2		
	20		18

The Hill School offers four courses of study in the Upper Forms in preparation for Princeton and Yale

1929–1930 Hill School Catalog Course Outline

1929, the annual tuition was $350 for day students and $1450 for boarders. There were additional fees for the medical and athletics departments; students bought their own textbooks.[77] School physicians were powerful and placed great emphasis on posture. A student was photographed in four standing postures upon entering The Hill and in his graduating year. For those boys who showed poor postural tendencies, "shadowgraph pictures" were taken about every six months.[78] Exposure to radiation was not a great concern.

The school's aims in 1929 were "to combine scholastic efficiency, consideration of each boy's individual needs, correction and direction of physical tendencies, attention to the formation of right habits of study, and maintenance of social and moral conditions favorable to the development of strong, manly character."[79] A pupil was under constant supervision of masters. This watchful care and close personal relations were to contribute to mutual confidence, sympathy, and manly cooperation.[80] Jim Michener was a master on the East Wing of Middle School. Since there were five floors with a resident master at either end of the upper four floors, he was one of eight middle school masters.

School Rules and Orders

There were general school orders and general school rules.[81] Orders addressed the daily schedule. The rising bell rang at 7:00 a.m. on weekdays and 8:30 a.m. on Sunday. Classes were held from 8:25 a.m. to 1:15 p.m. Afternoons were for exercise. Evening study hours, held in the schoolroom under a master's supervision, were 7:10 to 9:00 p.m. Lights went out at 10:00 p.m. Sixth formers had more latitude as their maturity dictated. Boys who violated orders received "marks."

Rules addressed leave (permitted over Sunday for urgent family or personal reasons), dismissal from school, Christmas and Easter vacations (mandatory time away from school), smoking (sixth formers could; lower formers needed parental permission and school approval), firearms (forbidden except under restriction of the Gun Club), and telephone calls (could be received only during specified hours). An appointment was necessary to meet with the headmaster. All edibles, other than a modest amount of fresh fruit from home, were contraband. Imbibing alcohol at school was forbidden. All radios were technically forbidden;[82] but they did exist, and one student believed Wendell okayed them by not confiscating them.[83] The illegal radios were crystal sets that the boys listened to after lights-out.[84]

Boys who violated rules received demerits. Fifty demerits resulted in dismissal. One alumnus recalled receiving 49 demerits, on the recommendation of the school's physician, for sneaking out of the infirmary where he was being treated for the flu. He left by way of the bathroom window and competed in an important pole-vault meet. The boys had been told that if they had a championship year, each would receive a gold track shoe for his watch fob. The school's doctor saw him at the meet and demanded his dismissal. Compromise was a single demerit less than that required for dismissal. He believed Wendell and Coach Colbath thought it pretty sporting of him to vault even though he was sick, but this doctor was so influential that they had to acquiesce. He could not talk with anybody for the rest of his senior year, and nobody could talk with him.[85]

Since the rule regarding alcohol was no drinking *at* the school, one alumnus felt Headmaster Wendell went a bit overboard when he expelled a boy who returned from Thanksgiving dinner at his parents' home with alcohol on his breath.[86] As the affected student told the story, he and his brother — also a Hill student—would often go the short distance home for Sunday dinner with the family, and they would take a couple of boys with them. On this occasion, it was Thanksgiving dinner; alcohol was served. They returned to school for the compulsory evening convocation—the annual sixth form show. One of the professors sat down in front of them, glanced around to check their identities, and turned them in to Headmaster Wendell. They were in Wendell's office Friday morning and off campus by Saturday noon. Their story got all over the east coast preparatory circuit. They were famous. The boy readily entered Gilman where the headmaster thought the entire episode ridiculous.[87]

The student dress code was rather strict: It dictated the required jacket or suit with tie for classes and the mandatory stiff collar for evening dinner, weekday evening chapel, and Sunday chapel. Everybody had shirts to which button-on stiff collars could be attached. One former student summarized: "I'd say it was a fairly strict dress code, and it was a good one."[88] Another alumnus expressed his approval and added: "A dress code is an important part of discipline. To relax that leads to sloppy manners and temperament." He also commented on teachers' attire during the Michener period: "They always had suits on. To me it's still a good point because it commands respect."[89] Of the dress code, Michener said: "It was indeed formal and I cannot recall ever appearing without full dress. This was, of course, especially true of the obligatory twilight religious services each weekday and the formal services with an outside minister on Sundays."[90]

School Life

Meals were served family style, as always. One student during the Michener years remembered: "The food was pretty—I don't want to say frugal—but I mean it wasn't embellished. It was good wholesome food but it wasn't prepared for your eye. There was a sameness; you had no innovation, no changes. Monday you had ham. Tuesday you had this. Wednesday you had that. You could tell the day of the week by what you were getting to eat."[91] Another student said, "I thought the food was pretty good. Everybody complained about it, but I've never been to a school yet where they didn't complain. If they don't complain, there's something wrong." He paused and continued, "Did you ever eat scrapple? That's the only thing I objected to. I never got used to it, and they served it quite often."[92]

On the extracurricular front, dramatics flourished with increased quality of productions and number of participants.[93] The Civic Club was now holding only occasional meetings. Michener does not remember politics being discussed, either formally or informally, during his two years at The Hill: "Absolutely not even mentioned."[94] However, a student during that time recalled morning exercises, called "Morning Ex." These were Mr. Rolfe's mandatory eleven o'clock Saturday morning meetings in which contemporary national and world events were presented and discussed—sometimes

The Dining Room in 1993 Is Virtually Unchanged From the Time Michener Ate Here
(Joy V. Bliss photo)

by prominent outside speakers, but most often by Rolfe.[95] Following the stock market crash of October 1929, no articles in the school's newspaper referred to the event. Another student of that time confirmed, "The financial panic of that early month went unheralded [at The Hill]."[96]

School publications faired as follows: *The Dial* continued its high quality; *The Hill School News* rose to its former height in 1930, when it won first place in interscholastic competition;[97] and because *The Hill Record* was in financial trouble, Judge Harold R. Medina, father of Standish F. Medina, class of 1933, agreed to underwrite it. The younger Medina reported that luckily the venture did not cost his father one cent as it turned out to be self-supporting;[98] however, he later admitted he helped support *The Record* by "selling and delivering 'hall feeds' from two places on High Street, which was a pain in the neck."[99]

Social events were planned for the boys. The 1929 autumn house party for upper formers is an elaborate example. Fifty-one girl guests arrived in a special train car and stayed from Friday until Sunday morning taking part in special meals, teas, dances, entertainment, and chapel services.[100] One alumnus reflected: "They did make a point of those social activities because you had no social life with girls as such, and I think they felt it necessary to have those meetings. They were, of course, heavily chaperoned in those days, which still, I think, is proper."[101]

On a smaller scale, the school had "Creams"—ice cream on Saturday nights. This social activity met with mixed student reviews; some thought it a clandestine method of taking roll-call.[102] Other activities were hikes, weekend camp, and much movie-going in Pottstown on Wednesday afternoons.[103] Although required to eat meals in the Dining Hall, students could also go off campus to the "Jigger Shop" where a big fellow by the name of Bock would sell them sodas and sundaes.[104]

The Thanksgiving holiday was only one day, and the boys stayed at school. The students went to study hall on Wednesday evening. On Thursday morning they gathered on the football field for intramural games. Students recall sack races, three-legged races, tugs-of-war, and sitting on a greased pole while trying to swat off the opponent. After Thanksgiving dinner, the afternoon was free; in the evening, they attended the rehearsed annual sixth form show. Regular classes resumed on Friday.[105]

Sports

Sports and the side benefits derived from participation in various sporting activities were integral parts of a Hill education. For a high school, the Hill athletic program seems gargantuan. The 1929 Hill School catalog boasted 25 tennis courts, nine baseball diamonds, six football fields, a quarter-mile cinder track, a 220 yard straight-away, a skating pond, gun traps, an indoor rifle range, a soccer field, and a nine-hole golf course. In addition, there were four basketball courts, three squash courts, two indoor tennis courts, a baseball cage, a partially covered one-eighth mile cinder track, and a swimming pool. There were also provisions for boxing, wrestling, and gymnastics. Unless unfit, all boys took part in required exercises four days a week.[106] An alumnus explained: "Compulsory exercise was dictated, for a well-conditioned body promoted health, well-being and a clear mind."[107]

The athletic department was large and the coaches powerful. The Hill emphasized character development; and the athletic director, Mike Sweeney, believed in character development through athletics. Other memorable coaches of the time were Chris Kogel, director of gymnasium, and Herbert "Fido" Kempton, head coach of football. Kogel, boxing and gymnastics coach, believed in strict discipline and good physical condition. In boxing the boys learned to absorb physical punishment—an excellent experience for college and later life. "He was great with younger boys and instilled in them competitive spirit and courage as well as boxing knowledge and skills."[108] For Kempton, physical condition was paramount. "He was a true drill master but was liked and respected by all."[109]

Edward C. Roe, class of 1931, star of football and boxing and active in other sports, reflected on the Hill program: "No where else in your academic training is *teamwork* and *discipline* and the ability to cope with physical discomfort taught as in sports. And to be a well-rounded student and be prepared for a successful college and then adult career, you must experience and learn these qualities of character."[110] Other outstanding preparatory schools were met in competition on the playing fields. "In visiting these schools to play, we met their students, saw their campuses and could obtain a more well-rounded experience, something the purely academic world of class-room, study-hall and library could not teach."[111]

About 25 masters assisted the boys as coaches in various sports.[112] During our 1993 interview, Michener said he did not coach at The Hill; however, toward the end of his second year there, the school newspaper reported that he had coached the fourth form (the previous year's interform champions) in far-fields baseball.[113] A student also remembered Michener as a coach in far-fields football.[114] After learning of Michener's activities in the far-fields, we asked him again about coaching and whether this sparked any memories. Michener replied, "I remember fourth form football very well, but not baseball. The Hill program in sports was exceptionally good, and I was proud of its accomplishments."[115]

Roe explained far-fields as a group of fields that were away from the varsity fields. There were football fields and baseball diamonds about a half mile from campus where the younger people practiced. The boys "came in" when they got more skillful and were able to make the varsity squad. When asked about Michener's coaching far-fields, Roe said: "Many younger professors were like we were; they started out there, and perhaps came back in. Everybody migrated as he got older and more experienced."[116]

> ### MUCH ENTHUSIASM SHOWN IN FAR FIELDS BASEBALL
>
> Spring is again calling the baseball fans of the School to the Far Fields. The teams are practicing under their respective coaches for the season which opens on April 21. The present Fourth Form, last year's interform champions, are working with Mr. Michener. They have an excellent pitching staff, including Wyatt, Francis, and Allen, but they will be handicapped by the loss of several players who have graduated to the squad. The Sixth Form is ably coached by Mr. Evans. For the past three years he has coached championship teams and hopes to duplicate his feat again this season. At the first practice of the Fifth Form, under Mr. Bristol, only six players showed up, and an urgent call was made for more players.
>
> So far the Fifth Form has been unsuccessful in the interform games and is hoping to make up for lost ground by an undefeated baseball team. The Third Form is under the supervision of Mr. Allison and hopes to celebrate its entrance into the league with a championship season.
>
> With all the material and enthusiasm that has been shown so far, this year's season ought to be a very close one and a very exciting one. At present the Fourth Form seems to be the strongest, but by the twenty-first, all the teams will be in much better shape for the opening games.
>
> **Hill School News, May 1, 1931**

Educational Program

Elsewhere, the Progressive Education movement was gaining momentum. The Hill's educational program was surveyed in 1926; and although few changes had been implemented by the time Michener arrived, the surveyor, a man from a bastion of Progressive Education, praised the school for its willingness to change. He was referring to a change from a traditional English school to a progressive institution.[117] Leading colleges were demanding change, and schools were finding they had to comply to compete.

During the Michener years, only English, other than science, made extensive changes in course content and teaching method through the inspiration of John Lester.[118] An English honors course was implemented; Lester placed Michener in charge of the lower school honors division.[119] He believed that Lester did this because of his success with fast learners—hence, the special reading classes.[120]

The rest of the departments held close to established patterns. The library was "languishing."[121] Although the 1929 school catalog describes the library as "large and valuable," comprising over 8000 volumes and always accessible to the students,[122] in reality, many of the books were gifts from collections that held no interest for students or faculty.

Master-Student Relations

More than an occasional ruckus broke out in the dormitories. The masters had clever ways of quelling these shenanigans. The boys accused two masters of sneaking up by traversing the hallways with one shoe off and one shoe on to give the impression of a slow walk. One master raced along in stocking feet (or sneakers) and would pounce in unexpectedly. The boys soon wised up to this tactic and spread sugar on the floor to create a bit of noise so they could hear his approach.[123] It was not unusual to accumulate a few demerits for roughhousing during the school years.

Students and faculty had a close relationship. One alumnus expressed this wholeheartedly: "I've always thought a great deal of Hill and the masters I had there, not only in academic fields, but there were a lot of good friendships you developed. When you got into college, your professors met you in class and very few of them developed a friendship or camaraderie. But at The Hill it was a little different. You got to know them and they'd invite you to their room, or if they were married, they had their own cottage or home, and you went there. There was more than just a pure scholastic relationship, just classroom alone. The same in athletics, there was an interest far and beyond just performing a sport. The relationship between the teachers and students was so close. They would tutor you if you had any difficulty in a subject, go over your exam with you, not only your own teachers, but others. If you had a problem, they would in most instances endeavor to help you. They lived on campus, and there would be one of them normally on hall duty or in the building."[124]

A number of young instructors taught at The Hill for only a short time. One alumnus said, "We had a lot of them pass through, as I recall they would stay one or two years, then they would find something else they preferred to do. I think Michener was one of them."[125]

Michener at The Hill

The 1929–1930 School Year

Michener arrived at The Hill in the fall of 1929, after his summer with Chautauqua. To better prepare Michener for his new career, John Lester had sent "textbooks and counsel"[126] during the summer months. He took up residence in the Hill School cottage-home of fellow faculty member Leonard A. (Bill) Rice, a colleague in the English Department.

Faculty Activities

On the light side, the faculty and their wives had frequent socials. Soon after Michener arrived, the faculty held an elaborately costumed "Mauve Decade" party. He attended. A science teacher was victorious in the spelling bee event, "thereby proving, as Mr. Michener, of the English Department, remarked, 'There is no God.'"[127]

The Hill boys poked fun at the faculty and lampooned most subjects in *The Hill School Snooze*, a parody on *The Hill School News*. In a November 1929 issue, the editors assigned contemporary song titles to faculty members. The song deemed appropriate for Michener was "Love Me or Leave Me."[128]

Why Girls Leave Home

Michener, Right, With Other Faculty Members. *Snooze*, Nov. 28, 1929

"THE DOVER ROAD" IS PRESENTED BY FACULTY

A. A. Milne's Charming Play Is Thoroughly Enjoyed By the Entire School

CAST DIRECTED BY MR. RICE

Second Faculty Production Smoother Than the First, But Acting Not So Sharply Characterized

The Dover Road, by A. A. Milne, was presented Saturday, March 8, in Memorial Hall. The cast:

The House
Dominic, the butler .... Mr. Michener
The Staff
Maid .... Mrs. Colbath
Footmen .... Mr. Tyndall Mr. Strachan
Mr. Latimer .... Mr. Rice
Guests
Anne .... Mrs. Ward
Leonard .... Mr. Hilkert
Eustasia .... Mr. Rice
Nicholas .... Mr. Laramore

The scene was the reception room of ....mer's house, a little way off the of ....
otherwise du.... ....
Rice, taking the rather uncongen.... part of Latimer, displayed mature mechanics and a fine voice. Mr. Laramore, as Nicholas, displayed all the quiet disillusion that one would expect from a week of the Latimer treatment. Mr. Michener suppressed himself very capably into a smooth, mechanical Dominic. The staff, played by Mrs. Colbath, Mr. Strachan, and Mr. Tyndall, showed a finished unobtrusiveness.
....ch for those who appeared. .... those who helped
Hitner

Hill School News, Mar. 13, 1930

When asked for an interpretation sixty-five years later, Michener wrote: "You startle me. No recollection whatever." [129] The same issue portrays Michener jauntily sporting walking shorts and garters in a faculty photograph captioned "Why Girls Leave Home."

In December 1929, the faculty presented *A Christmas Carol* to the school and its guests. Michener played the part of Jacob Marley. Bill Rice, whom Michener referred to as "the crusty master of English," [130] and in whose home Michener lived part of the time, directed the play and portrayed Scrooge. [131] In response to a question about the play, Michener wrote: "I had completely forgotten this episode, but the mention of Bill Rice's name brings it back with a gallop. He'd had a brief experience in the professional theater and its influence never left him. Since he was my housemother, as it were, and also a colleague in my department, I had close contact with him and enjoyed his rather airy memories of the stage. I've always loved *Christmas Carol* since those days." [132] One alumnus recently said, "I think that was the only time I ever saw it on stage. As I remember, it was very well done." [133]

Later in the school year, the faculty and their wives performed in a second play: A. A. Milne's *The Dover Road*. The *News* reported that Michener, cast as the butler, "suppressed himself very capably into a smooth, mechanical Dominic." [134] The *News* editors hoped faculty plays would become permanently established, but they were discontinued when Harold Conley, drama and speech coach, retired in 1949. [135]

The faculty also boasted a basketball team; Michener played center. The school newspaper reported a narrow loss for the faculty: "Mr. Michener stars as squad defeats faculty." [136]

1929 Christmas Book Published by Michener's English Classes

In December of each of Michener's two years at The Hill, he and the students in his English classes published a theme Christmas issue in which each member wrote a selection. The title of the 1929 issue was *The Christmas Book*, and its theme Shakespearean England. It was a professional 45-page book with green paper covers. James Michener wrote the "Foreword." All the editors, art editors, and business managers listed on the title page (illustrated) are found in the 1929 school catalog, third form. Both second and third formers contributed. Most were 13 to 14 years of age when they published *The Christmas Book*—quite an achievement for these boys.

Forty-four essays comprise the 1929 issue: third formers wrote 33 and second formers 11. In his foreword, Michener said these were boys in three of his classes. In 1993, after reviewing the student-author names, did he remember them? "I can visualize every one of them, every one. I know them all." [137] Titles of the first four entries give the flavor of the

"A CHRISTMAS CAROL" IS PRESENTED BY FACULTY

Messrs. Rice and Chancellor Give Excellent Portrayals of Leading Roles.

Instead of the regular song service last Sunday night, several members of the Faculty presented Charles Dickens' "A Christmas Carol" to the School and its guests.
There were four acts to the performance, all of which were splendid. Before the first scene, Dr. Lester read a short selection from the story and in between the following scenes he read various other parts to acquaint the audience with the plot.
The part of old Scrooge was portrayed splendidly by Mr. Rice. Mr. Bragonier, as his nephew; Mr. Michener, as his deceased partner; Mr. Chancellor as his clerk, and Mr. Abernethy as a charity worker, also did .... well.
.... of the play was built .... and shows his ....fully to ....

Hill School News, Dec. 19, 1929

MR. MICHENER STARS AS SQUAD DEFEATS FACULTY

Final Score 18-16 As Rauch and Munger Offset Desperate Playing of Faculty.

Between the halves of the Varsity game on Saturday, the first quarter of the Squad-Faculty game was played. It was completed when the Varsity had finished their game. The Faculty game was very fast and hard-played throughout, the squad finally emerging victorious, 18-16. Mr. Michener was the outstanding star of the game, although Munger and Rauch played very well.
The squad took the lead in the first quarter when Munger and Rauch scored goals in quick succession. Late in the period Mr. Evans sank a beautiful long shot to make the score 4-2.
Mr. Michener made a pretty long shot to start the second quarter and a moment later dribbled half the length of the court and scored to put his team in the lead. However, a basket by Irey, followed by one from Rauch, put the squad in the .... d at half.
.... ird period was somewhat .... two preceding ones. ....nted mostly

Hill School News, Dec. 29, 1929

booklet: "Queen Elizabeth," "The Life of William Shakespeare," "The Shakespearean Playhouse," and "A Shakespearean Christmas Eve." [138]

The yearbooks are difficult to locate. The only copy we found is a 1929 issue located at Swarthmore College. How did it get there? Michener: "I can't imagine how they got it. It must have been among my papers." [139] On the front cover, the Swarthmore copy is signed "M. H. Michener." We believe this signature, which is not in James A. Michener's hand, is that of Mabel Haddock Michener, his mother.

The Christmas Book

FOREWORD

The boys of three classes have written, corrected and arranged the essays and stories which follow. They have edited the book and managed its finances. They have studied the material for mistakes and from time to time they have reprimanded their own classmates for negligence. As master, I have been permitted to watch all this from a distance, and only occasionally have I been consulted, so that I can truthfully say to the editors and to the classes: "This is your book." I trust it will convey to parents and friends the Christmas Greetings of the boys, the best regards of The Hill and the real delight of the master.

JAMES MICHENER

EDITORS
Orin D. Bleakley, II
Walter H. Close, Jr.
William H. Ferde
Ralph MacM. Greenlee
Major Lee White, Jr.
Harry Fraser Wilkins, Jr.

ART EDITORS
John F. M. Davison
David G. Forman
George K. Stauffer

BUSINESS MANAGERS
James C. Agnew, Jr.
Foster Graesser
Jessee Spalding, III

DECEMBER, 1929

The Hill School
Pottstown, Pennsylvania

Foreword and Title Page from the 1929 Christmas Book

Michener Reviews Student Literary Efforts

Student literary works published in *The Record* were a tradition by 1929; it was a custom of the time to have members of the faculty and others review these writings. The reviews appeared in *The Hill School News.*

Faculty Reviewer Lauds Format and Precise Style of Christmas Record, But Criticizes General Theme of Stories

(By James Michener)

Michener reviewed the prose and poetry published in the December 1929 issue of *The Record*.[140] His rather lengthy critique appeared in *The News* the following month. In part, Michener wrote:

> Of the poetry, the [five] short pieces all have certain similar elements. Each treats of some aspect of misery; each is well composed . . . . It is pleasing to remark that each of the five again displays the remarkable feature of the book; a store of fine words used with consideration and with precise meaning.

> But here I would like to pause and summarize the articles so far considered. Each has as its major theme the thought of Death. . . . Through the whole book runs a strain of hopelessness and defeat. I, for one, question the legitimacy of such a totality of atmosphere. Death is beautiful, to be sure, but there are other themes upon which to turn for inspiration, and yet, from the whole of this issue I can extract no more than a handful of material which reflects anything but the defeat of purpose and the rejection of hope.

> This brings up the question of the purpose of a fine magazine like *The Hill School Record*. Is it not to be an expression of the School's thought; a cross section of the best literary effort, collected at appointed periods, for the delight of others? If that is so, is it just to offer the impression of defeat, hopelessness and misery, whereas, in truth, the School itself subscribes to no such doctrine. Instead, it is most jovial, most happy and most alive.[141]

Michener praised the illustrations; commended the lack of significant typographical errors; gave accolades to the beauty of the stories, themes and styles—"as favorable a comment as a reviewer could make." He concluded, "But too often, when beauty is the aim of an artist, vitality is lost, and it is vitality which should never be sacrificed, no matter what the effect gained thereby may be." [142]

Michener's comments on the appearance of the publication—format, illustrations, end pieces, introduction of color—are consistent with statements about craftsmanship he made in his memoirs sixty-two years later.[143] The physical beauty of a book was of lifelong importance to him, and it was this sentiment he conveyed at The Hill years before he even dreamed of working at Macmillan—or of writing books.

Summer 1930

In January 1930, Michener started to prepare a summer program. By written request, he asked Dr. Wendell to forward letters of introduction to the University of Chicago and Harvard University.[144] Wendell wrote to each school: "Mr. Michener is a man of unusual ability and literary trend and is a most highly valued member of our faculty. I commend him to your favorable consideration." [145] Michener said he received an invitation to do graduate work at Chicago but was unable to attend and has deep regrets.[146] Instead of attending summer school, he claims he lived at the Swarthmore home of Robinson, the criminologist whose son Walter was his boat-owning friend. Together they toured the Chesapeake, hence the novel by the same name many years later.[147]

Some confusion remains, since he mentions summer school grades in his August 18, 1930, letter to Wendell. As his summer activities ended, Michener wrote that he was heading to upper Pennsylvania for three weeks of sleep. In this letter, he also comments on The Hill's proposed system of examinations and grading. He added, "I am very anxious to get back to the Hill." [148] In Wendell's absence, Michener's letter was answered as follows on August 20, 1930: "We have read with interest your comments on the grading system, and shall consider them very carefully when all the letters are in. The faculty members have been most helpful in aiding us to reach the right decision. It promises to be a fine year. It won't be long now will it?" [149]

The 1930–1931 School Year

After the stock market crash in October of 1929, educational advances buoyed The Hill, but operating deficits pulled it down. Enrollment plummeted from an average of 430 to 357, and the number of masters was minimized.[150] However, school catalogs list tuition steady at $1450 until it increased to $1550 in 1934.[151] In spite of the times, Michener's salary rose to $1800 for his second year.[152]

Back at The Hill in the fall of 1930, the directory of Hill Masters lists Michener as living on 4 East Wing 43 of

---

The Hill School
Pottstown, Pa.
January 17, 1930

Mr. James I Wendell
The Hill School

Dear Mr. Wendell,

Would you bo so kind as to forward to the two gentlemen whose names are enclosed, letters of introduction for me. I wish to take summer work at their institutions, and I find that introductory letters are in order.

I thank you very much for your kindness.

Sincerely,

James A. Michener

Recommendations Requested for Summer School 1930

(1)   Mr. James Root Hulburt
Secretary of the English Department
University of Chicago
Chicago, Illinois

(2)   Mr. Philip P. Chase
Director of the Summer School
Harvard University
Cambridge, Massachusetts

SWARTHMORE COLLEGE
SWARTHMORE, PENNSYLVANIA
MATHEMATICS AND ASTRONOMY

August 18, 1930

Dear Mr. Wendell,

I am very sorry not to have been able to take the position with Mr. Collings that you obtained for me, but when I talekd with Tom I felt that it would be an imposition if I tried my hand at tutoring him in Latin. I just didn't know enough advanced work to be of much use, even though I did want to accompany them. I was able, however, to put Mr. Collings in touch with a man who seemed to have the highest qualifications. I want to thank you for your interest.

As for the proposed plan of marking, I am strongly in favor of it. I do not think we should go to the 90-100; 80-90; 70-80; 60-70 system of grading however. I think there is a lot to be said for the present system. My only other suggestion is more a question than an answer: If we go to this system, will it not be better to have mid-year exemptions? There will be found ample time for placing the unquestioned students in the passed group before the mid-term exams. I think that if we do turn to the monthly exams, we should put to use the results we obtain from them.

I am very anxious to get back to the Hill. I passed my summer work without notification, so far, of grades. I leave in the morning for a coal mining district in upper Pennsylvania, where I expect to sleep for three weeks.

Remember me to Mrs. Wendell and Mr. Finnegan.

Sincerely,

Jim.

Michener Comments on Grading

the Middle School.[153] His wards that second year remember his room as occupying the corner of the fourth floor. There were eight or nine rooms on the top floor, and the master's room was no different from that of any of the boys. Since radios were prohibited, the boys would gather in Mr. Michener's room to enjoy his record collection.[154]

1930 Christmas Book Published by Michener's English Classes

Late in 1930, Michener's students again published a yearbook (perhaps two) at Christmas. On December 17, 1930, Wendell wrote to thank Michener for the two booklets, "Epic England" and "The Poets," these the work of the boys in Michener's classes. Wendell wrote, "The articles are very interesting and surely such evidences of fine work must be a source of much satisfaction to you as well as to the contributors."[155] Michener recently said that Wendell correctly named the titles, and he believed Wendell referred to two publications Michener and his students put out in 1930.[156] We were unable to locate a copy of the 1930 issue(s), and as far as we can determine, these year-end publications ceased when Michener left The Hill.

Michener Reviews Student Literary Efforts

Twice during Michener's second year, *The News* carried his reviews of student contributions to *The Record*. In the first of these reviews, he extolled the virtues of prose over poetry as a medium that may be more readily and fairly evaluated.[157] The second review was a lengthy comment on style as it applied to the students' submissions.[158] Michener's poignant critique and well-chosen words were both professional and harsh. Did they challenge or silence a lad of 13? Michener was 23; his writing skillful.

Although he had primarily written poetry for his own high school and college literary publications, Michener told the young writers that it reassured him to see the majority choose

> *Mr. Michener is Faculty Member to Review February Issue of Record; Latest Number Has Much Noteworthy Prose*

prose over poetry for the February issue. As the two forms lend themselves to critique, Michener compared them:

> Contrary to the general belief, it is more difficult for a school paper to find good prose than it is to discover passable poetry. This is due to the fact that poetry can, if necessary, gloss over meanings with a symbolism of words that often leaves behind an uncertainty that was not meant. Because of this the majority of contributors to school papers prefer the medium of poetry; it can be criticized much less severely. It also has the added protection of a time-honored deference that critics do not always pay to prose. This reviewer feels that the stronger numbers of *The Record* have always been those in which stories and essays have dominated.

After addressing specific contributions, he continued:

> I hold no brief for prose as against poetry; the volume of Hill School verse is an ample proof of the fact that students here have time and again written fine verses, but this truth remains: that an individual writer faces a severer test of his own ability as a creative artist if he writes a large portion of his work in prose form. In that medium his ideas can be criticized more fairly by himself and by others. It is often possible to get away with questionable work if it is presented in poetic form, but if the author will attempt to put his ideas into prose, subjecting them to a careful scrutiny as to content and legitimacy, he will frequently be doing himself a favor that will possibly aid in his future development.[159]

Michener praised one student's prose as being "well thought out and careful; his poetry seems hurried, glosed [sic] over, written without a studied care. Perhaps that is exactly what the poet tries to achieve, that lack of finish, but in the majority of cases, it shows a lack of more than finish: a lack, perhaps, of attention."[160] Two writers whose prose received highest praise from Michener—Gilbert Macpherson and C. Walter Bühler—went into business careers: building and floor wax manufacturing, respectively. Neither wrote professionally.[161] Michener rated two poems the best of the issue. One was written by a third form student who later had a career in medicine. Although he had published medical articles, some later poems and a few anecdotes recalling the early years were written for personal enjoyment only.[162]

Michener reviewed all contributions. Positive comments balanced the negative, and overall, the review was harsher than the critique he wrote his first year at The Hill.

The April 1931 *Record* was the second of the school year and the last of the three issues reviewed by Michener.[163] He noted

> *Mr. Michener Reviews April Record; Praises "Chaos" and "The Quest of Sir Belaine"; Says Themes Are Too Forced*

that, unlike contributions to previous issues which made him suspicious that there was "too much care and not enough inspiration," this issue had evidence of inspiration but was lacking in care. The remainder of his critique centered almost exclusively on style:

> The summary of the whole extended criticism is this: If one deals with forced emotions (those, for example, that one requires in class rooms and from reading), one must write perfectly; the greater the emotion which prompts a person to write, the more liberties the author can take with style. This is certain, however, that a forced, decadent theme must have a perfectly organized plot and a similarly perfect style.

> The "*Record*" has a tendency to lean toward the forced style of writing, and it is because of this that I have made my criticism almost entirely one of style. If one is going to write of stilted things, one must not forget the second comma in the third line. As for myself, I think I much prefer spirited writing. . . . One can almost overlook the obvious faults in such writing, for the content carries the whole story along.[164]

Michener encouraged the students to write from actual experience. Those articles with themes based on personal experience were the ones he liked most and found best written.

Michener Remembers The Hill

Michener visited The Hill[165] on the occasion of the school's 100th anniversary celebration in 1951, but also in 1962, again in 1966, briefly, and in the 1980s when he was researching scenes for his book, *The Novel*, in which he speaks highly of the school. A fictional character attends The Hill, and Michener describes it as one of the best: "Tough discipline, fine teaching, a good mix for a lad."[166]

During our 1993 interview, when we asked about the physical layout of the school, Michener sketched a campus map. With an apparent love and aptitude for spatial arrangement, and a remarkable memory, he discussed each building and area, labeling as he went along. When finished, he said, "So it was a big installation—an odd one that was right on High Street. They kept it away from High Street as much as possible. We lived in that area, and I lived in that building here—the dorm."[167] He pointed to the middle school dorm on his drawing and said he had lived on fourth floor.

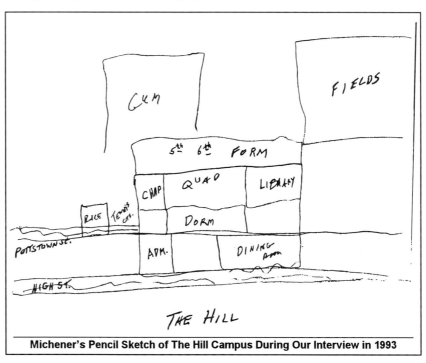

Michener's Pencil Sketch of The Hill Campus During Our Interview in 1993

"You say where did I teach? It's funny, I don't have a clue. It must have been on the ground floor of that building [dormitory]."[168] It was. The Hill School archivist recently spoke with some of the older masters, and they confirmed that the ground floor of Middle School had indeed been classrooms during Michener's two years at The Hill.[169]

"A remarkable fact about my time at The Hill was that I was a pretty gung-ho guy, and I came there under some difficulties. The preceding guy had been run off the campus; fine teacher—later had a splendid career at Hotchkiss, I think it was—so he was more than eligible but the kids got out of hand. ... It was touch and go with the new teacher. I was younger than some of my students. They, having gotten rid of my predecessor, sort of felt their oats. They were going to take a shot at me. ... It was very rough and everybody knew it, including the faculty. The faculty was not supportive; they said let the son-of-a-bitch sink or swim—let's see if he's really got it." Baiting of a new master was something of a sport—a tradition at The Hill. Michener added, "I felt myself that it was touch and go—that it was by no means sure that I was going to make it." [170]

Answering questions about teaching, he said, "I taught English, that was embracing both grammar and literature." Even though the school was large, Michener remembered the classes "tended to be small—about 15, 18." The role of English was "important. Very

Michener's Middle School Dormitory Room on the Top Floor, Right Middle School Classrooms on the Ground Floor (Joy V. Bliss photo)

important. We had maybe the biggest faculty because of the writing component. When anyone took a college board in science or anything else, if he couldn't write, he was a dead duck." Asked if he detected any students with literary talent, he said, "Not really. We weren't doing that kind of writing. We were doing 'answer-the-question' type of writing." [171]

In his first year of teaching, Michener made two changes. He obtained permission to incorporate *The Worst Journey in the World* into his curriculum; and, by accomplishing this, he got the students to read about Scott and the Antarctic, which he describes later. He reflected on his purpose for effecting the change: "Let's stop this crap about ancient knights; let's talk about somebody real, like your uncle." Asked if latitude with the curriculum was rare at that time, he remembered: "That was rare, but they were willing to listen. They knew I was a good teacher. I may not have been their ideal *type*, but they knew I was a very good teacher. They were willing to listen. As a matter of fact, I don't think I had any troubles at all making the switch." [172]

Michener then described the other change he made: "The other was—and I must have had a nerve beyond imagination, because I just came in September—to publish the yearbook each year. Every student I had had an essay in it. Some of them were heavily corrected by the professor, but we never went into that." These represented "a radical departure—nobody had ever done it before. It was highly appreciated by the students and their families." He later said: "In the class, the students had to do a lot of writing to try to master the tricks of the trade. It was with this in mind that I published the two yearbooks. I wanted them to have the experience of having written something, having it edited, and seeing it in print." [173]

The Feroe Press of Pottstown printed Michener's English classes' Christmas yearbooks for both 1929 and 1930. How was he able to have this class project professionally printed? "I had a boy in class named Feroe, tremendously nice kid, who by no means sided with me in the big wrestling match, but whose father had a printing plant. The Feroe Printing Company printed these two yearbooks. I don't know how we financed them, but they were damn good jobs." [174] The student was William; the father, Robert A. Feroe.

Robert A. Feroe began business by making paper boxes in 1911 and added a printing shop that evolved into The Feroe Press. Robert's seven sons, including Michener's student, William, all attended The Hill in the 1920s and early 1930s, [175] and they all joined the family business after college. [176] One of the sons, Melvin Feroe, closed the business and left Pottstown several years ago. His family did not have any copies of the English class yearbooks.

How does Michener rate The Hill's English program during his tenure in the department? "I mean they really taught you at Hill. Now, I'm only teaching the second and third form here—they've got these other teachers who are teaching the fifth and sixth form. So if I'm teaching at this level ... by the time the boy got through with us—five English teachers like me, and the others maybe better—he had an education that way exceeds many half-baked colleges when you graduate with an A. B. It's just a fact! ... I happen to think that the constellation we had in English at the time was pretty unusual; and if I was the low man on the totem pole, those kids were learning something." [177]

Does Michener remember his students? "You remember the distinctive students whether they were good or bad. They didn't have to get 'A' for me to remember them. They might have had some other attribute." [178]

Does he keep in touch with any of the students? "They keep in touch with me sometimes. I always answer the mail—very pleased to have reminders." [179]

Was this period at least in part responsible for his continued interest in teaching? "Not so much interested in teaching but interested in the intellectual process—interested in literature." [180]

At the time we met in 1993, he was 87 and continued to teach and work with graduate students.

Michener was 22 years old in the fall of 1929. Because they had fallen back and were catching up, some of the students were near his age or even older. Did his youth pose a problem when it came to discipline? Michener remembers the students as being very good about his age: "In other words, we settled that early. One of the first nights in chapel, I gave a senior a demerit. They said, 'You can't do that; he's president of the student body.' And I said, 'I just did it!' Everybody backed off—including me. I never did that again! I was very malleable. I could learn." He added, "I never bulled my way along, but I never backed off either. I was not a cause célèbre—ever. I just don't go that route." [181]

"There was a guy whose name I used to know well who later (chuckle) became some sort of an All-American football player at Illinois. He told me years later that he cried himself to sleep when I challenged him right off the bat and called him maybe an imbecile. He said he never got over it—that *I* had felt he might be an imbecile." He continued, "A couple have corresponded with me all through the years. I really took them on—head on." [182]

Michener related that a highly original German language master, George Bickel, took off one shoe and ran down the dormitory halls of his rather difficult floor giving the auditory impression that he was walking. In this furtive manner, the master could rapidly reach the scene of whatever disaster was in development. The students on Michener's floor accused him of doing the same. [183]

Asked if there were teachers at The Hill whose names he remembers, he said, "I can remember all their names if I had to. They were older men who made this their career; the younger men who were not going to had been phased out or phased themselves out. I knew them all—remember them vividly. That is, the ones I remember, I remember vividly. It would be at least two-thirds of them. I could list their names right now." He proceeded to do so. "Well, there were three Potts sisters. They were sort of the elite of the area. Three of our teachers married them: Colbath, Saunders, and Wendell. ... They formed the triumvirate and more or less let you know it in a subtle way. It was nothing invidious, but they were the 'in-crowd.' Then we had the older teachers like Rolfe, like Thomas, and Jasper Jacob Stahl—head of the sixth form. Daddy ['Pop'] Turner was the tough guy who could handle the study hall. Strachan, Shrigley, and Rice were the English teachers. Chancellor, Cowperthwaite, and Thomas were the classics teachers. Robins was the baseball coach; a very charismatic guy, whose name I don't remember, was the football coach." When we expressed amazement at his memory, he said, "Oh, I could go on with another twenty. ... Wherever I taught, I could do that." [184]

FACULTY
English
JOHN A. LESTER, M.A. (Haverford College) Ph.D. (Harvard University)
CHARLES L. SWIFT, M.A. (Dickinson College) (Yale University)
HAROLD G. CONLEY, Ph.B. (University of Chicago)
LEONARD A. RICE, B.A. (Tufts College)
G. A. CLEVELAND SHRIGLEY, B.A. (St. Stephens College)
MALCOLM STRACHAN, B.A. (Rutgers College)
JAMES A. MICHENER, B.A. (Swarthmore College)
The Hill English Faculty, 1929

When shown the 1940 book *Mike Sweeney of The Hill* [185] and asked if it evoked any memories, Michener replied, "He was Mr. Hill." Michener then looked at the frontispiece portrait and we all laughed when he remarked, " My God, he looks the same now as he did then." [186]

Of those who were phased out, Strachan and Shrigley "may have left a year or maybe two after [I did]. Strachan went to St. Paul's or Groton—I don't remember which. *Fantastic* advance. The others stayed on at Hill with great dignity—Rice and Chancellor and Lavertu in French and Thomas in Classics." [187] His voice trailed off as he reminisced.

What does Michener remember about the extracurricular program? "They would have a student play of one of the classics. They would have a faculty play of one of the classics. They would have a very active Saturday night entertainment program through the term—not every Saturday night—but they would bring in poets and writers and actors and so on." [188]

Michener "cannot recall a single field trip—*ever!* Certainly *never* any that I was affiliated with. Your job was to get into Yale, Harvard, or Princeton; and they did that rather well. ... A field trip? *Unthinkable.* I never saw a big bus on the campus." On further reflection, he continued, "I'm sure we didn't have one. I might be wrong on that, [they] probably rented one to take to a football game or a baseball game. I would suppose we had that. Field trip? No way." [189]

"Between the end of class and supper, you'd be out in the field knocking around. I might add, at my age, I was not able to coach. That would have come the next year. That was a very important job! [You] needed experience to establish yourself in the school." Just how important was the athletic program? "Sports were very important! You had to get right with the coaches or you were not going to be happy. There was no illusion that you were equal to the coaches, but it wasn't oppressive; they weren't gorillas, they were dammed good men." [190]

Is it the sports program that keeps alumni interested in the school? "Yes. That's a tragedy in American education. It's a never-ending struggle." [191]

Does Michener think the students remember him? "There's the factor here of selective remembrance. The fact that I, of the group of teachers, continued to be newsworthy, meant that you couldn't kid yourself that you remembered. I think there's a lot of that." [192]

"I would not think that at Hill or George School I ever attained the level of the beloved older teacher. I don't think anybody would ever come back to see me and say 'remember how we did this or how we did that?' I just don't think that happened. It happens in retrospect. Sometimes it surprises me that the memory is very clear and they're not faking it. But I think that's because I became well known as a writer, and they want to affiliate with me. I have *no memory* of their affiliating with me the way they did with certain teachers who were more on the scene. That's part of the problem; if I had stayed there eight years, I'm sure that they would have said, 'He was one of the top teachers.' *No way* any of these kids would remember me as one of the top teachers, because they only had me for one year." [193]

When asked why it mattered to a particular student whether he had taught one year or many, Michener had a ready answer: "There's another factor in that. You're in the dining room for four years. You're on the playing field for four years. You're in the dorm for three years, then you go to the big dorm, and life is very exciting there. I'm sure they remember those teachers." [194]

How did Michener benefit from his years at The Hill? "The critical facts about those two years in my life were that I was on duty 24 hours a day for six and a half days per week, and I just had a *lot* of spare time. I used that spare time to give myself an education in literature and music. I bought all the Red Seal records that were available in the city of Pottstown—maybe 400 of them—for fifty cents apiece, because it was the end of the Red Seal record business. I had an education in music that few people had." Those "two years were used by me to get my own education squared away. ... I read voraciously! I read everything in print. ... When I got on my own, I really studied. Those two years were invaluable to me." [195]

What was the structure that left him with so much spare time? "I was a dormitory master. I had to be in the dormitory from 9 o'clock until dawn. That kept me in one place—my place—with no interruptions from anybody. Except when they started to burn down the building, then I'd have to run out and put out the fire. They could be pretty raucous when they wanted to be." [196]

Did Michener feel like an outsider in The Hill system? "I doubt that I ever would have been promoted to the fifth and sixth form dorms. I wasn't a traditionalist. I'm not sure they would trust me. I'm not saying that invidiously, but I just wasn't a member of that team. I would not want to become like the two members I remember the most—I would never want to become like that. I think it would have been clear to the administration that I really was *not* their boy. I was as much an enrolled student at Hill as any of the other students. ...I don't think they would have wanted me to remain at Hill—certainly from the point of view of personality and other things. They knew I was a good teacher; I think they were happy to have me, but I don't think I would ever become part of The Hill hierarchy."[197]

In 1991, The Hill published a brochure listing the school's writers with extraordinary talent; "James A. Michener, Instructor of English at The Hill, 1929–1931," was the lone teacher included with ten notable former students.[198] Michener's words ring again: "I was as much an enrolled student as any of the other students."

Why did he leave The Hill after only two years? "I would think that the two years I was there, my tenure was very nebulous. They got rid of three younger English teachers: Shrigley, Strachan, and me—so I have reason to think, let's put it that way."[199]

Asked directly whether he was hired back for the next year, he said, "I begged the question by quitting and going to Europe. *Would* I have been hired back next year? This was the middle of the depression. Your guess is as good as mine." Later he added, "Everybody warned me against leaving a good job in the middle of the depression. That didn't deter me for a second. I sometimes *shiver* to think how badly wrong it could have gone. The fact is that it didn't, and I came out infinitely stronger."[200]

In the fall of 1930, Michener was a Pennsylvania candidate for a Rhodes Scholarship for the ensuing year. Dr. Wendell wrote a statement on Michener's behalf:

> We have found him a very keen teacher, an industrious worker, and I can say that he is the type of man that a school looks for, having in mind the necessity in time of replacing men who approach retirement. I can recommend Mr. Michener without reservation as a highly desirable candidate for a Rhodes Scholarship and I believe that, if selected, his work at Oxford will bear out in fullest measure my confidence in him.[201]

In this letter of strong recommendation, Wendell more than hints there may have been long-term employment for Michener at The Hill. Perhaps Michener's tenure wasn't as nebulous as he perceived. In spite of this fine recommendation, Michener did not receive the Rhodes Scholarship; instead, he was awarded a Lippincott Fellowship, sponsored by Swarthmore College. It could be applied to travel. He went to Europe.

The Students Remember Michener

Upon being questioned some sixty years after their association, a number of students do not remember Michener at The Hill even though they were either in his English class—and thus wrote selections for the class Christmas issues—or were his wards in the dormitory. One former student, C. Walter Bühler, claimed we were searching the wrong years for information about Michener's teaching. After several minutes on the telephone trying to convince him that Michener had reviewed his contributions to *The Record*, we referred him to page fifty-two of the 1931 *Dial*, which carries Michener's picture. There was a long pause, then he exclaimed, "I didn't realize he was there!" Bühler had so enjoyed *Caravans*[202] by Michener, he had taken an extensive tour of Afghanistan based on the strength of it.[203]

Another alumnus, Robert Biddle, later lived near Michener in Bucks County where they played tennis together, but he said he didn't remember much of Michener while at school other than to note that he had come out to watch him pole-vault. "He would just come out and watch the sport. He was interested."[204]

Michener was a dormitory master on the fourth floor of East Wing in 1930–1931. Approximately sixteen boys were in his care. The students described his room as a common room—no different from those of his young wards. It had a bed, basin, and a few chairs. The boys gathered in Michener's room during free time in the afternoons and after studies in the evening to listen to recordings from his large record collection. "He was good-natured about it."[205] One student recalled they listened to songs that were popular in the 1930s: "Little White Lies," "Dancing in the Dark," and "Stardust"; he remembered little or no classical music.[206]

When asked if Michener's youth made a difference when it came to discipline, the students said no. "He was fresh out of college when he came to the Hill School, and I guess it was his baptism by fire."[207] He stood up to it rather well.

Michener was "fair but firm. He was a good disciplinarian. You always knew that you were going to get a fair shake. People didn't try to take advantage of him; because, if he found them doing something they were not supposed to be doing, they also knew he would report them to the dean's office, and they would get some disciplinary action—like marks or demerits."[208]

Another student, William B. Watling, remembered that Michener was known as "Velvet," because he was soft-spoken and smooth. He also said, "Except for the fact that he was a master, he didn't seem that much older. I mean he didn't lord it over you. We used to play touch football, and he'd join in the playing. He seemed to be very well liked."[209]

Students remembered Michener's coaching far-field fourth form football with another master, Howard Vick Evans. When asked if it made any difference to the boys that Michener himself had not played football in high school or college, one student reasoned that it did not; because in those days, the students played the old single wing. The plays and formations were not very complicated, and basically it was more or less physical training—getting the boys in good physical condition. The coach didn't have to have a tremendous football background or any personal experience. Michener was described as a good coach: "He did a better than passing job."[210]

The Hill After the Michener Years

Michener left The Hill in the spring of 1931. Pioneering along the progressive education path halted with the resignation of John Lester in 1933.[211] Discipline by rewards and penalties remained; "petty rules and restrictions encrusted the system."[212] A renaissance in religious life came with the arrival of Rev. Howard L. Rubendall in 1937; he gave The Hill the structured religious life it was to retain.[213]

One evening in 1951, the Hill's dining hall was buzzing with guests as they celebrated the school's 100th anniversary. Toastmaster, Standish F. Medina, class of 1933, noted that, although there were thousands of preparatory schools in the United States, only a few dozen had reached the ripe old age of 100 years.[214] James A. Michener, an author of recent note, was in attendance.

However, there was unrest in The Hill's centennial year. Wendell, headmaster for 24 years, tendered his resignation, and it was accepted. The school had suffered through a depression, fires, a challenge to its tax exempt status, inflation, declining admissions caused by the uncertainties of two wars, an increasingly restive low-salaried faculty, chronic financial weakness, and a disciplinary system that was in need of overhauling.

Wendell's successor, Edward T. Hall, was headmaster for 16 years. During these years, The Hill was dedicated "to the pursuit of excellence," relations with Pottstown were strengthened, religious life was renewed, student responsibility was encouraged, faculty salaries and pensions were given top priority, the curriculum was revised to enliven teaching and course content (not toward the progressive and novel however), admissions criteria were tightened, poor achievers were dismissed, and endowment rose. Hall did not envision The Hill to be preparation for college, but rather to be an educational institution in its own right—like the great English schools."[215] During his tenure, "The Hill rose to a level of excellence and prestige it had not known since the days of John Meigs."[216] Hall surprised and bewildered the trustees, faculty, and students when he left The Hill for another school in 1968.

Archibald R. Montgomery III, followed Hall. The late 1960s and early 1970s were years of student unrest, protests, drugs, and liberalization of life styles. Montgomery understood and welcomed the turmoil confronting American youth. He was aware of the difference in life-style between contemporary youth and that of boys in a boarding school community. Hill students were protesting the disparity.[217] Despite resistance, change came; and students were allowed more freedom. At the same time, boys were showing a distaste for this type of school, which resulted in lowered enrollment in all boarding schools in 1970. Montgomery felt there was a place at The Hill for students of lesser intellect. The failure to resolve the conflict between granting freedom and maintaining standards contributed to the end of the Montgomery administration in 1973.

In 1973, Charles C. Watson was elevated from a ten-year career in teaching and administrative posts to the position of headmaster, a job he retained for twenty years. The turmoil of the sixties and early seventies was lessening everywhere. Through recruitment efforts, enrollment started to rise again in the mid-1970s. The endowment was large, and the school was financially strong. Improvements were seen in the quality of administration, faculty, and academic excellence of students; and physical additions and renovations were made.[218] Watson left Hill School for a position at a Virginia women's college.[219]

The Hill's tenth headmaster, David R. Dougherty, took over the helm in 1993. The Admissions Office, not the headmaster, now accepts applications and new students are admitted to all grades. The 1993–94 enrollment was 451 students.[220] Although the 1994–95 annual tuition was $20,000 for boarders and $13,400 for day students, the school provides substantial funds for financial aid in the form of both grants and loans.[221]

The newly expanded library houses close to 32,000 volumes. Renovated rooms on the library's third floor are devoted to the archives; and besides preserved documents, including school publications that contain articles relating to Michener, the staff continually processes memorabilia received from former students.

There are independent study projects for academic credit, advanced placement courses, and honors courses. There is also an underform writers' workshop with weekly critiques and seminars on literary theory and practice. The athletic program is still important; all boys participate in a program each term.[222]

Except for weekends when they eat buffet style, students have three meals each day in the family style that has existed since the days of Matthew Meigs. The Dining Hall is a stately stone structure with a high ceiling and dark wood; seventeen of N. C. Wyeth's American patriotic canvases, a donation of Mike Sweeney, decorate the hall. Faculty members, who sit at the head and foot of each long table, serve the students. On a rotating basis, each table has its assigned students who clear the dishes.

Academic dress—a shirt and tie, a jacket, trousers, socks, and "suitable" shoes—is mandatory for all classes, chapel, and in the dining room. In the mornings through lunch time, it is a requirement for the library, study halls, and public places. Town dress—shirt with a collar and sleeves, pants, socks, and footwear—is appropriate for afternoon laboratories and shop classes; for afternoons in the library, study hall, or in public; and to buffet meals.[223] In the 1990s, some would call this a strict code; but what a change it is from Michener's teaching years when the boys "ran frantically across the campus as the last bell pealed,"[224] tugging on that familiar stiff collar that was mandatory for dinner and chapel services.

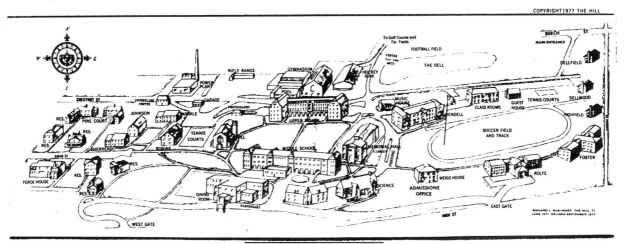

Campus Map 1993

THE TEXTBOOKS: TEACHING AND LEARNING

These are the textbooks Michener used at The Hill to teach and learn. We purchased them at the Oley auction 56 years after they had left his possession. He contributed commentary and notes on selected titles and typed the notes on his manual typewriter in his home office in Austin, Texas. Reproduced here are three previously unpublished poems which he wrote into the textbooks between 1929 and 1931; at the time, they described his feelings about the subject matter. His commentary in this section is taken from our taped interview;[1] quotation marks enclose his responses to questions. For reference, an annotated bibliography of these textbooks is appended at page 100.

Baldwin, James. *The Story of Roland.* New York : Scribner's, [C1883, 1930 by Scribner's; C1911 by Baldwin].

The signature, "James A. Michener," appears in ink above the half title on page (i). See the Introduction for a reproduction of this signature. Michener says he used this book at The Hill.

Bement, Howard, ed. *The Sir Roger de Coverley Papers : From The Spectator.* Chicago: Laurel, [C1925, 1930 By Laurel].

Bement taught English at The Hill from 1905–27.[2] There are no Michener entries, but he says he used this book at The Hill.

Blackmore, Richard Doddridge. *Lorna Doone: A Romance of Exmoor.* Ed. by Albert L. Barbour. 6th ed. New York: Macmillan, 1923 [C1905 By Macmillan].

The book is signed in ink: "Paul Reigner, Pennsburg, Pa." No Hill graduate has come from Pennsburg. There are no Michener entries, but he says he used this book at The Hill.

Boyd, James. *Marching On.* New York: Scribner's, 1927 [C1927 by Scribner's].

The signature, "Mr. Rolfe," appears in pencil on the first fly leaf. The same leaf shows pencil erasure; the bruised paper reads: "Hill School Library." "Extra copy" is written in pencil on the back of the front cover opposite the first fly leaf. There are no Michener entries, and he does not recall having or reading this book. Taken together, this information implies that the collection of books bought at the Oley auction might have come from a Hill School library deaccession.

Cherry-Garrard, Apsley. *The Worst Journey in the World : Antarctic : 1910–1913.* 2 vols. London: Constable, [C1922].

This is the only book in this bibliography that was not among the textbooks bought at auction in 1987. Michener replaced Tennyson's *Idylls of the King*, a standard text at Hill, with this book, probably the 1929 edition. 18cm x 11cm. Vol. 1: lxiv, 300 pages. Vol. 2: viii, 301-585 pages. Ten folding panoramas are included in this blue cloth hardcover edition.

> ## The Missing Jewel by James A. Michener

Glad as I was to see trustworthy old favorites like Edgar's handbook on diagramming and *Great Expectations*, I was grievously disappointed in finding that my favorite text of all was missing. During the winter term in 1930, I faced a disciplinary problem in my class which, if it had been allowed to run unchecked, might have ended my days as a teacher. An English class of older boys was finding their traditional textbooks boring and was beginning to take it out on me.

I was frightened lest they get completely out of control, a devastating situation in a tightly disciplined boys' school. Indeed, I had been given my job in 1929 because a young man teacher, who later had a splendid career in another school, had literally been run out of The Hill because his class had become fractious, a condition that could not be tolerated. But he seemed unable to resort to discipline; and one morning before he came to class, rascally boys had propped a heavy plaster cast against the top of his door so that, when he entered, the cast would drop noisily and shatter right before his eyes. Unfortunately, when he opened the door, he did so in his customary gentle manner, which allowed the circular base of the statue to roll along the top edge of the door and come crashing down one inch before his eyes. That did it. He resigned that afternoon, leaving a vacancy for me.

I was determined not to be so easily dismissed by an unruly mob of rascals, and boys from my dormitory still tell yarns about my going about at night wearing only one shoe, which allowed me to gallop down my hall making considerable noise with my one shoe and creating the illusion that I was walking in an orderly manner instead of rushing at breakneck speed to halt some shenanigan.

By one device or another, I was holding my own and it seemed unlikely that I would be run out of my classroom, but I wanted an even greater margin of safety, so I went to the administration and said: "The trouble stems from the book they have to read this term. They despise it, and they take their frustration out on me."

"What is the book?"

"Tennyson's *Idylls of the King*. They find it mushy. They call Lancelot Sir Drip."

"I found it mushy, too, when I was in their class. What do you propose?"

"I want to knock their blasé asses off their chairs. Give them a real challenge, about real men."

"What did you have in mind?"

"There's a new book out, new in this country at least. It's about the heroism of Sir Robert Falcon Scott's fatal trek to the South Pole in 1912. In a race against the Norwegian Amundsen to get to the South Pole, he lost by a few days."

"Didn't his attempt end rather poorly?"

"He and his entire group froze to death—or starved—or in the case of the great man Oates. . . ."

"Is he the one who knew that he was near death and walked out into the blizzard so that the others would have more food?"

"You have it right, Sir. I want to have my boys read about men like that. Something bigger than themselves—heroism in action."

"What's the name of the book? Who wrote it?"

"Apsley Cherry-Garrard's *The Worst Journey in the World*. He was a member of the base camp team. A very good book."

Although the Great Depression was already in full swing, hitting with powerful force families like those who could send their sons to The Hill, and funds were tight, the administration granted permission for me to order the books if I could get them wholesale, and when they arrived I told my boys as I handed each a copy: "You've been acting up a bit. And I'm fed up. I want you to read about how real men behave in adversity. You read this book, you'll remember it the rest of your lives."

It was a book like that. It told of the heroism that few men could match but that all would admire: the heartbreak of getting to the Pole on 17 January 1912 only to find that Amundsen had already planted a black flag there; the terrible march back to camp where supplies waited; the dropping off of the men one by one; Scott's farewell message to the Public as the gallant man lay dying. Even in 1931, it was cherished as one of the great letters of the English language:

> Had we lived, I should have had a tale to tell of the hardihood, endurance and courage of my companions which would have stirred the heart of every Englishman. These rough notes and our dead bodies must tell the tale.

When I read this letter to our class, the danger of rebellion faded.

Scott had a powerful effect on my students, and some have written in later years to tell me so; but he's had a more lasting effect on me. When I was stationed in New Zealand during World War II, I visited his monument in Christchurch and felt as if I were in touch with him. When it came time years later to write about the Arctic, I recalled the Cherry-Garrard book; and when in 1992 I finally got to Antarctica, I traveled with Scott at my elbow. But apart from the hero worship which he inculcated, he presented me with several difficult problems of assessment, one I have still not resolved.

Born into an elitist English family, he was a vain and arrogant man. When the time came to plan his dash to the Pole, he became fixated with the idea that real Englishmen would scorn using dogs to haul their sleds. They would pull their equipment on sleds, the way an honest man should, and not even information that Amundsen would be racing against Scott using dogs trained in Antarctic conditions, made Scott change his mind. And when the English learned that Amundsen proposed carrying only sparse rations on the gallop to the Pole and eating his dogs for sustenance on the way back, Scott dismissed the Norwegian with the terse summary: "The man's no gentleman."

I have reviewed every yard of Amundsen's sophisticated route to the Pole and compared it with Scott's far less clever routing. And when I had to calculate that Amundsen would have the speed of his dogs and the advantage of having the animals to eat on the return trip, while Scott's bone-weary men would be dragging those damnable sleds over rough wind-swept terrain, I had to conclude: "Scott must have been mad."

But today, after all these years, I still revere Scott as a noble man and find Amundsen quite to my disliking. I find myself muttering: "Any man could gallop down to the Pole if he encountered good weather and had his dogs to eat on the way back. It takes a real man to go down by dragging his sleds behind him and fighting every inch of the way, as a gentleman should."

You could categorize my experience with *The Worst Journey in the World* as "The Teacher Taught."

James A. Michener

Dickens, Charles. *Great Expectations.* London: Milford Publisher to Oxford UP, [1907, …1928].

Michener underlined text in ink and pencil and wrote the names of the characters in the story in pencil on the last fly leaf. He still writes out character lists in books he reads. He says he used this book at The Hill.

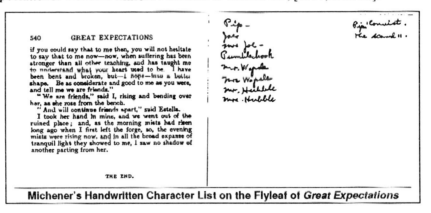

Michener's Handwritten Character List on the Flyleaf of *Great Expectations*

The Essential Dickens by James A. Michener

I felt a glow of warmth and well being when I found that the Albuquerque couple had salvaged a book which had exercised a profound influence on my thinking about these books which both pleased the general reading public and interested intellectuals concerned about the gravity of literature. *Great Expectations*, that almost flawless novel by Charles Dickens, was such a novel, and now, some sixty years after my discovery of the book, I am gratified to recall that I recognized its quality on first reading at a time when I knew much of the Dickens' oeuvre but not much about the man himself.

When I learned that in the winter term I would be expected to teach *Great Expectations*, I spent my Christmas vacation studying every aspect of the novel, and the more closely I followed the lines of narration and the development of the characters the more clearly I saw that this was not an ordinary novel but a masterpiece. I thought the opening chapter one of the two best beginnings of a novel I'd ever read, Thomas Hardy's wildly imaginative opening scenes of *The Mayor of Casterbridge* being the other. There a workman lifts his wife onto a bar table and auctions her off to the drinking customers.

The opening of *Great Expectations* was the more effective, I judged, because it served not only as the opening of the novel when Pip aids the escaped convict Abel Magwitch, but in the long middle of the narrative when Magwitch's fortune gained in Australia is converted into Pip's "great expectations," and utilized yet again at the close of the novel when Magwitch and Pip are once more struggling against the law. There is thus a satisfying roundedness to the novel, with all segments properly interrelated and each lending meaning to the whole. It is subtly constructed.

I was captivated by the brilliant manner in which Miss Havisham was introduced sitting in her disintegrating manor house with its remnants of her wedding cake with the spiders and mice running through the tunnels they had made, and she in the tattered dress she was to have worn on her wedding day, when a cruel-hearted bridegroom abandoned her without cause. She was a majestic old woman, intensely interesting to me, and understandable in her bitterness.

However, although I accepted her as a magnificent visual and moral invention, and understood her prolonged grief, I was completely unprepared when I read on to find that she was using her adopted child Estella, one of the most infuriating young women in literature, as a weapon to gain Miss Havisham's revenge on the male race: "Break their hearts, my pride and hope, break their hearts and have no mercy." Delectable Estella was being encouraged to demonstrate her ugly power by destroying defenseless young Pip.

I was shocked by this discovery of a truly evil intent, but I could believe that both Miss Havisham and her niece were capable of behaving in that manner. I was twenty-two years old that Christmas and just beginning to watch my colleagues of similar age picking and choosing and stumbling their way through the courtship and marriage process; and it seemed to me that most young men would, at some time in their lives, become entangled with some heavenly creature like Estella who would remain totally unattainable but always casting her spell upon the mind and memory.

But I must not throw the significance of this fine novel onto the shoulders of the other young men whose fortunes I was following with more than casual interest. I was myself embroiled in emotional setbacks and courtship disappointments, so that I was deeply involved in the misfortunes of young Pip. He and I were blood brothers.

This was true for another reason, too. Pip was an orphan and so was I. His problems were solved by his being taken into the home of his older sister and her husband. Mine were minimized by my being taken into the home of an almost saintly poor widowed woman who eked out a living by taking care of abandoned children. Pip had a rough time with the Gargerys; I found salvation with Mrs. Michener.

Therefore I followed young Pip with a magnifying glass, aware at every turn of the brilliant plot the extent to which the happenings might also apply to me. I must have taught *Great Expectations* with unusual intensity and ability to highlight incidents, for many students told me that they had started in class afraid of Dickens and that long, forbidding novel, but that I had made the book palatable and even enjoyable.

As I studied for my own self-protection as a teacher and taught as a cicerone for my students, I was increasingly aware of the almost shameless way Charles Dickens used any novel he wrote as a kind of vaudeville stage for the exhibition of his unique talents. I used the discovery to good advantage when teaching Chapter 32: Dickens was famous for his scenes of criminal life. The corrupt court of law. The shady lawyer. And especially the debtor's prison with its incredible mix of cutthroats, businessmen gone a little afoul of the law, and near maniacs who had better have been in an asylum.

"Let's look at him as he approaches Chapter 32. He is required to have his hero Pip waste some time prior to the arrival of the coach which will bring his beloved into the city. And I think we can hear Dickens talking to himself: 'Look here! I'm halfway through this novel and haven't yet had a good jail scene. The readers will expect it of me. So let's give them a stout one. Newgate itself! Yes, that's it. We'll have Pip visit Newgate on some pretext or other.'" And off he went, writing at breakneck speed to describe the famous prison, with a potman walking among the prisoners to sell them beer.

Early in the chapter he hits upon the fancy that lawyer's helper Wemmick is much like a gardener walking among his plants. And notice what he does with that simile, he wrestles with it like a dog gnawing at a bone. The jail becomes "Wemmick's greenhouse." On the next page it's Wemmick's conservatory: "You can see that he's having fun with us. He returns to topics he favors, sets a mimicking mood and writes inspired stuff. That's the way to think of Dickens."

But the novel had another influence on me that did not become significant till decades later, when I was myself a novelist. What secret did Dickens pass on to me, mysteriously, unstated, undefined at the time?

I became so identified with *Great Expectations* that I searched about for any information that would help explain the book and what Dickens himself thought of it, and I discovered to my amazement that when he reached the end of the story he was so perplexed as to what the final relationship between Pip and his beloved but unattainable Estella should be that he actually wrote two endings and circulated them to his friends, seeking advice as to which he should use!

Pip Loses His Girl

It was two years more before I saw herself. I had heard of her as leading a most unhappy life, and as being separated from her husband, who had used her with great cruelty, and who had become quite renowned as a compound of pride, brutality, and meanness. I had heard of the death of her husband from an accident consequent on ill-treating a horse, and of her being married again to a Shropshire doctor who, against his interest, had once very manfully interposed on an occasion when he was in professional attendance upon Mr. Drummle, and had witnessed some outrageous treatment of her. I had heard that the Shropshire doctor was not rich, and that they lived on her own personal fortune. I was in England again —in London, and walking along Piccadilly with little Pip—when a servant came running after me to ask would I step back to a lady in a carriage who wished to speak to me. It was a little pony carriage which the lady was driving, and the lady and I looked sadly enough on one another.

"I am greatly changed, I know; but I thought you would like to shake hands with Estella too, Pip. Lift up that pretty child and let me kiss it!" (She supposed the child, I think, to be my child.) I was very glad afterwards to have had the interview; for, in her face and in her voice, and in her touch, she gave me the assurance that suffering had been stronger than Miss Havisham's teaching, and had given her a heart to understand what my heart used to be."

When eminent critics, especially Sir Edward Bulwer-Lytton, austere author of *The Last Days of Pompeii, Rienzi* and half a dozen other bestsellers, urged vehemently that the above ending be thrown out and a better one provided, Dickens followed his advice and came up with this completely different conclusion, a reversal of all he had written before:

Pip Gets His Girl

The freshness of her beauty was indeed gone, but its indescribable majesty and its indescribable charm remained. Those attractions in it, I had seen before; what I had never seen before, was the saddened softened light of the once proud eyes; what I had never felt before, was the friendly touch of the once insensible hand.

We sat down on a bench that was near, and I said, "After so many years, it is strange that we should thus meet again, Estella, here where our first meeting was! Do you often come back?"

"I have never been here since."

"Nor I". . .

"I have often thought of you," said Estella.

"Have you?"

"Of late, very often. There was a long hard time when I kept far from me, the remembrance of what I had thrown away when I was quite ignorant of its worth. But, since my duty has not been incompatible with the admission of that remembrance, I have given it a place in my heart."

"You have always held your place in my heart," I answered.

And we were silent again until she spoke.

"I little thought," said Estella, "That I should take leave of you in taking leave of this spot. I am very glad to do so."

"Glad to part again, Estella? To me, parting is a painful thing. To me, the remembrance of our last parting has been ever mourning and painful."

"But you said to me," returned Estella, very earnestly," 'God bless you, God forgive you!' And if you could say that to me then, you will not hesitate to say that to me now—now, when suffering has been stronger than all other teaching, and has taught me to understand what your heart used to be. I have been bent and broken, but—I hope—into a better shape. Be as considerate and good to me as you were, and tell me we are friends."

"We are friends," said I , rising and bending over her, as she rose from the bench.

"And will continue friends apart," said Estella.

I took her hand in mine, and we went out of the ruined place; and, as the morning mists had risen long ago when I first left the forge, so, the evening mists were rising now, and in all the broad expanse of tranquil light they showed to me, I saw no shadow of another parting from her.

In later years professional critics have tended to prefer the first ending and to dismiss the gentler one as a weak kowtowing to popular taste. George Bernard Shaw was particularly sharp in his rejection: "Sentimental readers who still like all their stories to end at the altar rails may prefer this. They have their choice."

The novel was published with the second ending, a fact which would have a long-lasting influence on me. For as I studied the two endings I concluded with Shaw and those who felt that the balance of this great novel required the bittersweet, gloomy ending that matched the rain-sodden opening scenes in the moors, and I told my students: "Had I been writing the novel I'd have gone with the first ending."

But, when I went back and compared the two, I saw that the first was rather poorly written; there was no movement to the prose; there was no poetry, no warmth. It was arid, the hurried-up ending to a romantic tale, whereas the second version was obviously composed as the capstone to a novel. Time was taken to develop mood and image. A gentleness of emotion was shown between the two leading characters, and, yes, there was a gratifying finish to a compelling story. I could visualize Dickens receiving the adverse reactions of his friends to the first ending and taking an oath: "If they think it's too arid, I'll show them that I can still write with emotion," and he knuckled down and did so.

I have never forgotten the effect of that discovery of how a novelist sometimes works. Dickens, and Tolstoy and Hardy and hundreds like them, listened to their editors and modified the concluding passages of their novels, and if those immortals of the written word could subject themselves to superior criticism, so would I, if I ever became a writer.

I reached that august conclusion during Christmas vacation in 1929, and have adhered to it throughout the subsequent sixty-six years. I do not recommend that every writer listen to his editors and make alterations where consensus cries: "You can find a better ending," but I am relieved to know that many fine writers have listened, and restudied, and redrafted—usually to good effect.

James A. Michener

Drinkwater, John. *The Way of Poetry : An Anthology for Younger Readers.* Boston: Houghton, [^c1922 by Houghton, 1923].

The signature, "James A. Michener." appears in lead pencil and again in red pencil on the front end paper. In pencil, Michener wrote an unsigned poem on the inside front cover titled "Keats & Shakespeare." The many pencil marks in the margins were Michener's method of denoting memorized passages. He diagrammed a chronology of authors in ink and red pencil, which spans the last flyleaf and the inside back cover. The last time interval on the diagram is "1900–1930," which helps date Michener's usage. Michener says he used this book at The Hill.

Michener's Commentary

Michener slowly paged through *The Way of Poetry* and stopped.

"Oh this one. Yeah! I think we taught that the first year."

There was a long pause as he continued to look through the book.

"Hey, that's a lovely little poem" (voice trails off).

He looked at marginal parentheses in pencil at several passages on pages 206 and 207.

"I think those are all the things I memorized."

He turned a few pages and started reading from "Elegy Written in a Country Churchyard":

Full many a gem of
   purest ray serene
The dark unfathom'd
   caves of ocean bear;

He raised his head and with
obvious feeling recited from
memory sixty-four years later:

   Many a flower is born to blush
      unseen
   And (voice breaks) wastes its
      fragrance on the desert air.
   Some mute inglorious Milton
      here may rest,
   Some Cromwell guiltless of
      his country's blood.
   Some village-Hampden, that
      with dauntless breast
   The (with quavering voice)
      little tyrant of his fields
      withstood.

Before 1550	1550 – 1600	1700 – 1800	1800 – 1850
Chaucer Gower ballads romances	Wyatt, Green, Surrey, Marlow, Tichborne, Shakespear Spencer	Pope	Wordsworth Shelley Byron Keats
		1750 Chatterton Blake Goldsmith Gray Burns Moore	Coleridge Landor Hood Campbell Scott Clare Cunningham
1600 – 1650	1650 – 1700	1850 – 1900	1900 – 1930
Campion Marvel Carew Shirley Herbert Shirley Herrick Withery Heywood Wotton Jonson Drummond Lovelace	Milton Vaughan Dryden	Tennyson Browning Morris Rosetti Swineburn Arnold Whitman	109 111

Michener's Chronology Diagram From *The Way of Poetry*

With great emotion he sighed, "Ahhhhh. And that line *echoes in my heart!* But I used to know them all."

He found other favorite poems in the book, recited lines from memory, and ended by exclaiming, "My goodness this was a very good little anthology!"

Keats & Shakespeare by James A. Michener

I

Words tumble in profusion from the minds
That look upon the world's eternity,
And in the motely [sic] of their thought one finds
Harsh, chattering syllables that seem to be
Distorted echoes of the message sent
In prophecy by the omnipotent.

II

But from the welter of these babel sounds
Two voices speak with notes serene & clear—
In their sweet music beauty itself abounds
And all profane confusions disappear.

Edgar, Henry C. *Sentence Analysis by Diagram : A Handbook for the Rapid Review of English Syntax.* New York: Newson, [c1915 by Newson].

"Instructor in English, The Hill School   Pottstown, Pa." is printed below the author's name on the title page. A signature in ink, "J. Michener," appears inside the front cover. Michener says he used this book at The Hill.

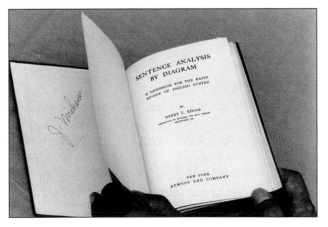

(Joy V. Bliss photo)

Analyzing a Sentence by Diagramming by James A. Michener

The author of this book, Henry C. Edgar, was remembered at The Hill as one of their outstanding teachers of English, and out of respect for him, the English department of which I was a member taught diagramming with more than customary enthusiasm. His book was an able introduction to the subject.

I had never been taught diagramming, had no understanding of what the procedure involved, and certainly no appreciation of how much a young writer could learn if, early in his career, he mastered the analysis of the two or three dozen standard English sentences. When I first saw the intricate patterns in Edgar and realized that I must within a few days explain those diagrams to my students, I panicked, but John Lester, the saintly Quaker who had hired me for the job at Hill, quietly instructed me, over a very long weekend in the mysteries of diagramming—at least the first six easy examples.

Spurred by that fortuitous introduction to the subject, I quickly made myself an expert in breaking down the English sentence, staying two assignments ahead of my students. I'm afraid I became so intrigued by the mathematics of the subject that I assigned my students far more work in sentence structure than they needed, but if they learned little from my excesses, I learned a great deal. My love for the English sentence started with Edgar, for when I completed his tidy little handbook I really understood both the complexities and the niceties of the sentence, of which I would probably write more than a million, counting the rewrites when I did not get the words properly distributed the first time.

If a scholar were to analyze a large number of my sentences, and the worksheets are available, on which I made my corrections, he would quickly note that one of my persistent habits is writing a run-on sentence like: "He hurried into the cellar, and, finding it cold, he knew he must find something to keep him warm." By the time I get to the end my long apprenticeship to the sentence warns me that this one would be more effective if I open it with a subordinate clause, so back I go, strike out the beginning and write: "Since the cellar to which he fled was surprisingly cold, he realized he must find something to keep him warm." Most rambling sentences can be strengthened by converting the first half into the subordinate mode.

If the young people in my classes—and I mean graduate students in their mid-twenties—have a major weakness it is that they often show no sign of having explored the wonders of the English sentence, and those who do exhibit understanding have quite often acquired it from studying Latin. Sentences sometimes ring with clarity like the sounding of a bell on a frosty morning: "Caesar, having built the bridge, crossed over it into Gaul."

It would be impossible, I suppose, to teach diagramming today. Too archaic, too tedious and not visibly of value to the young student, but those of us who explored the sentence form in this manner came away with a sense of structure that many writers today fail to acquire.

James A. Michener

Edwards, Boyd and Isaac Thomas, comp. and ed. *Mr. Rolfe of The Hill.* [Pottstown, Pa.: Hill School (Feroe Press)], [1929?].

This book is a collection of Rolfe poems and essays. Alfred Grosvenor Rolfe was Senior Master at the Hill School. Rolfe gave the book to Michener and autographed it in ink: "Merry Christmas from Alfred G. Rolfe. Dec. 1930."

Michener's Commentary

This book is *Mr. Rolfe of The Hill.* Was that a gift to you?

"Yes it was." Reflecting on his colleague, Michener added: "He was somebody! Wonderful man— 'Freddie' Rolfe."

Michener paused a long time while inspecting the book. When he spoke again, he commented on the publisher: "They were very good people—the Feroe Press people."

Hardy, Thomas. *The Return of the Native.* New York: Modern Library, n.d.

The preface by Hardy is dated July 1895. Michener signed, "J. Michener," in ink on the front end paper and on page 55. He says he used this book at The Hill.

> you've got is a dimant, so says I. Yes,' he continued, :o Grandfer Cantle, raising his voice so as to be heard :hrough the partition; 'her father (inclining his head :owards the inner room) was as good a feller as ever ived. He always had his great indignation ready against anything underhand.'
> ' Is that very dangerous?' said Christian.
> ' And there were few in these parts that were up-sides with him,' said Sam. ' Whenever a club walked te'd play the clarinet in the band that marched sefore 'em as if he'd never touched anything but t clarinet all his life. And then, when they got to :hurch-door he'd throw down the clarinet, mount the gallery, snatch up the bass-viol, and rozum away as if te'd never played anything but a bass-viol. Folk vould say—folk that knowed what a true stave was—
> ' Surely, surely that's never the same man that I zid tandling the clarinet so masterly by now!' "
> ' I can mind it,' said the furze-cutter. ' 'Twas a vonderful thing that one body could hold it all and tever mix the fingering.'
> ' There was Kingsbere church likewise,' Fairway re-ommenced, as one opening a new vein of the same mine if interest.
> Wildeve breathed the breath of one intolerably bored, nd glanced through the partition at the prisoners.
> ' He used to walk over there of a Sunday afternoon o visit his old acquaintance Andrew Brown, the first tarinet there; a good man enough, but rather screechy n his music, if you can mind?'
> ' 'A was.'
> eighbour Yeobright would take Andrey's me part of the service, to let Andrey have tp, as any friend would naturally do.'
> friend would,' said Grandfer Cantle, the ers expressing the same accord by the of nodding their heads.
> 55

Graduate Course by James A. Michener

The other textbooks to which I have appended explanatory notes were all examples of how I educated myself while attempting to educate my students. The relationship was a rich and rewarding one, the kind experienced by thoughtful teachers at every level of the educational system.

But the appearance of this next old book among the Hill texts takes the spotlight away from my students and throws it on me, for with this book and two of its siblings I used my spare time at The Hill to give myself an advanced education.

We beginning masters had an arduous schedule. For seven days a week we rose at seven, policed the large dining room at quarter to eight, taught our five classes through the day, served as assistant coaches on the playing fields and in the gymnasiums, then had to be in our dormitory, in charge of our active, imaginative scholars from nine till seven the next morning. One evening a week we were free to wander down into Pottstown from seven-thirty till eleven.

Actually, this left us blocks of free time, except that we had to be on the school premises, most often in the dormitory room in which we slept, each man in his own cubicle, of course. Throughout history men of all nations and cultures, when faced with empty time—in prisons, or concentration camps, or hunkered down in the Antarctic—have occupied themselves by constructing de facto universities in which they taught one another those basic courses in which they were expert. (I would help do this when idled on a South Pacific island in World War II, and I would write about a group of Englishmen doing it when icebound in the Arctic.)

This tendency to educate myself had manifested itself when I was a child, and now, with free time staring at me, I reverted to custom: I gave myself an intensive, advanced degree on the life of Thomas Hardy. In college I had heard such good reports about this strange man and his contradictory works—great novels, strong poems—that I had resolved that when time allowed I would get to know him.

From a secondhand store I bought the three novels which I had been told summarized his work: *The Return of the Native* (1878), *Tess of the d'Urbervilles* (1891) and *Jude The Obscure* (1895). From inter-library loan, I also obtained a biography and a copy of Somerset Maugham's recently published, *Cakes and Ale*, which was rumored to be a *roman à clef* detailing Hardy's difficult experiences with his wife.

From the opening pages of *Return*, the copy which now mysteriously returns to me, I was enthralled by Egdon Heath and the surrounding Wessex moorland. Hardy had not, as some studies report, invented this wonderfully effective name. He had revived it from the Saxon period of around A.D. 495 when it comprised many present-day counties like Dorset, Somerset and Hampshire, but he converted this ancient land into his own principality. Eustachia Vye cast her spell upon me, and I could identify with her target, Clym Yeobright. I was deeply interested in Diggory Venn, the reddleman, and his charming friend, Thomasin. But I was even more attentive to the way in which Hardy used the natural surroundings of his story; for the first time I realized that a dramatic setting, filled with meaning and overtones, could also be a character in a novel.

Like most young men my age, I fell in love with Tess Durbeyfield, daughter of a penniless village tradesman who learns, belatedly, that he and Tess might be related to their wealthy neighbors, the d'Urbervilles. He forces her to seek out the existing d'Urbervilles in hopes that they will aid her financially. Instead, the son Alec seduces and abandons her. She has comparable bad luck with other men and finally, in desperation, kills one of her betrayers. Her story ends with a religious summary which, because of its curious theology, reverberated around the world: "The President of the Immortals (in the Aeschylean phrase) had ended his sport with Tess." She still lives with me.

The last of the great novels, *Jude,* is an account of a young man much like me who stumbles and is pushed into such a chaos of tragedy, disillusionment and disaster, that I was aghast that a novel could parade such details. But the book had an effect on me of even longer duration than the others, because critics of the time were so repelled by Jude's deportment and the general tenor of the novel that they blasted it in a series of savage reviews. It was the general opinion in 1930 when I studied Hardy, that these destructive reviews caused him to stop writing novels—he certainly wrote no more—and turn to poetry.

When I finally found a book which printed his poetry, it was so far ahead of me in style and content that I summarized my research in one sentence: "The critics destroyed a fine novelist and replaced him with a mediocre poet."

In recent years, as I continue to study a man whose novels influenced my approach to art, I find that both my conclusions have been reversed by modern critics. They say his novels are heavy, too architecturally plotted, and laden with too much sentimental moralizing. But his poetry! They hail it as a harbinger of the future; it could be written and published today; and his ultimate fame will rest upon it, not on his dated novels.

They also prove that Hardy wrote much of this poetry not after the assassination of *Jude*, but years before. And that he did not quit writing novels because of what the critics said about *Jude*. He had given friends hints well before *Jude* was even written, that he would probably give up novel writing and concentrate on poetry.

These modern critics do not convince me. I think Hardy's three great novels are magisterial. I think his poetry does not warrant his inclusion in the noble procession of first-line English poets. And I'm satisfied that he gave up the novel because his last two, *Tess* and *Jude*, had been so excoriated.

I acquired from my intensive study of Hardy two guidelines for my own writing life: pay attention to the physical setting of your story; and never allow the critics to influence you down deep where it might do damage.

James A. Michener

Hawthorne, Nathaniel. *The House of the Seven Gables : A Romance.* Ed. Ernest Rhys. Ordinary ed. London: Dent, n.d.; New York: Dutton, [1907, 1930].

A Hill School student owner, "W. H. Nalty," stamped his name in blue ink inside the front cover, the first fly leaf, and the inside back cover; he also boldly printed his name in pencil on the bottom and fore edges. Michener wrote "End" in pencil on pages 38 and 66. He says he used this book at The Hill.

Hawthorne, Nathaniel. *The House of the Seven Gables: A Romance.* N.p.: Burt, n.d.

This printing of *Seven Gables* is different from that listed above. There are no Michener entries, but he says he used this copy at The Hill.

Hudson, W[illiam]. H[enry]. *Green Mansions: A Romance of the Tropical Forest.* New York: The
   Modern Library, Publishers, n.d.

Michener wrote in pencil "James A. Michener" on the back of the front end
paper. He says he used this book at The Hill.

The Bonus Books by James A. Michener

The unexpected appearance of one title among the textbooks gave me quiet, heart-warming pleasure, for it reminded me of one of the best ideas I ever devised in my teaching. I kept available three or four books which I had bought with my own money to use as bonus delights to reward students who were doing A work and who could read faster and with more comprehension than the average. I wanted them to read the maximum possible to refine their skills, and quietly lent them one of the novels I thought of as my bonus books. They were usually well received.

So when I spotted W. H. Hudson's fine novel, *Green Mansions* (1904), I could visualize my other bonus books and boys-about-to-be-young-men who had profited from them. This was the kind of book which comes along without drum beats or trumpet voluntaries to win a secure place for itself among the readers of that time. Such works lay no claim to long-lasting fame or permanent acceptance, but they win an honorable spot in the affections of those readers who, often by accident, become acquainted with them.

When I was in college (1925–29) a small book in this category reached a wide readership, especially among impressionable males, and left an indelible impression upon us. We never thought Hudson's masterwork a classic, nor did scholars like me expect it to find a place in what was already being termed *the canon*, that is, those books of unquestioned merit that ought to be read by all serious-minded adults and studied by anyone seeking an advanced degree in literature.

Green Mansions was something else, a wonderful fairy-tale novel written by a distinguished British naturalist who had not previously tried his hand at fiction. He devised a tale about a young Venezuelan gentleman of good breeding, Abel Guevez de Argensola, who lives in a kind of exile in Georgetown, the musty capital of British Guiana, in 1887, the time of the novel. This was an enclave not widely known in the rest of the world, but in our day familiar to everyone as Guyana, the remote place to which the demented religious leader, James Jones, hid the members of his religious cult and where he forced them all to drink poisoned Kool-Aid. In his travels through the jungle, Mr. Abel stumbles upon an unlikely adventure: he hears of a young woman of heavenly beauty and elfin-like charm named Rima, who is protected by a village elder named Nuflo, who lives in the jungle accompanied by animals and birds of exotic appeal. It is a love story of great delicacy, but also a depiction of jungle life as described by an expert. It ends in a scene so horrifying that to read it now, decades after the first time, still makes me shudder at the loss of this wonderful girl.

I believe that any young man between the ages of fourteen and twenty-four who reads of Rima without previous preparation or dry explanation will fall in love with her, for she is truly a magical creation, and her story a work of inspired imagination. Within the confines Hudson established for his novel, he wrote an almost perfect book. Young people who missed *Green Mansions* in those years when it first came out missed a work of elegance, vivid imagery, and deep emotional impact, but I am not sure that I would recommend it for today's teen-aged readers. It could be one of those books which had a bright success in its day, then retreated to the library shelves from which an occasional student retrieves it for an exciting historical read. I was careful as to whom I gave it; the boy had to have a free-wheeling imagination and a willingness to surrender himself to the Latin American jungle, but there were such boys, and they prospered from reading *Green Mansions*.

The second bonus book was a haunting tale, as gracious a love story as the 1920s provided. *Precious Bane* (1924) was written by Mary Webb, a determined scribbler from the almost-primitive English county of Shropshire on the Welsh border. She had offered an inattentive public five novels of rural life that sold poorly, and she might have quit trying except that a strange romance had for some years been pestering her so persistently that she had to write it down, almost as a last gasp. It dealt with Prudence Sarn, born of parents with no worldly goods and cursed by an unfeeling brother, Gideon, who treated her abominably and taunted her about never being able to find a husband because she had been born with a hare lip. "Hare-shotten lip," she called it. Her story, told in a heavy Shropshire dialect, tugs at the heart as she is forced to play Venus, the goddess of beauty, by rising stark naked in a display of rural magic. She is allowed to hide her misshapen face, but later, when the community sees her ugliness, the citizens condemn her as a witch and torture her on the ducking stool.

The novel closes with an ending that gained the author the praise for which she had longed. The weaver, Kester Woodseaves, finally sees Prudence for the courageous, adorable woman she has been through all her trials and he decides to marry her:

> "But no!" I said. "It mun be frummet, Kester. (It might be wrong.)
> You mun marry a girl like a lily. See, I be hare-shotten."

> But he wouldna listen. He would not argufy. "No more sad talk! I've chosen my bit of
>   Paradise. "Tis on your breast, my dear acquaintance."

> And when he said those words, he bend his comely head and kissed me full on the mouth.
> *Here ends the story of Prudence Sarn.*

Despite its ingratiating charm, this novel too might have died aborning had not a miracle intervened. Stanley Baldwin, Prime Minister of England, chanced to read the book and fell so under its spell that he wrote a four-page rave review for a later edition, which was so persuasive that readers had to buy a copy. Today, in 1995, it is little read, but in my early days it was a sensation.

Years later, after my return from Europe, I taught at the Quakers' well-regarded George School, like The Hill, in Pennsylvania. In my day it was engaged in educational experimentation, and I taught advanced students who were already reading books customarily reserved for juniors and seniors in college. For the ablest girls in my classes I provided as a bonus book, a wry, witty novel by Margaret Kennedy, an English writer with a style exactly suited to the bizarre household she wished to describe. *The Constant Nymph* (1924) tells of Sanger's Circus, the chaotic menage clustered about an amoral musical genius: "They were known as Sanger's Circus, a nickname earned for them by their wandering existence, their vulgarity, their conspicuous brilliance, the noise they made, and the kind of naphtha-flare genius which illuminated everything they said or did."

This brilliant novel, centered mainly in the Austrian Alps, but also in scattered locales like Florence and Brussels, gradually focuses on Sanger's fourteen-year-old nymph-like, gamin daughter Tessa as she progresses in her irresponsible way into her sixteenth year. Then she falls in love, desperately, with a young English musician, Lewis Dodd, already married to her cousin.

As the Circus moves about the vacation spots of Europe, Tessa grows ever fonder of Dodd, who at first dismisses her as a child. Because of her persistence he recognizes her ethereal quality, abandons his wife, and invites Tessa to leave England and cross the Channel with him. Fearfully seasick, she staggers ashore at Brussels and dies, not yet seventeen.

It was not a book to give a flighty child, but my students were an advanced group, and those who were obviously stable could read of a girl just a bit younger than they with control, perception and enlightenment. They profited from the reading.

For my boy students I had a powerful book I had picked up during my travels on the Continent, Nikolay Gogol's *Taras Bulba* (rewritten and enlarged in 1842). It tells of a heroic Ukrainian Cossack's protracted struggles against the neighboring Poles. It's a sinewy, sometimes brutal story of the kind of warfare that would plague this region for centuries, and anyone who read the novel in those years would have a background of understanding in the decades ahead.

One bonus book which proved popular with girls and boys alike was Edith Wharton's *Ethan Frome* (1911), that excellently crafted short novel about the New England married farmer, Ethan, who falls in love with the hired girl, Mattie, whose life he ruins in a sledding accident. I interrogated my boy students carefully: "Could you imagine yourself in Ethan's situation? At three different stages in his life? At the peaceful beginning of the story? When he crashes the sled? And during that long, terrible aftermath?" We had some penetrating discussions of Ethan.

But with the girl students I was equally inquisitive: "Could you imagine yourself as Mattie, falling in love with a married man? Would you have gone sledding with him? And after the accident, could you have sacrificed your own life to care for the two cripples the way Zeena did?" My students never read in a vacuum if I could prevent it.

My most amusing Bonus Book was one chosen, years later, by a pair of boys who did not normally like reading of any kind. They asked me if they could read *Love Story* by Erich Segal (1970), and since I knew the details of this spectacular popular success, I had to ask: "But why did you wish to read this book? Didn't you find it primarily for women?" and they explained: "But the hero is that keen hockey player, Oliver Barrett. All-Ivy league hockey team twice in a row and maybe this year, too." They did not remember much about Linda Cavilleri, Oliver's Italian girlfriend, except that at the end, she died.

I believe that reading should be not only instructive, monitory and representative of the culture of the period, but also enjoyable. In the most demanding curriculum there should be an interval in which one reads for the joy of it. I remember one time when I reached a hiatus in a very heavy work schedule, and somebody recommended that on a long airplane trip I read *Interview with the Vampire*, that elegant horror book so deftly written by Anne Rice about her lethal trio of New Orleans vampires. A more delightful vacation from arduous work I have rarely encountered.

These textbooks, rising like ghosts from the past, remind me of the principles by which I taught my students and myself, whether in high school, at the college level, or in post-graduate work at places like Harvard and Texas. I wanted my students to test themselves on materials more advanced than they might have chosen for themselves. I wanted them to project themselves into the lives of the characters about whom they were reading. I wanted them constantly to inspect, at the level of their understanding, the great works of the language. And at frequent intervals I wanted them to stop and enjoy themselves.

James A. Michener

Lewis, W. D., ed. *Tennyson's Idylls of the King : The Coming of Arthur : Gareth and Lynette : Lancelot and Elaine : The Holy Grail : Guinevere : The Passing of Arthur.* New York: Merrill, [C1911, 1912 by Merrill].

Michener wrote a longhand poem in ink on the first fly leaf titled "Ode to Tennyson" and signed "J A Michener." He added "Aurelius" and "Uther" in ink on the inside front cover. He drew extensive vertical lines in the margins and extensively underlined the text up to p. 147. And he made the following written comments, which are scattered throughout the book: "how sensual : How Tennyson," "awful," "I think that such a phrase is the most deadening thing imagineable [sic]. It is so rotten it cries aloud!," "what awful rot," "Longfellow," "I'm afraid I prefer the barge of Anna Xristy," and "Ιεσου Χριστωζ." The title page names Lewis as principal of the William Penn High School for girls, Philadelphia.

106   *IDYLLS OF THE KING*

In battle with the love he bare his lord,   245
Had marr'd his face, and mark'd it ere his time.
Another sinning on such heights with one,
The flower of all the west and all the world,
Had been the sleeker for it; but in him
His mood was often like a fiend, and rose   250
And drove him into wastes and solitudes
For agony, who was yet a living soul.
Marr'd as he was, he seem'd the goodliest man
That ever among ladies ate in hall,
And noblest, when she lifted up her eyes.   255
However marr'd, of more than twice her years,
Seam'd with an ancient sword-cut on the cheek,
And bruised and bronzed, she lifted up her eyes
And loved him, with that love which was her doom.

Then the great knight, the darling of the court,   260
Loved of the loveliest, into that rude hall
Stept with all grace, and not with half disdain
Hid under grace, as in a smaller time,
But kindly man moving among his kind.
Whom they with meats and vintage of their best   265
And talk and minstrel melody entertain'd.
And much they ask'd of court and Table Round,
And ever well and readily answer'd he;
But Lancelot, when they glanced at Guinevere,
Suddenly speaking of the wordless man,   270
Heard from the baron that, ten years before,
The heathen caught and reft him of his tongue.
"He learnt and warn'd me of their fierce design

Michener's Commentary

Michener looked over his poem "Ode to Tennyson."

"I don't know—I just got fed up with *Idylls of the King*—I couldn't take anymore. So I not only rejected it, I did something about it!"

We all laughed. The three poems he wrote in the textbooks were criticism. Did he ever think of being a critic?

"No, I took literature very seriously. I would never consider myself a literary critic. I'm not addicted enough to the canon. I'm something else."

Ode to Tennyson
(after teaching him for some time)

The furies play about your whitened head
and drop away in mortal anguish tried,
For they have naught to do with living dead

nor with the ageing many who have sighed
and with old tears bewail'd an ancient past.
not furies touch your pages; life had died

Before it sees your fingertips, and fast
Into the realms of unreality
Your painless, tiring music fades. At last

This old senescence dips into the sea
of your half-tiresome tears and leaves the earth
no richer and no poorer. It would be

Salvation to your soul if honest mirth,
or ugly gentleness, or full-mouthed gales
of laughter played on your white, empty birth,
Giving the passion that retreats & pales.
                    J A Michener

My Failure by James A. Michener

A wave of deep regret floods over me as I see this handsome book, so carefully printed, its lyrical words so carefully explained by notes from some earnest Philadelphia high school teacher. It occasions this mournful reaction because it represents one of my first deplorable failures as a teacher.

I was required by The Hill syllabus to teach Alfred Lord Tennyson's *Idylls of the King,* it having been decided by both the faculty and the Board of Trustees that the noble ideals exemplified in the *Idylls* were those that a school like ours should inculcate in the bosoms of the untamed young men we had in our care. It was hoped that they would come out of such a class with a sense of nobility, integrity and moral purity. We had learned that our graduates who had done well in *Idylls of the King* also tended to do well in Princeton, Yale and Harvard while those who did poorly also did poorly in lesser colleges like Cornell, Brown and Penn. I was determined that my boys should master the *Idylls* and adopt them as life patterns.

But even before class started, I was aware that I was not adequately prepared to teach the revered verses of Lord Tennyson, so I did what I had always done in high school and college when faced by an intellectual challenge, and would continue to do through my life: I dug down and gave myself an intensive graduate course of Tennyson, a poet I had missed both in school and college. I read the *Idylls*, analyzing each passage as I went. I searched out the major criticisms, and read two biographies of the great poet, whose reputation in 1930 stood almost at its apex.

I found to my surprise, and perhaps disappointment, that I could generate no sympathy for Tennyson, whom I disliked as a man, nor for his poems, which I felt to be the work of a minor poet. At the end of my enforced education, I realized with some dismay that I would start my forthcoming class ill prepared for the job of instructing my young firebrands in the glories of knighthood and the adventures of the Arthurian court.

Apparently my distaste for Tennyson and his cardboard figures betrayed itself to my students because we had not got far into the course before it was apparent that they were not going to acquire from their reading of the *Idylls* what they were supposed to get, and would have got had they had an inspired master who had a feeling for turrets, gonfalons and jousts. I was not qualified to lead them into those elysian fields. In my notes to an earlier book, not represented in the cache found among the treasures by the people in Albuquerque, I explain how I sought permission from the school authorities to junk the *Idylls* and take my sneering boys into the real-life terrors of Antarctica.

What is important now, as we bid an almost scornful farewell to Tennyson, is his effect on me in later years. In the winter of either 1930 or 1931, I penned the *Ode* that I copied onto one of the book's blank pages, and it well expresses my feelings at that moment, but sometime later John Lester, the head of our English department and the man who had brought me to Hill, told me that he feared I had undervalued Tennyson, and that he, Lester, judged the long poem, *Locksley Hall*, to be not only a sensitive evaluation of modern society but also one of the finest explorations of how a young man faces, or ought to face, life. He advised me to study it carefully, not adding that he suspected I might be in need of just such a poem.

I followed his advice, and soon I was immersed in those impassioned, explosive, and alluring fifteen-syllable lines. I would, for many years as I traveled backwaters of the world, find myself chanting almost defiantly:

Comrades, leave me here a little, while as yet 'tis early morn;
Leave me here, and when you want me, sound upon the bugle-horn. …

As I read on, I found that Dr. Lester was correct, this was a poem which spoke with force and insight to young men of my age, and had special merit because of its capacity to look far beyond the obvious present, and in that aspect Tennyson spoke particularly to me, for I too speculated constantly about the future:

For I dipt into the future, far as human eye could see,
Saw the Vision of the world, and all the wonder that would be;
Saw the heavens filled with commerce, argosies of magic sails,
Pilots of the purple twilight, dropping down with costly bales;
Heard the heavens fill with shouting, and there rain'd a ghastly dew
From the nations' airy navies grappling in the central blue; …

Did I, as I pondered these prophetic lines, suspect that within the decade I would be a member of America's "airy navy" grappling with Japan "In the central blue?" How powerfully he spoke to me!

But I could accompany Tennyson only so far, for even at that early date I was repelled by the insinuations of his closing couplets which scorn the defeatism of his young hero who decides, broken-hearted, to flee England and settle in Asia where: "I will take some savage woman, she shall rear my dusky race." And the dreadful, condemnatory line near the end, when he comes to his senses and comes home to England: "Better fifty years of Europe than a cycle of Cathay."

I was about to spend years in the South Pacific tracking European and American men who as beachcombers had "taken some savage woman" who had reared the dusky offspring. I too was destined to marry a woman of a different color, and as for "fifty years of Europe" being superior to "a cycle of Cathay," I would be a principal witness of both the rise of Japan to a position of world leadership and the simultaneous decline of much of Europe.

I cherish *Locksley Hall* for what it says to young men; I reject most of its later ideas, but I know I would have cheated if I had not read it and memorized much of it.

And then, when I was in my seventies, much traveled and weary, a literate neighbor said: "When I see you I'm reminded of that wonderful poem by Tennyson."

"What could that be?"

"*Ulysses.*"

"Never heard of it," and had long had a copy at hand, which he read to me, and for the first time I heard those words which so perfectly summarized my life. I will not quote them here, they're a personal message between Tennyson and me, but they're worth looking into.

How strange that this poet, whom I rejected with such venom, should have worked his way back into my life with a poem I needed at age twenty-three and another appropriate for seventy-three! I think the lesson of this is that if I had not been of such strong and individual judgment as to reject Tennyson in the *Idylls* I might not have been sensitive enough to accept him in *Locksley Hall* and *Ulysses.*

Linn, James Weber, ed. *A Tale of Two Cities by Charles Dickens.* Boston: Ginn (The Athenæum Press), [^c1906 by Ginn].

Michener signed the book in ink inside the front cover: "J. Michener." He says he used this book at The Hill.

Michener's Commentary

Do Michener's favorite authors and poets tend to be twentieth century or classical?

"I follow contemporary writing as well as I can, and when I get a vacation I might grab five or six books and read them to catch up. But I was educated in a classical vein. I never back off on that."

Does he feel that a classical background is important?

"I'm not sure it is for everybody. But for some of us who have the great sweep of human life in our cameras, I guess you need something more."

Do classical authors offer him some forms or solutions to writing that are valuable?

"I think what they offer to me is accrued knowledge that has been built up around them."

Miller, George Morey, ed. *The Victorian Period.* New York: Scribner's, [^c1930 by Scribner's].

Two of the front end papers are inscribed in ink: "John J. Weinberger : Hill School : March 20, 1931." Michener added marginal pencil marks for passages he memorized. He used this book at The Hill.

Reynolds, George F. and Garland Greever. *The Facts and Backgrounds of Literature : English and American.* New York: Century, 1920 [^c1920 by Century].

His bookplate, printed "Ex Libris : James Michener," is tipped in inside the front cover. He printed his name in pencil in an uneven hand on the fore edge: "DHS MICHENER"; the initials stand for Doylestown High School. Michener made many marginal marks in ink including the underlining of his initials, the

JAM portion of "J. A. M. Whistler" on p. 303. Michener's brief notes in ink are scattered throughout the book: "Drama—See P. 46," "Painter's-Pallace[sic] of Pleasure : Hollinshed's-Chronicles : Plutarch's-lives," "Cont. on 64," "Cont on 65," "American Tragedy" written in after Dreiser's play, *The Genius*, and "and Hayley."

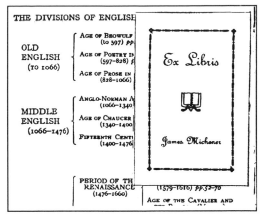

Michener's Bookplate From
The Facts and Backgrounds of Literature

Michener's Commentary

When asked about the pre-printed personalized bookplate in *The Facts and Backgrounds of Literature*, Michener answered: "I had that printed up in college, and it appeared in quite a few hundred books. And I would have kept it [Reynolds] with me as a handbook."

Shakespeare, William. *The Merry Wives of Windsor.* Ed. Fred P. Emery. New York: Macmillan, 1928 [^C1913 By Macmillan].

Michener inscribed an untitled poem in ink on the inside front cover; there is no evidence of rewriting. The text contains margin marks and underlining in ink; there are notes in Michener's hand on pages 75, 76, and 78. He wrote on the last fly leaf: "1. Host of Garter [Inn]. : 2. Arrangements for the elopement. : 3. Herne's Oak. : 4. [left blank]." The end papers are illustrated with scenes from old England; Michener traced in ink some of the scenes' figures. While looking at this with Michener, we asked him if he was a doodler; he said, "No." This was the only doodle found in these textbooks. Michener says he used this book at The Hill.

[Untitled] by James A. Michener

Many a time my sides have ached
From laughing at this foolishness,
But still there's something wild and gay,
And ever new and ever fine.

Michener's Commentary

You apparently enjoyed *The Merry Wives* judging from the words you chose for your poem?

"Right. Yeah. (Reflective pause). I liked that very much. I've always written poetry at a rather sophomoric level, but I read a great deal of it because I just love the rhythms of the English language. Memorized a lot of it."

Does it have the musical content that you like?

"Yep. My poetry certainly influenced my prose."

How?

"The balance and the conciseness and the way they can express things so beautifully."

Reading Should Be Fun by James A. Michener

The last of the books to which I add my notes illustrates that reading should also be fun. Few English classes have had more fun than mine did at The Hill when we studied *The Merry Wives of Windsor* together and laughed at the way in which Mistress Ford and Mistress Page bamboozled lecherous Sir John Falstaff into dressing like a woman and subjecting himself to all kinds of insults.

I must have taught that class in 1931, and I cannot vouch for what my students learned except that Shakespeare could be rowdy when he wished. But I learned something that saved me later from making a Falstaff-like ass of myself. I was engaged in a public brawl with Dr. Albert C. Barnes, the irascible art fancier in suburban Philadelphia who had a multi-million-dollar collection of French impressionist paintings which he would allow few to see. By what I deemed a clever ruse, I sneaked in to his mansion disguised as a coal miner from Pittsburgh. Unfortunately he learned about my deception and declared war on me.

At the height of our imbroglio, he commissioned one of his henchmen to visit me with the proposal that he, the henchman, would take me to his mother, who served as charlady at the Barnes mansion, and she would dress me in woman's clothes so that I could pass as her helper and thus weasel my way back into the forbidden mansion. Of course, Barnes would be lying in wait and when I appeared in drag, he would burst forth with a bevy of Philadelphia cameramen to photograph me in my folly.

I listened attentively as the henchman developed the strategy, then typed out a note for the Doctor: "I read *Falstaff* years ago. Think up something original. See you in your museum one of these days." Then he really mounted a vendetta against me, so furious that in the end I had to beg for mercy. But Falstaff didn't win all his battles either.

That's why teaching and reading and living with the old tales can be so much fun. I'm glad someone rescued these antique books.

James A. Michener

Tatlock, John S. P., and Percy MacKaye. *The Complete Poetical Works of Geoffrey Chaucer : Now Put Into Modern English.* New York: Macmillan (Norwood), 1923 [C1912, By Macmillan].

In this book, Michener signed just "Michener" in ink on the inside front cover and wrote "Line 1761- : 3042" on the inside back cover. He says he used this book at The Hill.

THE GEORGE SCHOOL TEACHING YEARS: 1933–1936

Securing A Teaching Position

After leaving Hill School in the spring of 1931, Michener lived, roamed, and studied in Europe for two years on a Lippincott Traveling Fellowship.[1] By his own account, this was an eye- and mind-opening experience.[2] He saw the new political movements in Europe that ultimately led to World War II in which he eventually played a part. As he traveled, he also experienced the art, music, and literature of Europe. Importantly, he was not greatly affected by the hard depression felt in the United States.[3] The freedom and travel of those two years mirrored his future career.

In 1933, before his Fellowship came to a close, Michener sought employment in the United States. He applied to George School, a private Quaker high school, by letter dated January 15, 1933. He stated his educational qualifications and added, "My letter to you is not a feeler, but an application for a job on your force."[4]

Mr. Walton, Head of School, acknowledged receipt of Michener's letter and said an English vacancy was unlikely but a history position was probable.[5] Walton would contact Michener's references, including Dr. John Lester, but wished to know why Michener wanted a Quaker school. Sensing success, Michener quickly replied by cable from Scotland that he was "anxious to join you am working in American history at present."[6] Two days later, to fulfill Walton's earlier request about his interest in a Quaker school, Michener wrote a full letter of reply in which he summarized his Quaker past (graduating from Swarthmore and rejoining the Friends Meeting there), mentioned his acquaintanceship with George School while growing up in neighboring Doylestown, and confided that he wanted "to live in Friendly circles."[7]

Writing to Michener in Scotland, Walton acknowledged both

> End Cottage
> Boarhills, Fife
> January 15, 1933
>
> Mr. George Walton, M.A.
> George School
> Newtown, Pa.
>
> Dear Mr. Walton,
>
> I am a graduate of Swarthmore College, Class of '29, studying at present in St. Andrews University, Scotland, and I am writing to you to apply for a teaching position.
>
> I graduated with Highest Honours from Swarthmore, in English and History, and taught for two years at The Hill School, under James Wendell and Dr John Lester. After that I came here for a year's work in English, during which year I was awarded a fellowship from Swarthmore.
>
> I am a Quaker and orginally lived in Doylestown. I have, of course, close knowledge of your school, and no doubt many of the people at present with you, or recently removed, have a close knowledge of me.
>
> I think I am qualified to teach either History or English, and I am pretty certain of the English. I have had experience with young people, and have coached athletic teams. In Swarthmore I played basketball, and at Hill I coached football and baseball. In Scotland I have been playing rugby and cricket.
>
> For references I refer you to Dean Walters, now of Cincinnati; to Drs. Spiller and Hicks of the Swarthmore English Department; to the men at Hill; to Sir James Irvine and Professor George Duncan here, and to your own Dr. Miller.
>
> I resigned from Hill, after a good rise in salary, and have reason to believe that I could return when a vacancy occurred, but I would greatly prefer, almost to exclusion, work in a Quaker school.
>
> My letter to you is not a feeler, but an application for a job on your force. I hope that it will be possible for me to get it.
>
> Sincerely,
> James A. Michener
> James Albert Michener

Application for Employment at George School

Michener's cable and full reply, and stated he was delaying the final decision on the position at George School until late May or early June. Mentioning that three other members of the Society of Friends were also vying for an appointment, he asked Michener for his "reaction to the plan for improving secondary education through a new type of cooperation of school and college, as proposed by the Progressive Education Association in the enclosed clipping."[8] George School's membership in this association points out how liberal the school was towards implementing new ideas in education. Michener became a member of the Progressive Education Association while at George School,[9] because the chance to develop new ideas in teaching appealed to him. It still does.[10]

In a detailed five-page typed letter, Michener replied to Walton's request for comments on improving secondary education. He stated his views on advanced education: "Student and teacher [must be] aware of direction in their work. This direction—and not the individual classes—is the important thing. ... The significant weakness of the Swarthmore [Honors] plan was that it tried to arrive at no reasonable synthesis; the correlation was lacking. ... However, both at Hill and at Swarthmore, I was practically convinced that it is unwise to inflict all subjects on all students. ... I approve of fitting a small number of students for a career of scholarship. ... I don't think students with high Intelligence Quotients should be rewarded in any way but by being allowed to do more work than the others. My lasting impression of my work at Hill is this: that it's more dangerous to hold back a brain than it is to invite it forward. The corollary of this self-obvious theorem is that able students should be allowed to do all the work they are so eager to do, but always with a clearly outlined direction in mind."[11] He then summarized his qualifications for teaching. Three days later he sent Walton his summer plan.[12]

On April 10, 1933, at Michener's request, Dr. John Lester of Hill School sent Walton a letter recommending Michener for the teaching position. It was a glowing endorsement. In part Lester wrote: "Jimmie's forte is with the better minds in our schools, and while he was here I placed him in charge of our honor divisions in the lower school. Here he did excellent work, and in fact fitted in extremely well. ... He is personally an interesting and charming lad and I became very fond of him while we were working together."[13]

Walton wrote to Dr. Lester and described the four Friends candidates for the George School position including Michener; he asked Lester's opinion of Michener. Walton: "Our committee went over the [Michener] correspondence last night. One of them called him a humanist, not fully sympathetic with the religious ideals of

---

End Cottage
Boarhills, Fife
February 24, 1933

Mr. George Walton
George School
Newtown, Pa.

Dear Mr. Walton,

I want to teach in a Quaker school because I am a Quaker, both by birth and by conviction. My parents, through moving into a non-Quaker district, became practising Presbyterians, but while at Swarthmore I rejoined the Friends Meeting.

I prefer Quaker schools because I've had the opportunity of seeing several systems in operation, and have found none that betters the Friendly ideal of education. I prefer teaching in a residential school because I like the life of an educational circle.

I had an excellent four years at Swarthmore, making the friendships I now wish to resume. I want to live in Friendly circles, and, if marriage is an economic possibility within the next few years, to make a home in the same surroundings,

George School is naturally attractive to me, since I have been acquainted with it from my school days in Doylestown. My brother played against your teams when I was just starting sports, and I accompanied him frequently to Newtown. Later on, of course, Twining was there, and when I reached Swarthmore, I was in constant touch with George School graduates.

Finally, I am an ardent alumnus of Swarthmore; the college was admirably good to me in many ways, and I know that its good points are strangely the property of Quaker ideals. Dean Walters, when I last saw him, reassured me as to this idea of mine, and after being in Europe for two years, the belief has grown even stronger.

Sincerely yours,

James A. Michener

Reasons for Requesting a Job at a Quaker School

End Cottage, Boarhills
April 14¾ 1933

Dear Mr. Walton,

I've been seeing my professor and am now able to advise you as to my plans for the next few months. I am at present living near St. Andrews and attending the university. I shall stay here definitely until I hear from you. Then I shall go to the British Museum in London until the first of June.

After that I hope to travel to Germany, thence to Italy and back to a French seaport, boarding a vessel for home about the third or fourth of August.

If it is either necessary or advisable for me to return to America sooner, I can leave here the first week in June. At your discretion, I have permission to leave my work at the university immediately, go to America and return for the summer months. This latter course naturally entails expense; but very little inconvenience. I shall be only too glad to cross, if it will enhance my opportunities of teaching at George School next year.

In speaking with my professor, I discussed work at George School, and we came to the conclusion that you would be doing your students much good if, in the last year, or the last semester of the last year, you gave either:

a. a short course, with textbook and magazine-newspaper work, on "The State of Europe since 1918"

b. or a series of lectures, with maps, on the same subject.

I suggest the latter merely because I know how crowded the last year is; but on the other hand, the good students will by that time have acquired their college entrance credits, and will also have probably satisfied the faculty as to their right to graduate, so that such an addition might possibly entail no hardship.

That it would do a lot of good seems obvious, and if either of the alternatives can be fitted into your system of work, I recommend it to very heartily. Such a course might be made quite vital.

Yours,

James A. Michener

Michener's 1933 Summer Plans

Friends. Is this the true reading of him as thee knew him during his days at the Hill School? … We were all impressed by his superior mentality. Is he well balanced?"[14] Walton's daughter had known Michener at Swarthmore, and she wondered why he should be hired.

Walton also asked The Hill headmaster, James I. Wendell, for his opinion of Michener and received this swift response: "Frankly, I think you will make no mistake in taking him."[15]

However, Dr. Lester's reply of May 22, was a non-endorsement of Michener, which strongly contrasted with his endorsement six weeks earlier. Lester: "To be quite frank, I cannot see Jimmie in the position that you are trying to fill."[16]

Michener, still in Scotland, secured the George School English Department position in late May 1933 in spite of Lester. He wrote a happy undated letter to Headmaster Wendell at The Hill, mentioning Walton's cable of acceptance. He thanked Wendell for discussing his qualifications with Walton and added: "I hope to see you when I return in the fall, and I thank you again for your assistance in the difficult task of getting a job."[17]

In 1994 we sent Michener a copy of John Lester's letter of non-support for a possible explanation. After reading it for the first time, he wrote: "You astound me! Never heard of this about-face, but Lester was a convinced Quaker and may have felt that a job in a Quaker school ought to be reserved for young men who had made a similar commitment. The existence of this letter, in the depth of the depression when it would have been easy for George School to drop me and hire a real Quaker, is a major discovery. George School showed courage in sticking with me, and I pray they never regretted the decision."[18]

THE HILL SCHOOL
POTTSTOWN, PENNSYLVANIA

DEPARTMENT OF GUIDANCE
JOHN A. LESTER, PH. D., DIRECTOR

May 22, 1933

Dear George:

This is an answer to thy letter of May 18th. Before I proceed I want to tell thee that C. D. Mendenhall has been elected for membership on the Committee of Tests and Measurements of the Educational Records Bureau, and it will be a great pleasure to me to welcome him on that committee when it meets early next year.

I want to be completely frank and helpful if I can with regard to the substance of thy letter. Jimmie Michener's main interests are intellectual. He played basketball; he was an incentive to a certain group of boys of similar type of mind. His strong point would be in working with a group of able boys. On the other hand Jimmie is not a person to make any Quaker contribution to the new curriculum. I think that member of thy committee who called him a humanist was right; and at the same time I think that thy daughter's comment, while acute and penetrating, would not quite be just of the Jimmie of today. He has undoubtedly made growth. To be quite frank, I cannot see Jimmie in the position that you are trying to fill. It is one of very great importance in view of the service that Quaker schools may be able to do in the next ten years. I cannot, then, say that Jimmie is just the man for you, and I shall be very much interested if thee has a chance to have a personal interview with Herbert Abraham.

If I can help further please let me know.

Thy friend sincerely,

John A. Lester

George A. Walton, Principal,
    George School,
        George School P.O., Pa.
JAL:S

John Lester's Non-endorsement of Michener

George School

George School was built on verdant farm land south of Newtown, Pennsylvania. The funds for the school came from the will of Hicksite Quaker, John Malin George (1802–1887).[19] To promulgate their values, the Hicksite Quakers established Swarthmore first and George School second, both in rural settings. Both schools offered guarded education that demonstrated and implemented Quaker ideals including daily services in a Meeting House. After six years of planning, fund raising, and constructing the first building, called "Main," George School opened for inspection as a private high school on August 18, 1893.[20] Unlike The Hill, George School admits male and female students. George School and Swarthmore have the same motto: "Mind the Light."

"Main" as It Appears Today (Joy V. Bliss photo)

The school grew on its 227 wooded acres under the leadership of heads of school George Maris (1893–1901) and Joseph Walton (1901–1912). George A. Walton, son of Joseph, led the school from 1912 to 1948,[21] a span that includes Michener's three teaching years. Student board and tuition costs during Michener's tenure were $700 per year.[22] Enrollment had risen to 327 in 1933; the largest Senior class in its 40-year history graduated—136. Michener's starting salary during the depression was $1200.[23] Athletics always played a part in a day at George School. Space and facilities were ample. From the inception of an athletic program at George School until the present day, the subject of competitive sports, and whether they are in tune with noncompetitive Quaker ideals, has been weighed pro and con.[24]

As they were 100 years ago, meals are served in Main. Michener ate there, since "board" was part of his compensation. We ate lunch in old Main, the original 1893 building; it serves as a constant reminder of long service. This atmospheric legacy exists because George School, unlike The Hill and Swarthmore, has been fortunate indeed to have escaped major fires. Students and faculty have always eaten their meals together but in a way different from that practiced at Hill School. Students have no seating assignments; the atmosphere is relaxed and enthusiastic; and the dress code, casual.

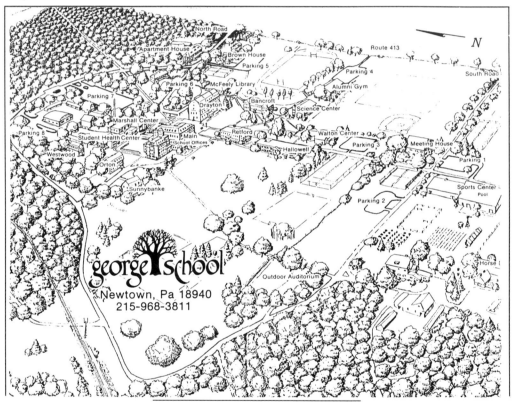

George School Campus Today

Michener taught English IV in Bancroft Hall[25] (see the above map). Near Bancroft Hall is the library, named after Richard H. McFeely, successor to Walton and Head of School from 1948–1966.[26] McFeely, also from Swarthmore College, taught history at George School during Michener's years there.

The 1993–94 enrollment was 528, of which 15 percent were Quaker and 10 percent were foreign nationals, evidence of the strong humanitarian outreach programs sponsored at George School.[27] Since 1978, The Head of School has been David Bourns.

Bancroft Hall Today (Joy V. Bliss photo)

Teaching and Learning at George School

1933–1934 School Year

Michener's presence on campus in the fall of 1933 and his position in the English Department were announced on page one of the opening number of the school newspaper, *George School News*.[28] Not only was he mentioned first in the list of new faculty, but a second front page article announced that he had written the play "Phiz the Whiz." Herbert Abraham, also a new faculty member, was one of the Friends vying with Michener for a George School position and the applicant recommended highly by John Lester of The Hill. Abraham got the history teaching job Walton had originally suggested for Michener.

In addition to his teaching position, Michener was one of a staff of five men in charge of a dormitory of one hundred boys where his influence was strong.[29]

Judging from the number and content of Michener news items in the *George School News* over the next three years, he returned from Europe with a much broader perspective and was a more active teacher than he had been at The Hill. We asked Mr. Michener what difference time had made. He said, "When I got back to George School, I was on a whole new kick. I would say that the shift from Hill School to George School with the two-year break in there was almost ordained. ... I don't think I would ever [have] become part of the Hill hierarchy   at George School I would have. Oh, no, George School was a revelation!—run by Quakers, half the committee women, very liberal, very avant-garde, even though Pennsylvania conservative. Strange school—I enjoyed it. But, I'm not saying it was more important to me than Hill School was—because of what I did for myself at Hill School. I might have been a very shallow person had I gone right to George School." He mused softly, "Might have been."[30]

Micelli Marionettes

The marionette partnership of James Michener and William Vitarelli, the intern in industrial arts who was mentioned in the "Phiz the Whiz" news article, lasted at least through Michener's first two George School years, and their close association continued later in life.[31] Besides manual training instruction, Vitarelli started a puppet making and performing club—the Marionette Guild. He also contributed at faculty musical functions, built some of the sets for student and faculty plays, and was assistant track coach. Michener helped with the construction of the marionettes and the performances. They formed the Miccelli (or Micelli) Marionettes, the name being derived from Michener plus Vitarelli and variously spelled with one or two c's. George School still stores one of their large marionette stages.[32]

In December, the *George School News* announced "A Midsummer Night's Dream" as a forthcoming production of the Marionette Guild.[33] Michener contributed the script. He also wrote the scripts for the spring marionette shows. For the spring 1934 show, in addition to three scenes from Shakespeare, the evening's entertainment included a fairy tale in verse, "The Princess Who Could Not Dream," written by Michener.[34]

VITARELLI STARS IN FACULTY PLAY "PHIZ THE WHIZ"

Three Moorestown Musicians Give Instrumental and Vocal Selections

"Phiz the Whiz," a two-act play, presented by a group of three faculty, and musical selections by members of the Moorestown Men's Glee Club comprised the program on Saturday evening.

"Phiz the Whiz," written by James Michener, English instructor, included William Vitarelli as "Phiz," the scientist who seeks to destroy crooners; Mildred E. Maxfield, as "Celia," the scientist's daughter, and the author as "Larry," the reporter who tries to get a story on the scientist's invention.

Representing the Moorestown Glee Club were Joseph Conway, marimba artist; Prescott Herr, '22, baritone, and Mary Martin, pianist. Selections by Mr. Conway included "I Love You Truly," "Mighty Like A Rose," and "Love's Old Sweet Song." Mr. Herr sang among others, "The Two Grenadiers," "Little Coon's Prayer," and by request "Chloe," and "On the Road to Mandalay." Both artists were accompanied by Miss Martin.

George School News,
October 11, 1933

STUDENT GROUP PLANS TO STAGE MARIONETTES

Mr. Vitarelli and Mr. Michener Aid in Work on "Miles Standish"

A marionette show, "The Courtship of Miles Standish," is to be presented by a group that has been chosen by William Vitarelli, interne in manual training, and James A. Michener, English instructor, sometime before Christmas.

The group that is presenting the production has had one meeting in which they named the following positions:
Setting and Staging: Donald Rockwell, '35.
Puppet Making and Manipulating: John Alexander, '35, John Price, '35, Alfred Moon, '35.
Dialogue Revision: Alfred Moon, '35, John Alexander, '35.
Scenery: Jean Price.
Costuming: Margie Pirman, Mr. Michener and Mr. Vitarelli will advise and assist all the departments.

George School News,
October 18, 1933

TWELVE ADDITIONS MADE TO FACULTY THIS YEAR

Dietitian and Assistant to Dean of Girls Among Newcomers

James A. Michener, A. B. (Swarthmore) teaches Junior and Senior English. This position was held formerly by Margaret A. Gist.

Herbert J. Abraham, A. M. (Oxford) is instructing American history and international relations in the place of Henry Burnell Shafer.

Elisabeth M. Harvey, A. B. (Goucher) teaches mathematics and history, and Anna P. Gullette, A. B. teaches history and general language.

Mary Jane Anderson, B. S. M. (Oberlin) has taken the directorship of music, which was held previously by Clees McKray.

M. Elizabeth Maxfield, A. B. (Swarthmore) is executive secretary and teaches a class in second year French.

Felicia Anderson, Columbia, Mo., fills the place of dietitian, vacated by Jessie Middaugh.

Mrs. Jo Wilder Abraham, assistant dean of girls, will act as Miss Allen's aide in matter of discipline and hospitality.

Stevenson W. Fletcher, Penn State, B. S., on interne here last year, teaches general mathematics and 1st and 2nd year algebra.

The internes are as follows: Rees J. Frescoln, Jr. (English); Eleanor E. Jones (history); Charles P. Rogers (mathematics), and William Vitarelli (manual training).

George School News,
October 13, 1933

MARIONETTE GUILD BEGUN

A marionette guild is being formed by James A. Michener and William Vitarelli, and as soon as perfection is attained by this guild, the play, "A Midsummer Night's Dream," will be presented at George School.

The construction of the marionettes themselves is being done by John Alexander, John Price, and Edgar Alexander. Marjory Pirman, dressmaking; Jean Price and Fritz Rockwell, scenery and settings; while Mr. Michener has the literary side, and Mr. Vitarelli supervises all construction and manipulations. Staging and lighting is done by Tom Sharples, John Alexander, John Broomall.

Any one interested in constructing marionettes may join the guild.

George School News,
December 14, 1933

The George School Marionette Club Rehearsal with Michener at Center Stage (George School photo)

The 1934 school annual, published at the end of Michener's first year of teaching at George School, included a faculty panorama photograph taken at the front entrance to Main and listed Michener as an English teacher.[35] The Miccelli Marionettes received accolades: "This clever group of students and teachers achieved such a high

Hobby Groups Active During Year

The Micelli Marionettes, directed by James A. Michener, teacher of English, and William Vitarelli, interne in manual training, have delighted the school audience with several splendid productions. On March 17th they presented "A Midsummer Night's Dream"; on April 28th, particularly for the Progressive Education Conference meeting at school that day, an original play by Mr. Michener, "The Princess Who Could Not Dream"; and on June 2nd, a six-part program, including "The Princess," a marionette orchestra, and a play by Carolyn Groves, '35, "Hard Times in Heaven." Over forty students have assisted in making the puppets, working back stage, and speaking the lines. Special mention should be made of the unusually excellent and effective stage sets used and of the careful artistry of each of the productions.

Another interesting and active hobby group has been that in local history, under the leadership of Walter H. Mohr, head of the history department. In addition to the more obvious study of the early development of the community, the assemblying of scrap books, and the like, they unearthed an old cocoonery in the nearby woods and had the experience of real pioneers in examining its curiosities.

***George School Bulletin*, June 1934**

MICCELLI MARIONETTES IN SHAKESPEAREAN SCENES

Jean McVaugh and Barbara Wetzel to Produce Original Drama

The Miccelli marionettes will present a varied program either some Saturday night or as an informal Friday night entertainment during the spring term, according to James A. Michener, instructor in English. They will give three scenes from Shakespeare: the Village Scene from "Midsummer Night's Dream", the Balcony Scene from "Romeo and Juliet", and the Drinking Scene from "Twelfth Night". Students are carving and dressing the puppets, painting and staging the sets.

Also an original fable written by Jean McVaugh will be produced entirely by students with no faculty participation. Barbara Wetzel will probably direct.

A fairy tale in verse, "The Princess Who Could Not Dream", by James A. Michener, instructor in English, is being prepared for presentation at that time.

***George School News*
April 12, 1934**

degree of success that a professional puppetress [sic], upon seeing their work, remarked that they were the best marionettes he had ever seen in a high school. This group is seriously considering making a tour to Cape May [New Jersey] during the [Friends] Conference this year."[36] Sanctioned hobbies were also described in the Annual: "The Friday night hobbies consist of: … Marionettes—sponsors, James A. Michener, William Vitarelli."[37] Even the alumni publication, *George School Bulletin : The Georgian*, in June 1934, contained an article about the Micelli Marionettes performances for the school year and pictured Michener and the students making puppets.[38]

Sharing Memories

In Scotland studying at St. Andrews, Michener hiked across the country more than once. As he hiked, he photographed the countryside. Twice, the *George School News* reported the ways he used knowledge gained in Scotland on his return to

*Mr. Michener Possesses Collection
Of Old English, Scottish Ballads*

The Bowdoin College Library

First, he shared what he had learned about Scottish music. A long article described [musi]cian, and sociologist who collected a large number of Gaelic ballad records that [...] tribal legends of 13th century Scotland. These ballads, which he used in the [...]d the basis for essays he had written for the *Glasgow Herald*.[39] Second, the *News* [...] photographs he had taken of Scottish moors, locks, and glens to help describe for the [...]tures in Scotland.[40]

[...]r reported another talk given by Michener but on a different topic; he was a lecturer [...]nia, where he spoke on "Boyhood Along the Delaware."[41]

Sports

Sports were, and still are, an important part of training and energy release at George School. Michener participated in numerous ways. He was a representative to the Eastern Board of Basketball Coaches.[42] He and Stevenson Fletcher were assistant basketball coaches in charge of the two training tables during meals in Main.[43]

Michener also played on the faculty basketball team with great success; he was high scorer with 21 points in a February 1934 game. The faculty consistently beat the varsity team during the year.[44] He participated in other sports. As George School Cubs baseball coach, he chose the team for the 1933–34 season.[45]

Tennis was a sports activity for Michener as well; however in the spring of 1934, the *George School News* printed an article announcing that James A. Michener, English instructor, was recovering from back strain from a tennis match and was back in classes after five days but was still spending evenings recovering in the school infirmary.[46]

Literary

The last issue of the *George School News* for the school year lists Michener as a guest at a picnic and advisor for the newly appointed *News* editor for the coming year.[47] The intended activities of the teachers during the coming summer were also described in the issue; Michener was staying at George School to teach English classes.[48]

When asked if he produced literary publications at George School similar to the Christmas issues his classes published at The Hill, Michener said: "No. George School didn't really require it. They had a much more liberal curriculum."[49]

Summer 1934

According to the *News*, Michener stayed at George School during the summer of 1934.[50] Besides teaching English, he remained an active participant in marionette performances. The *George School News* described the Cape May Friends Meeting Conference appearance of the Micelli Marionettes: "This summer, the Micelli Marionettes, sponsored by J. P.[sic] Michener, English instructor, and William Vitarelli, mechanical drawing instructor, gave several performances in public outside of George School."[51]

[...]TING
[...]ch of
[...] Shane.
[...] James
[...]y at-
[...]astern
[...]s and
[...]ege at
8 P. M.
The meeting was held to make the new basketball rules for the ensuing year. Frank Macguire, Dean of Stroudsburg Teachers College, read and interpreted the rules.

**George School News,
December 14, 1933**

FACULTY DOWNS VARSITY QUINTET BY FINAL RALLY

Michener Nets 21 Points; Euler and Farquhar Each Get 15; Final Score 54-51

In a hard, fast game on Saturday night the faculty basketball team defeated the boys' varsity team by a narrow margin, 54-51.

During the first few minutes the faculty and the varsity fought hard to gain a lead, but it was only toward the close of the first quarter that the varsity succeeded in pulling ahead. The game ended [...] faculty fighting to close [...] the 17-9 score. [...]sity sco[...]ggle in the early game ended. [...]rter the fac[...]

Because of the [...]ntu on teams there were numb[...]pped the faculty scoring twelve from foul shots and the vars[...] n'ne.

The game was divided into eighths, because of the unusual length of the quarters, which were of ten minutes' duration.

Summary

Varsity	G.	F.	P.
Euler, f.	6	3	15
Cann, f.	4	2	10
Waddington, c.	0	1	1
Farquhar, g.	7	1	15
Jamieson g.	2	2	6
Westerfield, f.	2	0	4
Total	21	9	51

Faculty	G.	F.	P.
Sensenig, f.	2	5	9
Michener, f.	8	5	21
Fletcher, c.	6	1	13
Sutton, g.	1	0	2
Shane, g.	1	1	3
Swayne, f.	3	0	6
Total	21	12	54

**George School News,
February 28, 1934**

MICHENER CHOOSES CUBS

Michener States Cubs Working Hard for Game with Lambertville

After three and a half weeks of practice, the Cub baseball team has been chosen by James A. Michener, cub coach. The members of the team are: Catcher, Edward Thatcher, '35; pitchers, Charles McCall and Harry Keen, '37; first base, Lewis Brown, '34; second base, Edgar Wagg, '37; short-stop, Horace Sinclair, '34, and John King, '35; third base, William Cooper, '36; left field, John Wende, '35, acting captain; center field, Murray Hoffman, '34; right field, William Haines, '34; substitutes, James Taylor, Francis Worley, '34; Richard Smith, '36; John Rothrock, Robert Willetts, '37.

Mr. Michener stated, "The team has had so far an excellent season. They are practicing for their one outside game of the season with Lambertville."

Acting Captain Wende states that the school team expects to emerge victorious.

**George School News,
May 2, 1934**

MICELLI MARIONETTES FILL HEAVEY SUMMER SCHEDULE

Cape May, Langhorne, Newtown and Gimbel Brothers on List

This summer, the Micelli Marionettes, sponsored by J. P. Michener, English instructor, and William Vitarelli, mechanical drawing instructor, gave several performances in public outside of George School. One of the first engagements was at the Cape May Conference. They set up their stage on the boardwalk and ran skits daily for one week. The students who participated in these performances were Miller Eves, '36, John Price, '35, Barbara Wetzel, '34, Sara Atkinson, '37, and Betty Brick, '36, while William Vitarelli directed the undertaking.

The next engagement was filled in Newtown, followed by runs in Lansdowne, Langhorne and a return to George School for a family reunion which met there.

Through the success of these engagements, agents of Gimbel Brothers' Department Store in Philadelphia interviewed Mr. Vitarelli and asked him to bring his Marionettes to their toy department for their Education Week, September 1 to 8.

**George School News,
October 3, 1934**

Traveling away from campus with the marionette show while at the same time fulfilling teaching duties apparently put some strain on Michener's schedule. The George School archives contain a typed letter of complaint from Mrs. H. Spenker addressed to Michener's boss, George Walton. Michener had been taking his dinners with Mrs. Spenker but failed to notify her of absences that were to start July 30. Mrs. Spenker asked Walton to show Michener the letter as a double method for obtaining the two dollars due. According to her letter, Michener had verbally promised to pay but had failed to do so.[52]

1934–1935 School Year

Michener started his second year in the English Department by experimenting with education. He described his ideas in a letter to Walton.[53] He was glad to take junior rather than senior class students so that he and his pupils would not be forced to focus on preparing for college board tests. This freedom from preparing for tests allowed him to ensure that students had a memorable class and fun besides.

Faculty Activities

Michener responded quickly when the religion instructor, leading by example, listed his "ten best books" in the *George School News*,[54] and suggested that other teachers might like to do the same. Michener's list was in the very next "Correspondence" column.[55] None of the titles in his list match the titles of the Hill School textbooks, although two other books, *Tess of the d'Urbervilles* (1892) and *Taras Bulba* (1842), are mentioned in his notes, *Graduate Course* and *Bonus Books*. Thomas Mann's book was the most contemporary book in the list—1927. No preferences are suggested since the list is in alphabetical order.

October 8, 1934

Dear Mr. Walton,

The impending inquiry concerning the objectives of George School interests me very much. I've been thinking about the subject most of the summer.

As a result of my conclusions, I have definitely turned my back on objective tests this year. Last year I taught for the E.R.B. and for the College Board, in an effort to reassure myself that if those tests were important, I could comfortably work toward them as legitimate objectives.

I satisfied myself regarding that, and although I would enjoy preparing students for College Boards, which to me are very fine tests, I have been quite pleased to take all Junior work this year. This eliminates the College Board as an objective.

In the E.R.B. tests I made a careful study of the results, and found that my classes rated satisfactorily in the part over which I never taught a lesson, and far above average in the particular field which I was stressing. The field itself was of very little ultimate importance. I have this analysis of the school, by departments and by subjects, and it is illuminating.

This year, with your permission, I would like to disregard the E.R.B. tests, too, as the ultimate objectives of teaching. Since the testing committee will be here shortly to decide upon legitimate tests for whatever teaching programs we have arranged, I'd like them to arrange a test to cover the objective I am trying to establish.

I'll describe, for want of a better term, as voluntary participation in a vital experience. My secondary objective is that the students have a good time in class. I am endeavoring to direct all my work at these two points, and I hope that you will approve, and that you will do all you can to test the efficiency of the program.

I would also like to be exempted from the objectives of the E.R.B., not because I'm afraid of adverse results, because I doubt if they will be adverse, but because I want to feel free to move in directions that I haven't even seen, so far.

If the results are not satisfactory by midyears, I suspect that some intensive drill would pull my classes over the danger line of most of the objective tests.

Sincerely,

James A. Michener

Michener's Ideas About Testing

The faculty not only taught, but also provided "culture" for the students. A lively report is given of the fun-filled faculty play, *Hay Fever* by Noel Coward. According to a student reporter, the performance took on the look and feel of a "wild and wooly [sic] farce."[56] The reporter continued: "The result was that more unbelievable things took place between eight and ten that have not been seen here in years. … The students enjoyed it, and the visitors refrained from booing. The chief result of the evening can best be summed up in the words of the senior member of the English Department [Michener] when he said, 'Now the students won't have to peek into the Leed's [sic] Room to see how the faculty acts out of class.'"[57] The Leeds Room, reserved for faculty functions, was in the southwest corner of Main during Michener's tenure.[58,59]

Marionettes

Marionette shows continued with ever-increasing popularity under the leadership of William Vitarelli.[60] "George School Marionettes" became the troupe's

---

Correspondence

To the Editor of the News:

Last week Mr. Miller submitted to you his list of the ten best books in the George School Library, and at the same time he added the suggestion that other teachers might like to do so. Books to me, as the unfortunate students in my classes know, are synonymous with novels, so I submit below the ten that I think are preeminent. I refer to and select from only the books in the library.

E. Bronte, Wuthering Heights.
Butler, The Way of All Flesh.
Conrad, Victory.
Gogol, Taras Bulba.
Hardy, Tess of the d'Urbervilles.
Mann, Magic Mountain.
Maugham, Of Human Bondage.
Thackeray, Vanity Fair.
Tolstoi, Anna Karenina.
Turgenev, Fathers and Sons.

James A. Michener

George School News, October 24, 1934

new name. Although the 1935 annual lists Michener with the "Micelli Marionettes,"[61] he is not mentioned in connection with marionettes in any *News* articles for the 1934–35 school year, so perhaps Micelli was no longer an appropriate name. As reported in the *News*, Vitarelli wrote material for several of the shows. The successful puppet shows were becoming known outside the school. Vitarelli, without Michener, took the marionettes on a tour of several eastern states during the summer of 1935. Another metric of his success was financial: "With all new equipment, dolls and stage, and a Packard roadster and trailer recently purchased by Mr. Vitarelli, great enjoyment is anticipated."[62]

Sports

During this second year at George School, Michener was again the assistant coach in both baseball and basketball. Stevenson Fletcher was promoted to head basketball coach. Besides coaching, they both played on the faculty basketball team, which continued its dominance over the varsity team. Fletcher played center; Michener, forward.[63] Michener was also in charge of basketball Intramural League affairs, and, with the help of Birkenshaw Mendenhall, instructor in mathematics, he picked the year's all-star team. *The Georgian*, July 1935, ran an article written by Michener that detailed the 1934-35 basketball team—"A Famous Five."[64]

A Famous Five

By JAMES A. MICHENER, teacher of English

Because the 1934-35 Varsity Basketball Team ranked with the "great" teams of 1908, 1917, 1925—
Because one of its members was hailed by referees as "the finest school boy center in the district"—
Because it was the first team coached by Steve Fletcher, a George School basketball star himself—
And because it inspired exceptional interest and development among the younger boys—
Assistant Coach James a Michener has written of its season.

THE boys' basketball team had a good year, winning twelve of its fourteen games. The team lost to Lawrenceville, Friends Central, Frankford, and Chestnut Hill, but each of the defeats was close, and they were so spaced that they never spread their gloom into a definite losing streak. The game with Lawrenceville was probably the best of the year, for it was a tough struggle all the way to the final whistle, which found the teams tied. In the overtime play, a weakened George School team was forced to bow.

Two weeks later the Buff and Brown team tasted the glory of into a thrilling overtime game and winning. To those of ...lestown, this year's team will always ...oyles-

The Georgian, July 1935

Faculty Quintet Trounces Varsity

Michener High Scorer for Teachers With 13 Points Out of 45-16 Total

Piling up a large lead in the first sixteen minutes of play, the faculty continued its long winning streak at the expense of the George School varsity by trouncing the schoolboys 45-16 on the George School floor Saturday afternoon.

By winning, the faculty snapped the four-game winning streak of the varsity dribblers. The ultimate victors got off to a 19-6 lead in the first quarter, and though they slowed down considerably in the second half, were never in any danger of being overtaken.

Jack Talbot, Jim Michener, and Steve Fletcher each counted six times from the floor for the faculty, while Michener also scored on a free shot to lead in scoring with thirteen points. Charley McCall the losers' forces in scoring goals and the same

George School News January 30, 1935

Teaching and Commentary

Topics related to education occupied much of Michener's time. He continued as a member of the Progressive Education Association and was on the English language committee. When the Association held a weekend conference in New York in May, Michener attended.[65]

For the ensuing school year, Michener was offered a new job teaching history at George School. In his written response to Walton's idea of a move to the history department, he stated his interest "in making a wise synthesis of English and social studies."[66] In our interview, Michener said of this period, "I found at George School that I was a little bit tired of correcting papers and other things, and I changed from English to history—re-educated myself. A few years later I was teaching history at Harvard. Because I had such a *fantastically* strong education that history was just a collateral."[67]

One of the consistent themes throughout Michener's life has been his interest in inter-relationships among various fields of study: art, music, literature, poetry, history, and sociology. For years, Michener has sought to bring elements and methods from many disciplines together in his teaching and writing.[68] (The "Miss Smith" referred to in the reproduced letter of March 28 was Constance Smith, English intern during the 1934–35 school year.)

Instructors at Meeting

Shane, Michener, Mohr, Mendenhall Attend Curriculum Conference

Four George School faculty members attended a conference of the Committees on Secondary School Curricula of the Progressive Education Association, held on Saturday and Sunday at the Hotel Roosevelt, New York City, to hear the tentative reports given by the committees on present curricula.

Three of the teachers who attended are committee members Joseph B. Shane, instructor in mathematics, and James A. Michener, English instructor, are members of the committees dealing with their respective subjects; and Walter H. Mohr, history department head, is on the Social Studies Committee.

C. Birkenshaw Mendenhall, instructor in mathematics, also attended the conference.

George School News May 15, 1935

The 1935 annual lists Michener as English Instructor for the second year, and he is pictured in the faculty panorama.[69]

The final issue of the *News* for the school year came out June 10, 1935. "The Prompter" column includes a Michener comment on dramatics at George School: "The final innovation in dramatics that might be mentioned is one that was barely hinted at during the course of the year. Students were speaking more, as in the peace assemblies, meetings, and informal groups. This brings to mind the suggestions made to us by several teachers this year. Wouldn't it be possible to have more speaking on the part of students? Some good poetry is being written in George School. Some good themes are being thought out.

ʰ while. Might
₁ hear them?
..sh Instructor."[70]
..elight is the
...ngdon Swayne's starring role
in a student melodrama[71] in the same *News*
issue in which Michener's summer plans
were announced.[72] Mr. Swayne is the
present day George School historian and
archivist, and although he has since come
to know Michener, he does not remember
him from their mutual campus days.
Kingdon has a long association with
George School. His father, Norman, taught
science at George School from 1909–1950[73]
and played faculty basketball with
Michener.[74] All of Norman's children
attended George School; Kingdon was born
on campus, grew up on campus, and
graduated in 1937.[75] Although Michener
was not Kingdon's teacher,[76] that Kingdon,
of all people, has no memory of Michener
from the George School years, indicates
that Michener was not yet the memorable
man he would become.

Faculty members' summer plans were
also printed in the *News*: "Instructors Will
Paint, Play, Ponder, Plod—at Home and
All Over the Map."[77] Michener planned to
attend "Virginia State" (University of
Virginia at Charlottesville) to study history
in preparation for the next school year. It
indeed proved to be a historic summer
for Michener.

Summer 1935

In Virginia at summer school,
Patti Koon quickly captured
Michener's attention. His undated
letter to Walton at George School,
sent from Virginia in late June or
early July, summed up the
relationship and Patti's attributes with
obvious zest, zeal, and exuberance.[78]
He inquired about George School's
living accommodations for his bride
and himself for the coming year.
Walton answered that he and Mrs.
Walton planned a motor trip to
Charlottesville soon to visit him.
Michener's suggestions for a place for
the couple to live at George School
were denied. Walton wrote, "Living
off campus is also a possibility if you

Dear Mr. Walton

When you first spoke to me on the subject of teaching
History, I was naturally surprised, but upon thinking it over for about
a week, your suggestion looks very good to me. I would therefore like to
apply for that position, formally.

There seems to me to be a big future ahead for the
social sciences, especially in view of the modern trend toward social
legislature. That's one reason why the idea appeals to me.

Secondly, there's a lot of work to be done in making
a wise synthesis of English and the social studies. I'd appreciate having
a try in this field.

Thirdly, at the last meeting of the Commission on
Secondary Education, I got the job of working up the bibliography of
literature dealing with sociological conflicts, and, as a side line,
literature dealing directly with American History. This work is planned
to cover a two year period, and it would fit in nicely with similar work
at George School.

And finally, I still think that Miss Smith has a lot
to offer the school, and I would be very pleased if anything I could do
would be helpful in making it possible for her to return next year.

Sincerely,

James A. Michener

Early Comment on the Synthesis of English and Social Studies

Davis 214
University
Charlottesville, Va

Dear Mr. Walton,

The girl in question is twenty-one and the
daughter of a Lutheran minister in South Carolina. She graduated
from the University of South Carolina last year. She was tennis
champion for four years, basketball forward for four years,
hockey forward for four years and was captain of each sport for
the last two years. She took her degree in music and is accomplished
on the violin. She resembles your daughter Pusey in many ways.

She was voted the best liked girl in the university, and I believe I am the third fellow to propose to her
since summer school began. She graduated with a very good scholastic record, and is personally abstemious and very honest.

Strangely enough, she led the movement for the
disbanding of girls fraternities at college and was still highly
successful. She's a tomboy and adorable.

Since athletics, music, independence, and hard
work characterize her, I thought I better act fast, so we are
planning to get married as soon as everything is convenient. There
is no rush, but I imagine it will better for both of us to get
married before the winter.

You are the first person either of us is speaking
to, for we would like to come to George School together in the
autumn. Naturally, I've been thinking like the devil for the past
week and a half before writing you, and several possibilities come
to mind.

(Continued next page)

can manage within your present salary." Walton continued the letter with eloquent and fatherly advice:

> But let's not hurry. Love does not reach its height in possession, but in sharing,— through understanding. Time and some experience are necessary to gain understanding. Love expresses itself in words, glances, and caresses, but do they mean the same thing to both parties? It takes time to learn this language so as to get the fullness of its meaning.
>
> Marriage brings inevitable contact with persons and things in each other's environment, and often carries responsibility for some of these. Time is needed to get acquainted."[79]

Michener quickly replied with a gracious thank you letter. In part he said, "Patti and I are trying to go so slow that your advice falls on fertile ground, but at such a time a locomotive seems to be crawling."[80] He asked Patti to write to introduce herself and enclosed her handwritten two-page letter with his. She tells of being a Lutheran minister's daughter, loving Jim, participating in athletics and coaching, and being willing to help at George School and gamble on the living quarters there.[81]

The blossoming romance generated a quick succession of events. Patti's father, Reverend S. P. Koon of Lone Star, South Carolina, wrote to Walton and asked for an account of Michener's character.[82]

Walton responded with a detailed, three-page letter, much of which describes events of Michener's life already documented here; however, some new items and summations are of interest. Michener was transferring to the George School History Department; the summer school at Charlottesville was preparation for his new position which started in September. At George School, Michener had been assistant master in a boy's dormitory, just as he had been at The Hill. His salary for 1935–36 season was board and room and $1300 cash. Walton's statements to Rev. Koon of a more personal nature include these:

- "He is an original, resourceful, brilliant, unconventional teacher, a great

---

Letter from Charlottesville (continued)

First, I'm sure we could live together very comfortably and happy in Baron's room on Fourth. Neither of us will be very strong on cash, so we won't be cluttered up with furniture. There appears to me to be ample room there for one year of married life, and since I am springing this all on you so suddenly, I have no wish to inconvenience you. The only question seems to be the introduction of a faculty wife above the second floor, but my own guess is that it would work fine.

Secondly, how about Wheeler's, where Mifi roomed this winter? I know this would entail another shift for Drayton, and about that I can say nothing, for I don't know your plans. I naturally would be willing to meet whatever financial differences were necessary.

Thirdly, couldn't Charley Rogers' suite be made into a livable quarters for newlyweds? I'm sure we could fix it up admirably. The location would be good, too.

I'm sure Patti--she swears she was christened that by a musical mother--will be an addition to George School, and she'll make a wonderful third baseman for the faculty ball club. I have absolutely no intention of trying to rush things, Mr. Walton, but our interests are so nearly identical that I am quite eager to get started on the long journey.

This letter is quite private to you and to Mrs. Walton, and I only wish Patti were there to speak for me, for I think she would be much more eloquent in her bob-haired silence than I am on a typewriter.

History progresses nicely, and I am at present chairman of the social activities committee for the university. George School has been heard of a lot about here, but Quakers are considered a mild kind of freak.

Sincerely,

Jim Michener

Davis 214 University
Charlottesville, Va.
July 5, 1935

Dear Mr. Walton,

That was a fine letter you sent me, and I appreciate it. Patti and I are trying to go so slow that your advice falls on fertile ground, but at such a time a locomotive seems to be crawling. We talked music, art, politics, family, North and South, grammar, and athletics for four days before I kissed her. She broke my glasses for doing so, and when I discovered that I wasn't a bit sore about the three dollars, I decided it must be love.

Your plan to come South is good, for I imagine that if you were line up Frescoln, Fletcher and me, with our prospective wives, you wouldn't be able to say which had chosen a girl more suited to his needs and his personality. I think Patti's fully aware that in marrying me she will be marrying into a group where community living is a real problem. She's always been the minister's daughter and has accepted that responsibility very well. She's been brought up quite strictly, and has worked hard. Since we alone are not the only consideration, I've asked her to write you by way of introduction, for it may be that you will be able to utilize her athletic ability at the school.

Knowing your work this summer, this letter does not call for an answer. I'm just glad that you wrote as kindly as you did. It makes a person feel good.

Sincerely,
Jim.

P.S. I like the idea of Orton as you mention it. We couldn't get there before September anyway, and I don't think we'd even be conscious of dampness.

inspiration to our more brilliant students, and, contrary to one's natural expectations, very inspiring and helpful teacher to slow students. He has prodigious physical and nervous energy."

- "Students who dislike him dislike his over-enthusiasm."
- "New ideas take hold of him with great force. After the enthusiasm has spent itself, he is quite ready for another departure. This has proved true as regards teaching schemes."
- "I think his attitude towards women is as fine as anyone could desire."
- "He is one of our able young men who is marked for a more rapid promotion than some others."
- "I do feel emphatically that they should take time to get thoroughly acquainted before they marry. It takes longer than he realizes."[83]

James A. Michener, age 28, and Patti Koon were married 17 days later, July 27, 1935.[84]

1935–1936 School Year

We learn little about Michener's teaching of History IV (sophomore students) during the 1935–36 term.

First, a radical change occurred in the production of the *George School News*. It went from a polished, typeset newspaper to *The News*, a rough typewritten and mimeographed sheet. The opening number states that the *George School News* was "extinct." We found only one Michener news article for the year: He played a part in the year's faculty production— "Rivals" by Sheridan. Interestingly, Michener played multiple parts: "The rollicking Mr. Acres, the unique Fag, the adamant Sir Anthony, and gallant Jack Absolute to the rainbow of perfection and the immense enjoyment of a sympathetic audience."[85]

Second, living off campus with a new bride may have contributed to the lack of additional details that year. Michener hinted at this in his letter to Walton on March 30, 1936, in which he said in part, "Another year in the country would be a hardship."[86]

Although Michener happily accepted a

THE PINE GROVE PARISH
REV. S. P. KOON, D. D., PASTOR
LONE STAR, S. C.

July 8, 1935.

Mr. George A. Walton

George School, Pa.

My dear Sir,

        Please give me information concerning Mr. James A. Michener who is now a student at the University of Virginia. I shall be glad to have you speak of his present position, character, ability, reliability, disposition, etc. I shall be glad for any information that will help me to really know him. I hope that you can get a reply to me by July 15. If you cannot do this, then write me at New Market, Va. as I expect to be there about ten days visiting my son, the Rev. Lewis Koon. Thanking you for any information you may give me, I am

        Very sincerely

        S. P. Koon

JAMES AND PATTI MICHENER
GEORGE SCHOOL, PA.

March 30, 1936

Dear Mr. Walton,

        I am very glad to accept a teaching position at George School for the following year.

        I was sorry to see that no provision was being made to find a place for Patti and me on the campus. We have looked at the past year as a kind of salutary test of our determination. We both hoped very much to live on the campus next year, for we felt that we had discovered to our own content that our marriage was to a permanent and hilarious thing.

        We're both very happy at George School, and there is no thought of leaving, of course. Another year in the country would be a hardship, but it would be bearable, since each of us has always looked at the "long-view" of things. We have never spoken to anyone this year, in spite of badly nipped ears and wet feet. In fact, we derived some pleasure from the contest against an abominable winter.

        I'm sure you understand the many questions that rise in everyone's mind from year to year. I have very few, really. I comment on this one merely because it seems quite pressing. The change in department seems to have profited me. I like history and English both, and the combination is one rich in teaching potentialities.

        Sincerely,

        James A. Michener

Accepts a Teaching Position for the 1936–37 School Year

history teaching position for the following year, ultimately, he didn't fill it. At the close of the 1935–36 term, the 1936 annual summarizes the year's changes for Michener:[87] He is listed as a History IV instructor and in charge of the Music hobby group, which he founded. William Vitarelli's name, alone, appears as advisor for the marionette group.

POSTLUDE: COLORADO STATE COLLEGE, HARVARD, MACMILLAN, AND WW II

Colorado State College—Greeley

Although Michener had accepted a position for a fourth year of teaching at George School, an unexpected opening in the Social Science Department at Colorado State College in Greeley prompted a letter of inquiry from the director of the department, William L. Wrinkle, to George Walton, Head of George School.[1] Based upon reports Wrinkle had had about Michener, he requested Walton's evaluation of him. Since the position in the laboratory school carried with it the possibility of a dormitory directorship that would include services of both husband and wife, Wrinkle also asked Walton to comment on the qualities of Patti Koon Michener.

Wrinkle's letter arrived late in the summer—a time when school administrators become deeply concerned over sudden vacancies. Walton quickly scrawled longhand notes on Wrinkle's letter in preparation for a reply. In part he wrote: "I would not want to see him undertake the directorship of either of my boys' dorms. Not systematic, unreliable in routine detail. Not indifferent to duty but absorbed. ... Obligations of community social life, immature tardiness, forgetfulness, and hesitation to enter into planning of social events are faults to be observed. No moral faults. High estimate of versatile scholarship and original inspiring teaching methods." His notes about Patti were uncomplimentary. His actual letter of reply is less critical but pointed out two of Michener's weaknesses: keeping up with routine responsibilities and appointments, and needing discipline to see a job to completion.[2] Walton mentioned that Michener had been granted a raise at George School for the 1936–37 school year, but he did not express his feelings regarding dormitory duties associated with the position at Greeley, nor did he mention Patti. The softer reply implies that Walton had accepted Michener's inevitable departure from George School.

Michener got the position at Greeley, which included teaching in addition to studying toward a master's degree in social science. After the school year was underway, Michener wrote to Walton about his life out West.[3] He and Patti lived in a dormitory with about 30 boys; he had 90 high school students in social studies and 15 college students in teacher training work. They had joined a progressive Congregational Church in Greeley. He added that they missed George School and now better appreciated the fine education students got there. In January, Michener wrote to tell Walton about his nice raise in salary; he credited this to having "learned much of my education from you and your school."[4] After he had left the school, Michener further continued his connection with George School by writing an article for the *Georgian* in which he warmly and graciously pointed out the facets of George School he liked best—a faculty of high caliber for a secondary school and the substantial freedom given to each teacher. His only negative comment was that he felt it was a mistake to have a school board with no faculty representatives.[5]

Michener continued at Colorado State College, earning his master of arts degree in 1937.[6] He stayed on at the college for two more years and wrote sociology articles, participated in sports, experimented with education methods, became much more active in politics, and involved himself in a local free idea discussion group at Angell's restaurant.[7] Michener said of the time: "At a critical point in my life, I moved to Colorado, which was one of the best things I ever did, for the grand spaciousness of that setting and the freedom of political expression that was not only allowed but encouraged, converted me from being a somewhat hidebound Eastern conservative into a free spirit."[8]

Harvard

In early 1939, Michener got an offer to teach and study towards a Ph.D. at Harvard. He continued to keep in touch with George Walton at George School, whom he clearly respected. He told Walton about his new position in a letter dated January 16, 1939. Walton replied, saying in part: "Your letter of January 16th has remained unanswered, though I should at once have wired you my congratulations about the opening at Harvard. May it rise to your fondest expectations!"[9] Higher education was certainly generating opportunities for Michener. He taught at the Harvard School of Education from 1939–1940 on a leave of absence from Colorado State College.[10] A scholarly result for the year was the book, *Unit in the Social Studies,* written with H. M. Long.

COLORADO STATE COLLEGE
OF EDUCATION · GREELEY
January 16, 1939

Office of the Secondary School

George Walton
George School, Pa.

Dear Mr. Walton,

Good luck has been hounding my steps for the past
two months. Tonight I sent a wire finally accepting a job at Harvard.
I am going to teach there in the graduate school for two summers, and
become a student once more during the regular school year, teaching
one course on the side. I need not tell you what a thrill this is
to me, especially as I shall be working with a man whom I have come
to respect as a great man in my field.

I am especially pleased with my goo luck since I
was able to choose between three of the great national universities.
The choice has been difficult for me, since it has meant severing
my connections with Greeley, but there are times when one must be
willing to make a gamble.

In leaving I have perhaps done you a disservice;
I have strongly recommended Herbert Abraham for my job. Today we received a disclaimer from Herbert, but my employer is unwilling to
accept that answer, and is writing in the morning to press the claims
of this school. After my recommendation---given in absolutely glowing terms---the men here want him. I tell you this because I am now
finished with the case entirely. The problem is entirely one for you
and Herbert to settle, and it may well be that Greeley will have
little to offer in competition with George School.

For myself, I look forward to work at Harvard with
great delight mingled with trepidation. I came to Greeley to take my
place among social studies men who had been years in the field. I now
go to Harvard to consort with men who have probably forgotten more
about the field than I shall ever know. It seems a long time since
that March afternoon when you asked me in the faculty room if I would
be interested in changing my department. I think that move marked
you as a real administrator, for I have been very happy in the field
and have achieved more satisfaction in it than I ever could have in
English.

I'll conclude with a statement I have often used
out here in educational meetings and which I passed on to Walter Mohr
as a Christmas present: "The perfect social studies curriculum would
consist of three big rooms with Walter Mohr in one, teaching students
the beauty and dignity of historical truth, while illuminating that
truth with mellowed wisdom; with Dick Mc.Feeley in the second teaching
the sound doctrines of citizenship, fellowship, and general community
usefulness; and with Herbert Abraham in the third, teaching the ultimate commonality of social aspirations the world over." You'll understand me when I say that I really know myself to be by far the least
of that remarkable social studies department you had in 1935-36.

Sincerely,

Jim Michener

Notifies Walton That He Accepted a Position at Harvard

Macmillan

Michener did not complete the Ph.D. degree, choosing instead to work as a textbook editor for Macmillan Publishing Company. After Michener started work at Macmillan, he received written comments from George Walton[11] about "Progressive Education," the America-should-be-tough article he had written. Walton, the friendly Quaker, hoped that Germany would crumble from within, but he saw war looming. Michener, also a Quaker, had different ideas based on his experiences in Europe; he felt the Nazi regime would continue to rise.

Michener's work inside the publishing industry turned out to be crucial to the development of his future career.[12] He saw how authors were made and broken and how economics and mathematical dexterity influenced publication of literary works and textbooks for education. Was he interested in mathematics? He replied, "I always carried a slide rule with me. I knew the proportions of the slide rule were arranged according to a logarithmic scale. I've always thought in proportions. It [editing at Macmillan] was formative as a mathematical exercise. Making, producing, and publishing a book requires a mathematical perspective. Later, I wound up an advisor to NASA. I wound up on the Board supervising astrophysics at Harvard. Proportions and logarithms. Strange, strange, very strange."[13]

In his book, *The Novel*,[14] Michener recounts the business creativity required in the publishing industry. In the book, he is recognizable as the plain but persistent Pennsylvania author, Lukas Yoder. Yoder is a multi-talented "triple threat": books, painting, and polished speech. Yoder, ultimately successful at writing and art, donates money to a local university to improve the education of writers. He, like Michener, realizes philosophically that the publishing house that he has helped make famous is financially strong enough to support the next generation of struggling writers.

November 3, 1941

James A. Michener
Textbook Department
The Macmillan Company
New York, N.Y.

Dear Jim:

There was one more word that I wanted to say yesterday about your article for "Progressive Education", but no opportunity occurred. Is it not true, as Herbert Hoover and many others have pointed out, that the Nazi movement will in time be destroyed from within? Your opportunity to get acquainted with ardent young Nazis in the formative stages of the movement was much more extensive than mine, but I had enough to make me understand your reference to their devoted spirit and high resolution. I could see it even as late as December 1938, but in strong contrast with their violence and injustice towards the Jews. Since then, they have tried to conquer Europe. Leonard Kenworthy, after spending last year in Germany, reports that their policy of encouraging violent antagonisms among traditionally opposed groups already appears to have been sowing the wind. A whirlwind is ready to be reaped.

I am not opposing the trend of your article that the spirit and purpose of democracy must be as ardent and self-sacrificing as that of Germany, but wish there were a little more emphasis upon a foundation of moral soundness, both in principle and practice.

This is admittedly a pacifist approach but, if true, how can we dodge it?

Hoping to see you often, I am

Truly your friend,

George A. Walton, Principal

Walton Comments on Michener's Progressive Education Article

While at Macmillan, Michener applied to the U.S. Army for war service. He asked George Walton for a recommendation and mentioned that Patti was planning to join the WAACS.[15] Walton promptly replied and enclosed the recommendation, "To Whom It May Concern," in a sealed envelope. He said, in part: "He is a man of reliable character and brilliant mind, energetic, original, and full of initiative. His colleagues respect his ability, were stimulated by his originality, and sometimes felt obliged to restrain his impulsiveness. His pupils admired him as an excellent teacher."[16]

JAMES A. MICHENER
EIGHT WEST THIRTEEN
NEW YORK CITY

September 30, 1942

Dear Mr. Walton,

The Unites State Army is considering me for a job with them and have suggested that I ask one former employer to tell them what he thinks of me. I am eager to get whatever work is available, either through a commission or through the regular ranks.

Will you please send me, in a sealed enveloped addressed "To Whom It May Concern", a confidential statement which will be seen only by the commanding officer in charge of my case? I must submit your sealed envelope along with my other credentials. I shall greatly appreciate your kindness in helping me out, as you did several times in the past.

(Continued ⇒)

I hope you don't think I was trying to steal Rees away from you. He happened to be visiting me when Gilchrist, an old and close freind of mine, wrote to me about a vacancy he had on his staff. I was aware at the time--and Rees confirmed my opinion--that many obstacles would lie in his way, even were you to deem it possible to release him. I felt obligated, however, to inform him of the possibility of the job, since he would have been very good in it and since Gilchrist needed a man like Rees. I hope that Patti (who plans to join the WAACS) and I shall see you before the autumn is too old.

Sincerely,

James A. Michener

Requests a Recommendation for the Army

World War II

Instead of serving in the Army, Michener joined the Naval Reserve. When he wrote to James Wendell at Hill School on Navy stationery in the spring of 1943,[17] he mentioned meeting several Hill School men who were also in Navy uniform. Wendell replied warmly: "To be sure, I think all of them [Hill boys], with few exceptions, regret that they cannot go on into college, but they realize there is a job to be done and the quicker they get at it the quicker it will be over. … We have had a good year at The Hill despite general conditions, much better than we had reason to expect would be the case when the term began in the autumn."[18]

In his mid-thirties and married, Michener normally would not have seen active duty, but in 1944 he went on his first Navy tour of the South Pacific. After a second tour, which the Navy requested and which involved writing part of the service history of the war, he was discharged in 1946 as a lieutenant commander. The Navy has given him awards and recognition and has never forgotten his services.[19]

In his autobiography, Michener tells in detail how he wrote short stories in the South Pacific about the ethnic clashes of World War II.[20] After the war, he returned to his day job as editor for Macmillan and at night turned the war stories into his first novel, *Tales of the South Pacific*.[21] He submitted the manuscript to his employer, Macmillan. Due to delays and paper scarcity, they did not publish the book until 1947. A Pulitzer Prize followed quickly and so did money from his financial interest in the smash Broadway hit musical, *South Pacific* by Rogers and Hammerstein, which is based on the book. Michener resigned from Macmillan in 1949, never to hold another salaried job.

Because his native abilities and good fortune provided him with such a broad base of experiences, training, and skills, his continued literary success was assured. Michener was well prepared, and it paid huge dividends.

UNITED STATES NAVY

May, 1943
Tuesday Night

Dear James and Marnie Wendell,

The other day I had to take a paper to another section of the Aeronautics bureau here, and when I delievered it, a fine looking young man asked me if I weren't a former teacher of his? I was, and he was Paul Griffiths, now a lieutenant, junior grade, in naval aviation.

"You must come over here with me," he said. "I may have a surprise for you." And around the corner was Lt. senior grade Walter Close with a service stripe across. his heart.

At my Naval Training Base I played basketball one day with a handsome, very rough, laughing, good sport. "Don't we know one another?" I suddenly demanded. Of course we did, for the big fellow was Albert Snook, whom I had in the very first class I ever taught in any subject anywhere.

And again, I bumped into an officer, and it was Tommy Campbell, who used to sing so beautifully with his brother Bill when they were together at The Hill. He looked efficient and clean in his naval uniform.

Another time a group of us were at a club in New York and still a fifth chap came up. He was Harry Fox, looking fine and chipper. I think he told me that Fred Allen had also joined the Navy.

So the old school has been much in my mind as I see the splendid crop of naval officers you have helped produce, and I have seen but one very small part of the total group. All that I meet speak with affection of the school and of their growth there. You must be proud that so many of them are doing what they can in one of the great services.

Sincerely,

James A. Michener

AFTERWORD

We share here impressions, opinions, and miscellanea gained from our research: visiting Swarthmore College, The Hill, George School, the Michener Art Museum; interviewing Mr. Michener; and reading the many items relevant to this period of his life.

Driving to Austin to interview him, we mused at length about Mr. Michener and his home office. What we found surprised us. Located on a shady side street, his home was a comfortable 1960s brick ranch that blended well with similar homes in his quiet neighborhood. We were ushered from the front door to his office. A large cereal box on the breakfast table added to the unpretentious atmosphere. After a perfunctory greeting, Mr. Michener was ready to begin. A large meeting table upon which we spread the textbooks occupied the center of the spacious room. A manual typewriter was on his desk at the far end of the room, as were books borrowed from the University of Texas-Austin library relating to the notes he had been writing for this book. Adding to the quiet atmosphere of the room was the lush vegetation of the backyard visible through the many picture windows. It was amazing how few books there were on his many wall-shelves.

Sitting around the table, we got better acquainted as he asked many questions about the textbooks. We had anticipated a half-day session, but by noon, the interview on the formatted questions sent in advance had not begun. It pleased us that we would continue after lunch and would join him at his favorite cafeteria, the Marimont. Mr. Michener rode in our station wagon and we learned that he is a cautious rider: In advance, he announced the turns and local traffic pitfalls. Back at his office, it was mid-afternoon when his wife poked her head in the door and reminded "Cookie" that he needed to rest. He did not heed her reminder but continued until all questions were answered. At five o'clock when the interview came to a close, Mr. Michener walked us from the office, through the garage, and to the driveway waving a friendly farewell as we drove away.

Although frail, his self-motivation, fine memory, mental vitality, and focused interest in the future were most inspiring. Despite his age, he has kept up with the times—except perhaps in one area, the computer. The manual typewriter is still his favorite, and there were three in the room. He still types his copy on a typewriter and has a computer-generated draft produced and saved by others on his staff. He tried the computer but did not find it to his liking.

We found that he was *still* teaching and learning at age 87. He established and endowed writers' programs at the University of Miami and the University of Texas-Austin where his teaching was selective. He said, "I'm not so much interested in teaching, but interested in the intellectual processes—interested in literature. I have always affiliated with very bright students. Even today—I mean, whether I'm here [in Austin] or in Florida—they've already been weeded out. They're all knowledgeable and they're very exciting. I don't want to deal with people at the least common denominator. I want them to get up there a little bit. That's my constant ambition: raise their sights." His views on education are strong: teach the intelligent and willing; remove those who continually cause disruption and discipline problems. He advocates sending children to the best school to be found and afforded—public or private.

During his lifetime, he moved many times, eight in Doylestown alone. Throughout his writing career, he has been a global transient and even purchased homes in some of the settings of his numerous books. Yet, from his correspondence during his formative years and our interview, we learned that he continued to keep in touch with many of his far-flung acquaintances. We think his energy and thoughtfulness in maintaining these communications, in spite of a hectic writing schedule, are two of his many strong attributes. During our interview, the telephone rang several times, and we learned firsthand just how busy he is. There was laughter all around when he remarked, "John and I just sit here and answer the phone!" He referred to John Kings, his secretary and coordinating editor.

We soon learned that the story of his formative years is also a glimpse at private education and its methods in the 1930s. Written communication between schools was remarkable. The number of letters sent, received, and fortunately saved is impressive. We now understand good communications were partly due to the education system of the day, which rated students and teachers personally rather than as a percentile from a barrage of sophisticated achievement tests.

There are interesting contrasts among writings from the late 1940s. The depression, poverty, and World War II forged hopeful stories from James A. Michener and literature about an alternative life-style from the counter-culture. Both sought to describe social and ethnic interactions. Michener's characters move forward in spite of obstacles, and in the long-term, outcomes are positive. Representing the counter-culture, one voice of the beat generation, Jack Kerouac, described the post-war human condition and experience at the same time Michener started writing popular historical fiction. Kerouac published his first book, *The Town and the City*, in 1950.[1] The beat world of menial work, poverty, protest, drugs, homosexuality, and sex stands in stark contrast to Michener's world of liberal Quakerism, humanism, scholarship, and civil obedience. Yet, the two writers began working at nearly the same time and gained a loyal readership.

One biographer argued that Patti Koon was a poor marital partner.[2] After reviewing the information available from Michener's formative years, we disagree. We feel that the 14-year marriage is what he needed and wanted then. They had music, sports, and energy in common. Their mutual lack of social graces was not a point of division or of great importance.

The purchase of the textbooks at the Oley auction drew us to Michener's writings. As we read more and more for background information, we found his books very easy to read. Story lines and characters are often complex and interwoven, yet the words flow smoothly and effortlessly. By his use of vivid compound adjectives and powerful adverbs, crisp dialog springs to life. Evident in his prose is the influence of music and poetry, which he loves, and sentence diagramming. Our new understanding of his formative years has added immensely to our appreciation of his writing.

By any standard, Michener has been a major contributor to Swarthmore College. Although he is appreciative of his years at The Hill and at George School and contributed a taped interview for the George School centennial,[3] he has not rewarded them financially. We asked him about this difference, he said, "They would want to have a lot of interaction—but I just can't do it. They have both made very honorable overtures. I feel indebted to both of them. I have the happiest emotional relationships with them. But I learned (chuckles) more than I taught— especially at The Hill. We sort of have to let it go at that." We find it understandable that Michener would repay his alma mater but not former employers.

We visited the James A. Michener Art Museum in Doylestown to learn more about Michener's hometown and legacy. The museum uses much of the structure of the 19th century Bucks County Jail and is an intriguing blend of new and old. Although the building is primarily an art museum, Michener memorabilia are on display in a small alcove to the left of the entrance. This office-like setting contains a complete array of Michener first editions on loan from collector Jeffrey Gregorie. Our visit was short, but during it we observed several people walk in expecting to find a "Michener Museum" and walk out disappointed. We think this alcove attracts a wide variety of people interested in Michener, the person, and warrants expansion. We recognize his desire for Quaker plainness and his sensitivity to his surname, but publicizing at the museum the *process* of his rise to literary success could serve as a valuable educational tool.

James A. Michener Alcove, Michener Art Museum (Joy V. Bliss photo)

By his own account, Michener was a foundling placed in the care of Mabel Haddock Michener. He talked at length about his feelings for his name: "See, I'm different from other people in that. That is *not* my name. It was just an agreed-upon solution to a legal problem. It bears no relation to reality. So I think differently about that. I've been very reluctant to have any buildings named after me; I've avoided that—fought it. I don't want prizes named after me. I'm not very much indebted to the name." When we mentioned that he had put a lot into the Michener name, he said, "Well, I'm sometimes aware of that and wished to hell I hadn't. Wish that I'd taken something else. When I started to become known, I would get anonymous letters pointing out that I was *not* a Michener. Who in the hell did I think I was parading under their name—with bitterness you cannot imagine. They would feel that someone like me should stay down at this level where he belonged—tip his hat to his betters. I never identified one of them. But they were rather good for me because they kept me from flying too high. It kept me on a fairly steady keel." Michener balanced the good and bad aspects of his relatives' gibes. We found that he weighs positive and negative factors in many situations and as a consequence has developed a skillful diplomacy.

James Albert Michener settled on his signed name quickly. During the time he lived in Doylestown, his name is found written in various ways: "J. Michener," "James A. Michener," "Jimmie," and "James Michener." During the Hill years, we see from his textbooks and correspondence that he used all four of the above, plus "J. A. Michener." Clearly though, "James A. Michener" was by then the most prevalent usage and still is. Friends call him "Jim"; Mari, his wife since 1955, called him "Cookie." Looking at the schoolbooks with him, we asked about his signature. He answered: "I can't imagine myself today writing 'J. Michener.' I sign my name maybe a thousand times a year, at least. It just doesn't look like me at all. I can't remember in the last 15 years ever signing 'J. A. Michener.' If I take the trouble, *occasionally* I'll sign 'James Michener'—then I'm not happy with it. Might be somebody who has a special book or something." By the time he was at Hill School, did "James A. Michener" sound the best to him? "Pretty much, yes. I am surprised in these textbooks that the name I settled on—James A. Michener—is almost identical to the way I sign it today. Very similar." He compared his 1929 signature with his 1993 signature and commented, "The 'A' varies a bit but there's always that break between the 'Mi' and the 'ch.'"

He continued, "I sign my name so often, that if I had my way I'd have Abe Ax as my name!" Everyone laughed, and then he added, "Or Al Ax!—Jeez I do sign it a lot."

Our interview was over and Mr. Michener sat looking nostalgically at the textbooks. He closed by saying emphatically: "*My, but this is an amazing resurrection.*"

The End

The Authors Discussing the Textbooks With Mr. Michener

ACKNOWLEDGMENTS

The authors would especially like to thank James A. Michener for granting us what turned out to be a full-day recorded interview at his home in Austin, Texas. We thank John Kings, Michener's secretary and coordinating editor, for planning both telephone and personal interviews and for taking photographs. Deborah Brothers, State House Press, and Leo John Harris, Pogo Press, gave us valuable publication ideas.

The following two people were most helpful in furnishing us with early Michener records and material and for answering our endless questions: Lauren A. Chapis, Hill School librarian and archivist, and Kingdon W. Swayne, George School archivist and historian. The illuminating tours they gave of their beautiful campuses aided us in gaining a clearer picture of the two schools. We also thank Odie Lefever, Development Office, George School, for her help.

We extend a sincere thank you to the following Hill School Alumni: Robert Biddle, III (1933), Frank Bissel (1933), C. Walter Bühler (1932), Ernest S. Burch (1933), David P. Close (1934), William P. Davis (1933), Carl Ferenbach (1933), Mr. and Mrs. Melvin "Teb" Feroe (1928), Paul L. Griffiths (1933), Standish F. Medina (1933), John W. Nicholson (1933), Alexander H. Revell III (1943), Edward C. Roe (1931), George K. Stauffer (1933), William B. "Spike" Watling (1933), and Major Lee White (1933). Our interviews and correspondence with them were extraordinarily helpful filling in details of Hill School life during the time Michener taught there. We must say a word about the Hill School Alumni. We found them to be a gracious, well-spoken, and gentlemanly group of successful men. Visiting with one after another, we soon decided that it was as though they had come from the same mold. As far as we could ascertain, the only common denominator, other than age, was their years of Hill training. We think this speaks very well for The Hill.

Our visit to the James A. Michener Art Museum in Doylestown was very informative. We thank Bruce Katsiff, Director, and Brian Peterson, Curator of Exhibitions, for a tour of the facility and much useful information about Michener. We especially enjoyed learning how they assembled the alcove containing Michener memorabilia. In the alcove are photographs by John Hoenstine showing Michener in front of the eight Doylestown childhood homes in which he lived. We thank Mr. Hoenstine for pointing out his favorite Michener picture, which we have reproduced with permission.

Pam Cressman, librarian at Central Bucks West High School in Doylestown, provided photocopies and lent originals of relevant Commencement issues of the *Torch*.

Michael Durken, archivist for the James A. Michener papers, and Edward Fuller, special collections, were quick to supply requested information from the McCabe Library at Swarthmore College. They were most helpful and gracious when we visited the library to search through the school publications for evidence of Michener's campus activities.

We also thank Mrs. Hazel Allgyer, bookkeeper for the Oley Auction House, for determining the consignors of the Michener textbooks.

Mr. and Mrs. Melvin Feroe provided much useful information about both the Feroe Press and relevant books published by the press for The Hill and sent a gift copy of John Lester's, *A Spelling Review*.

To our proofreaders, Kathryn Lindell, Dorothy Logan, and Charlotte Norwood, we say a heartfelt thank-you.

PHOTO AND DOCUMENT CREDITS

Bucks County Historical Society, Doylestown, Pa.: Microfiche copies of the *Bucks County Intelligencer*.

Central Bucks West High School, Doylestown, Pa.: Permission to reproduce portions of the *Torch*.

George School, Newtown, Pa.: Permission to reproduce documents, the marionette photograph, and portions of the yearbooks, newspapers, and other relevant school publications that they have published and copyrighted.

The Hill, Pottstown, Pa.: Permission to reproduce documents, portions of the yearbooks, newspapers, and other relevant school publications that they have published and copyrighted.

James A. Michener Art Museum, Doylestown, Pa.: Copies from the Michener clipping file.

John Hoenstine, Photographer, Doylestown, Pa.: Copyrighted photographs of Michener at 81 N. Clinton, Doylestown.

John Kings, Michener's Secretary and Coordinating Editor, University of Texas-Austin: Permission to reproduce Michener's portrait.

Swarthmore College, Swarthmore, Pa.: Permission to reproduce documents, the photograph of Robinson House, portions of the yearbooks, newspapers, and other relevant school publications that they have published and copyrighted.

REFERENCE LIST

Introduction

1. A Grove Day, *James Michener*, 2nd ed. (Boston: Twayne, 1977); John P. Hayes, *James A. Michener : A Biography* (Indianapolis: Bobbs, 1984); and George J. Becker, *James A. Michener* (New York: Ungar, 1983).
2. James A. Michener, *The World Is My Home: A Memoir* (New York: Random, 1992).
3. James A. Michener, *Tales of the South Pacific* (New York: Macmillan, 1947).

Purchase of the Michener Textbooks

1. James A. Michener, *Report of the County Chairman* (New York: Random, 1961).
2. James A. Michener, letter to G. L. Dybwad, 16 Oct. 1987.
3. Hazel Allgyer, letter to G. L. Dybwad, 7 June 1993.
4. James A. Michener, personal interview, 24 May 1993.
5. Ibid.

The Doylestown High School Years: 1921–1925

1. "Opening School," *Bucks County Intelligencer* 25 Aug. 1921: 7.
2. James A. Michener, letter to the authors, 7 May 1994.
3. James A. Michener, *The World Is My Home : A Memoir* (New York: Random, 1992) 412.
4. "Local Brigade Teams Won One and Lost One," *Bucks County Intelligencer* 9 Mar. 1922: 3.
5. "Brigade Claims Junior Championship of Town," *Bucks County Intelligencer* 30 Mar. 1922: 1.
6. Michener, *World Is My Home* 484-85.
7. Michener, letter to the authors, 7 May 1994.
8. "Doylestown's Schools Will Open on Tuesday," *Bucks County Intelligencer* 7 Sept. 1922: 7.
9. "Junior Tennis Crown Being Fought For Now," *Bucks County Intelligencer* 28 Sept. 1922: 6.
10. Michener, *World Is My Home* 412.
11. Michener, letter to the authors, 7 May 1994.
12. "Coach Gardy Explains What Team Needs," *Bucks County Intelligencer* 19 Oct. 1922: 4.
13. Ibid.
14. "Gardy's Quintet Won From Jenkintown High," *Bucks County Intelligencer* 21 Dec. 1922: 4.
15. Michener, letter to the authors, 7 May 1994.
16. Michener, *World Is My Home* 412.
17. Doylestown High School, *Torch* 8.2 (1923): 3.
18. Doylestown High School, *Torch* 8.3 (1924): 2.
19. Doylestown High School, *Torch* 8.4 (1924): 11-12.
20. Michener, *World Is My Home* 123.
21. Doylestown High School, *Torch* 8.5 (1924): 10.
22. Michener, letter to the authors, 7 May 1994.
23. Ibid.
24. Doylestown High School, *Torch* 8.2 (1923): 18 and 23.
25. Doylestown High School, *Torch* 8.4 (1924): 24.
26. Michener, letter to the authors, 7 May 1994.
27. Doylestown High School, *Torch* 8.4 (1924): 18-20.
28. Michener, letter to the authors, 7 May 1994.
29. Doylestown High School, *Torch* 8.3 (1924): 7.
30. Doylestown High School, *Torch* 8.5 (1924): 20-21.
31. "List of Grade Pupils in Doylestown Boro. Schools as Given by Dr. Carmon Ross," *Bucks County Intelligencer* 11 Sept. 1924: 8.
32. "Fifty-Six Graduated From the High School," *Bucks County Intelligencer* 25 June 1925: 1.
33. Doylestown High School, *Torch* 9.4 (1925): 10-11.
34. "Swamp Sellersville in First Game Here," *Bucks County Intelligencer* 11 Dec. 1924: 1.
35. "Doylestown a Winner," *Bucks County Intelligencer* 5 Feb. 1925: 1+.
36. "Got Off to Poor Start," *Bucks County Intelligencer* 26 Feb. 1925: 1.
37. "Perkasie's Flying Start Won the Game," *Bucks County Intelligencer* 19 Mar. 1925: 1.
38. Doylestown High School, *Torch* 9.4 (1925): 38.
39. "High School Students Give Boys' Week Talks," *Bucks County Intelligencer* 7 May 1925: 7.
40. "County Seat Seniors Left for Washington," *Bucks County Intelligencer* 7 May 1925: 1+.
41. Doylestown High School, *Torch : Commencement Issue : 1925* (June 1925).
42. Michener, letter to the authors, 7 May 1994.
43. Ibid.
44. "Michener Won Prize," *Bucks County Intelligencer* 18 June 1925: 4
45. Michener, letter to the authors, 7 May 1994.
46. "Fifty-Six Graduated From the High School," *Bucks County Intelligencer* 25 June 1925: 1.
47. *Thirty-Third Annual Commencement [Bulletin] : Doylestown High School : 1925*, 23 June 1925.
48. Ibid.
49. "Sousa At The Grove," *Bucks County Intelligencer* 13 Aug. 1925: 6.
50. Michener, letter to the authors, 7 May 1994.

The Swarthmore College Years: 1925–1929

1. Richard J. Walton, *Swarthmore : An Informal History* (Swarthmore, Pa.: Swarthmore College, 1986) 1.
2. Ibid 3.
3. Ibid 4.
4. Ibid 6.
5. Ibid 7.
6. Ibid 10.
7. Ibid.
8. Ibid 13.
9. Ibid 16.
10. Ibid 21.
11. Ibid 25.
12. Ibid 26.
13. Ibid 28.
14. Ibid 29.
15. Ibid 31.
16. *Swarthmore Phoenix* 15 June, 1925: 1.
17. Ibid 38.
18. Ibid 39.
19. "Two Out of Five Open Scholars Are Chosen From Pennsylvania," *Swarthmore Phoenix* 15 June 1925: 1.
20. "The Freshmen," *Swarthmore Phoenix* 23 Jan. 1926: 4.
21. "Sentiment on Rules for Freshmen Given in M.S.G.A. Meeting," *Swarthmore Phoenix* 16 Mar. 1926: 1.
22. A. Grove Day, *James Michener*, 2nd ed. (Boston: Twayne, 1977) 17. John P. Hayes, *James A. Michener : A Biography* (Indianapolis: Bobbs, 1984) 35. George J. Becker, *James A. Michener* (New York: Ungar, 1983) 4.
23. "New Freshmen Course in Table Manners Offered," *Swarthmore Phoenix* 29 Sept. 1925.
24. Hayes, *James A. Michener* 34.
25. "Men's Fall Handicap Tennis Matches Draw Big Crowd of Entries," *Swarthmore Phoenix* 29 Sept. 1929: 1+.
26. "Freshmen Basketball Team Victors in First Two Games," *Swarthmore Phoenix* 19 Jan. 1926: 5.
27. "Collection Cuts," *Swarthmore Phoenix* 13 Apr. 1926: 6.
28. "Chi Omega and Phi Delta Theta Take First Honors," *Swarthmore Phoenix* 28 Sept. 1926: 1.
29. "Honors Students' Averages," *Swarthmore Phoenix* 8 Mar. 1927: 4.
30. "Annual Production of Freshman Show Proves Financial Success," *Swarthmore Phoenix* 20 Apr. 1926.
31. "Phi Delta Theta Wins Over Kappa Sigma in Interfraternity Finals," *Swarthmore Phoenix* 11 Jan. 1927: 5.
32. *Portfolio* Nov. (1926): 30.
33. *Portfolio* Mar. (1927).
34. Becker, *James A. Michener* 4.
35. James A. Michener, personal interview, 24 May 1993.
36. "Five Interfraternity Basketball Contests Open Season This Year," *Swarthmore Phoenix* 6 Dec. 1927: 3.
37. *Portfolio* Oct. (1927): 15-17.
38. *Portfolio* Mar. (1928): 10-12.

39. "Lion and Kangaroo Produce Show With Twenty Lively Acts," *Swarthmore Phoenix* 22 Nov. 1927: 1-2.

40. "Little Theater Club Gives Unusual Drama as Spring Production," *Swarthmore Phoenix* 1 May 1928: 1-3.

41. "Michener Promotes Spirit By Speech At Mass Meeting," *Swarthmore Phoenix* 30 Oct. 1928: 5.

42. "Losing Streak Ends As Basketball Team Downs Ursinus Five," *Swarthmore Phoenix* 19 Feb. 1929: 5.

43. "Swarthmore Defeated by Main Line Quintet in Mediocre Struggle," *Swarthmore Phoenix* 5 Mar. 1929: 1+.

44. "Delta Upsilon and Phi Psi in Final Round of Basketball Tourney," *Swarthmore Phoenix* 5 Mar. 1929: 3.

45. James A. Michener, "Personal Opinion," *Swarthmore Phoenix* 12 Mar. 1929: 4.

46. "Roaring Garnet Lion Prepares Snappy Acts For Hamburg Carnival," *Swarthmore Phoenix* 20 Nov. 1928: 3.

47. "Swarthmore Celebrates as Talented Thespians Revel in Novel Roles," *Swarthmore Phoenix* 27 Nov. 1928: 1+.

48. "Cast of Senior-Junior Play 'Twelfth Night' Chosen After Tryout," *Swarthmore Phoenix* 5 Mar. 1929: 1.

49. "Five Original Plays To Be Given By Curtain Theater," *Swarthmore Phoenix* 7 May 1929: 3.

50. "Beatrice Beach Wins First Award in 1929 One-Act Play Contest," *Swarthmore Phoenix* 14 May 1929: 1-2.

51. "M.S.G.A. Nominations For Second Semester at Regular Meeting," *Swarthmore Phoenix* 8 Jan. 1929: 3.

52. "Literary and Dramatic Criticism," *Swarthmore Phoenix* 19 Mar. 1929: 4.

53. *Portfolio* Oct. (1928): 8-10.

54. "Students Launch Campaign to Aid Endowment Drive," *Swarthmore Phoenix* 23 Apr. 1929: 1-2.   "Student Body Unanimously Backs Endowment Drive," *Swarthmore Phoenix* 30 Apr. 1929: 6.

55. "Parrish Halls Reverberate With Grads' Voices as Army of Alumni Invades College," *Swarthmore Phoenix* 3 June 1929: 1.

56. "James Michener Chosen to Deliver Ivy Oration Baccalaureate Sunday." *Swarthmore Phoenix* 19 Mar. 1929: 1.

57. "Ivy Orator Expresses New Valuation of College Life," *Swarthmore Phoenix* 3 June 1929: 7.

58. "Phi Beta Kappa," *Swarthmore Phoenix* 3 June 1929:1.

59. "Swarthmore Confers One Hundred Twelve Degrees on Students," *Swarthmore Phoenix* 3 June, 1929: 5.

60. *Halcyon : 1930*, 239.

61. Hayes, *James A. Michener* 41.

62. *Halcyon : 1927*, 141.

63. James A. Michener, *The Fires of Spring* (New York: Random, 1949).

64. Hayes, *James A. Michener* 34-44. Becker, *James A. Michener* 4-7.

65. Michener, personal interview, 24 May 1993.

66. James A. Michener, letter to George A. Walton, 11 April 1933, George School Archives.

67. Michener, personal interview, 24 May 1993.

68. "Michener to Graduate," *Bucks County Intelligencer* 31 May 1929: 6.

69. "Swarthmore Chautauqua to Get $5,000,000 Endowment," *Phoenix* 8 Mar. 1927: 5.

70. "Swarthmore Chautauqua to Build Large Studio," *Swarthmore Phoenix* 27 Apr. 1926: 1.

71. James A. Michener, *The World Is My Home : A Memoir* (New York: Random, 1992) 243.

72. "Literary and Dramatic Criticisms," *Swarthmore Phoenix* 19 Mar. 1929: 4.

73. James A. Michener, letter to George A. Walton, 11 Apr. 1933, George School Archives.

74. Walton, *Swarthmore : An Informal History* 40.

75. Ibid 47.

76. Ibid 49.

77. Ibid 50.

78. Ibid 55.

79. Ibid 61.

80. Ibid 63.

81. Ibid 77.

82. Ibid 83.

83. Ibid 90.

84. Ibid 91.

85. Ibid 94.

86. Ibid 102.

87. Ibid 113.

88. Ibid 140.

89. Ibid 143.

90. Ibid 122.

91. Swarthmore College, Office of Public Relations Press Release, 25 Sept. 1991.

92. Julie L. Nicklin, "Colleges That Helped Spawn Michener's Career Are the Beneficiaries of His Philanthropy," *Chronicle of Higher Education* 13 Jan. 1993: A27.

The Hill Teaching Years: 1929–1931

1. James A. Michener, personal interview, 24 May 1993.

2. Ibid.

3. Ibid.

4. James A. Michener and McFeeley, telegram to James I. Wendell, 2 Mar. 1929, Hill School Archives.

5. John A. Lester, letter to James I. Wendell, 4 Mar. 1929, Hill School Archives.

6. Paul Chancellor, *The History of The Hill School : 1851–1976* (Pottstown, Pa.: Hill School, 1976) 135.

7. Lauren A. Chapis, letter to the authors, 23 Mar. 1994.

8. James I. Wendell, letter to James A. Michener, 12 Mar. 1929, Hill School Archives.

9. James A. Michener, *The World Is My Home : A Memoir* (New York: Random House, 1992) 447.

10. Ibid.

11. Ibid.

12. Michener, personal interview, 24 May 1993.

13. "Four New Members Added to the School Faculty," *Hill School News* 11 Oct. 1929: 2.

14. *1851 Circular*, reprinted in *Hill School Bulletin*, Sept. 1980: 11.

15. Chancellor, *History of The Hill* 9.

16. Paul Chancellor, et al., *A History of Pottstown Pennsylvania*, (Pottstown, Pa.: Historical Society of Pottstown, 1953) 71.

17. Chancellor, *History of The Hill* 3.

18. *1851 Circular* 11.

19. Chancellor, *History of The Hill* 12.

20. Ibid 5.

21. Ibid 14.

22. Ibid 13.

23. Ibid 11.

24. Ibid 15.

25. Ibid 71-2.

26. Ibid 23.

27. Ibid 72.

28. Lawrence Rhodes. "The Hill School in Retrospect," *The Hill School Bulletin*, Sept. 1980: 18.

29. Chancellor, *History of The Hill* 35.

30. Ibid 134.

31. Rhodes, "The Hill School in Retrospect," 18.

32. Ibid.

33. Chancellor, *History of The Hill* 38.

34. Lauren A. Chapis, letter to the authors, 10 May 1994.

35. Chancellor, *History of The Hill* 46.

36. Ibid 50.

37. Ibid 47.

38. Ibid 49.

39. James A. Michener, letter to the authors, 7 May 1994.

40. Chancellor, *History of The Hill* 155.

41. Boyd Edwards and Isaac Thomas, comp. and ed., *Mr. Rolfe of The Hill*, (Pottstown, Pa.: The Hill School, 1929?) 10.

42. James Hilton, *Good-bye, Mr. Chips*, (N.p.: Little, 1934): 12.

43. Chancellor, *History of The Hill* 83.

44. Ibid 85.

45. Ibid 88.

46. Ibid 106-07.

47. Ibid 115-16.

48. Ibid 117.

49. Edward C. Roe, personal interview, 14 Apr. 1994.

50. George K. Stauffer, telephone interview, 22 May 1994.

51. Chancellor, *History of The Hill* 135.

52. Ibid 149.

53. Michener, letter to the authors, 7 May 1994.

54. Chancellor, *History of The Hill* 149.

55. Roe, personal interview, 14 Apr. 1994.

56. Michener, personal interview, 24 May 1993: 37.

57. Roe, personal interview, 14 Apr. 1994.

58. Chancellor, *History of The Hill* 135.

59. Ibid 139.

60. Ibid 64.

61. Ibid 63.

62. Ibid 65.

63. Michener, letter to the authors, 7 May 1994.
64. John A. Lester, *A Spelling Review : For Preparatory Schools and High Schools* (Pottstown, Pa.: Lester, 1922).
65. Michener, letter to the authors, 7 May 1994.
66. Chancellor, *History of the Hill* 142.
67. *The Hill School Catalogue For the Year 1929–1930*, (Pottstown, Pa.: Hill School, n.d.) Frontispiece.
68. Ibid 37.
69. William P. Davis, telephone interview, 22 May 1994. William B. Watling, telephone interview, 19 May 1994.
70. Frank Bissell, telephone interview, 22 May 1994.
71. *Hill School Catalogue For the Year 1929–1930*, 37-38.
72. Ibid 37.
73. Ibid 8-19.
74. *A Tradition of Excellence*, (Pottstown, Pa.: Hill School, 1991).
75. Michener, personal interview, 24 May 1993: 28.
76. *Hill School Catalogue For the Year 1929–1930*, 30 and 44.
77. Ibid 39.
78. Ibid 25.
79. Ibid 20.
80. Ibid.
81. Ibid 31-32.
82. David P. Close, telephone interview, 10 Apr. 1994.
83. Standish F. Medina, letter to the authors, 19 Apr. 1994.
84. David P. Close, telephone interview, 17 May 1994.
85. Robert Biddle, III, telephone interview, 31 May 1994.
86. Standish F. Medina, letters to the authors, 24 Mar. 1994 and 19 Apr. 1994.
87. Stauffer, telephone interview, 22 May 1994.
88. Close, telephone interview, 17 May 1994.
89. Roe, personal interview, 14 Apr. 1994.
90. Michener, letter to the authors, 7 May 1994.
91. Roe, personal interview, 14 Apr. 1994.
92. William B. Watling, telephone interview, 19 May 1994.
93. Chancellor, *History of The Hill* 137.
94. Michener, personal interview, 24 May 1993: 43.
95. Close, telephone interview, 17 May 1994.
96. Standish F. Medina, Toastmaster's address, 100th Anniversary of Hill School, Pottstown, 1951.
97. Chancellor, *History of The Hill* 137.
98. Medina, Toastmaster's address, 1951.
99. Medina, letter to the authors, 19 Apr. 1994.
100. "Autumn House Party Proves Great Success," *Hill School News* 12 Dec. 1929: 1-2.
101. Roe, personal interview, 14 Apr. 1994.
102. "Inquiring Reporter," *Hill School News* 12 Dec. 1929: 4.
103. Medina, letter to the authors, 24 Mar. 1994.

104. Roe, personal interview, 14 Apr. 1994.
105. Medina, letters to the authors, 24 Mar. 1994 and 19 Apr. 1994. Close, telephone interview, 17 May 1994.
106. *Hill School Catalogue For the Year 1929–1930*, 25.
107. Edward C. Roe, letter to the authors, 21 Apr. 1994.
108. Edward C. Roe, letter to the authors, 19 May 1994.
109. Ibid.
110. Roe, letter to the authors, 21 Apr. 1994.
111. Ibid.
112. *Hill School Catalogue For the Year 1929–1930*, 26.
113. "Much Enthusiasm Shown in Far Fields Baseball," *Hill School News* 1 May 1931: 2.
114. David P. Close, telephone interview, 20 Apr. 1994.
115. Michener, letter to the authors, 7 May 1994.
116. Roe, personal interview, 14 Apr. 1994.
117. Chancellor, *History of The Hill* 139.
118. Ibid 141.
119. John Lester, letter to George A. Walton, 10 Apr. 1933, George School Archives.
120. Michener, letter to the authors, 7 May 1994.
121. Chancellor, *History of The Hill* 141.
122. *Hill School Catalogue For the Year 1929–1930*, 23.
123. John W. Nicholson, telephone interview, 31 May 1994.
124. Roe, personal interview, 14 Apr. 1994.
125. Nicholson, telephone interview, 31 May 1994.
126. Michener, letter to the authors, 7 May 1994.
127. "Faculty Holds Novel Mauve Decade Party," *Hill School News* 14 Nov. 1929: 1-2.
128. "Faculty Song Guide," *Hill School Snooze* 28 Nov. 1929: 7.
129. Michener, letter to the authors, 7 May 1994.
130. Ibid.
131. "'A Christmas Carol' is Presented by Faculty," *Hill School News* 19 Dec. 1929: 2.
132. Michener, letter to the authors, 7 May 1994.
133. Bissell, telephone interview, 22 May 1994.
134. "'The Dover Road' is Presented by Faculty," *Hill School News* 13 Mar. 1930: 2-3.
135. Lauren A. Chapis, letter to the authors, 19 May 1994.
136. "Mr. Michener Stars as Squad Defeats Faculty," *Hill School News* 19 Dec. 1929: 2.
137. Michener, personal interview, 24 May 1993: 8.
138. Hill School English Class, *1929 Christmas Book* (Pottstown, Pa.: The Feroe Press, 1929).
139. Michener, letter to the authors, 7 May, 1994.
140. *Record* [Hill School], 39.3 (1929).

141. "Faculty Reviewer Lauds Format and Precise Style of Christmas Record, But Criticizes General Theme of Stories," *Hill School News* 23 Jan. 1930: 1-3.
142. Ibid.
143. Michener, *World Is My Home* 278.
144. James A. Michener, letter to James I. Wendell, 17 Jan. 1930, Hill School Archives.
145. James I. Wendell, letters to University of Chicago and Harvard University on Michener's behalf, 17 Jan. 1930, Hill School Archives.
146. Michener, letter to the authors, 7 May 1994.
147. Ibid.
148. James A. Michener, letter to James I. Wendell, 18 Aug. 1930, Hill School Archives.
149. Hill School Administration Office, letter to James A. Michener, 20 Aug. 1930, Hill School Archives.
150. Chancellor, *History of The Hill* 142.
151. Lauren A. Chapis, letter to the authors, 22 Feb. 1994.
152. Chapis, letter to the authors, 23 Mar. 1994.
153. "Directory of the Hill Masters," *Hill School News* 10 Oct. 1930: 3.
154. Close, telephone interview, 17 May 1994.
155. James I Wendell, letter to James A. Michener, 17 Dec. 1930, Hill School Archives.
156. Michener, letter to the authors, 7 May 1994.
157. "Mr. Michener is Faculty Member to Review February Issue of Record; Latest Number Has Much Noteworthy Prose," *Hill School News* 12 Mar. 1931: 2+.
158. "Mr. Michener Reviews April Record; Praises 'Chaos' and 'The Quest of Sir Belaine'; Says Themes Are Too Forced," *Hill School News* 1 May 1931: 3+.
159. "Michener is Faculty Member to Review," *Hill School News* 12 Mar. 1931: 1-3.
160. Ibid.
161. Walter C. Bühler, telephone interview, 26 Apr. 1994.
162. Nicholson, telephone interview, 31 May 1994.
163. "Mr. Michener Reviews April Record," *Hill School News* 1 May 1931: 3+.
164. Ibid.
165. Michener, letter to the authors, 7 May 1994.
166. James A. Michener, *The Novel* (New York: Random, 1991) 276.
167. Michener, personal interview, 24 May 1993.
168. Ibid.
169. Chapis, letter to the authors, 23 Mar. 1994.
170. Michener, personal interview, 24 May 1993.
171. Ibid.
172. Ibid.
173. Ibid.
174. Ibid.
175. Chapis, letter to the authors, 19 May 1994.

176. Chancellor, "Feroe Paper Box," *History of Pottstown* 115.
177. Michener, personal interview, 24 May 1993.
178. Ibid.
179. Ibid.
180. Ibid.
181. Ibid.
182. Ibid.
183. Michener, letter to the authors, 7 May 1994.
184. Michener, personal interview, 24 May 1993.
185. Michael F. Sweeney, *Mike Sweeney of The Hill*, (New York: Putnum's, 1940): Title page.
186. Michener, personal interview, 24 May 1993.
187. Ibid.
188. Ibid.
189. Ibid.
190. Ibid.
191. Ibid.
192. Ibid.
193. Ibid.
194. Ibid.
195. Ibid.
196. Ibid.
197. Ibid.
198. *A Tradition of Excellence*, (Pottstown, Pa.: Hill School, 1991).
199. Michener, personal interview, 24 May 1993.
200. Ibid.
201. James I. Wendell, letter on Michener's behalf, 28 Oct. 1930, Hill School Archives.
202. James A. Michener, *Caravans* (New York: Random, 1963).
203. Bühler, telephone interview, 26 Apr. 1994.
204. Biddle III, telephone interview, 31 May 1994.
205. Close, telephone interview, 20 Apr. 1994.
206. Close, telephone interview, 17 May 1994.
207. Ibid.
208. Ibid.
209. Watling, telephone interview, 19 May 1994.
210. Close, telephone interview, 17 May 1994.
211. Chancellor, *History of The Hill* 143.
212. Ibid 144.
213. Ibid 145.
214. Medina, Toastmaster's address, 1951.
215. Chancellor, *History of The Hill* 189.
216. Ibid 205.
217. Ibid 207-8.
218. John Markle, Jr., letter to Charles C. Watson, 24 Feb. 1992, Hill School Archives.
219. Chapis, letter to the authors, 22 Feb. 1994.
220. *The Hill School : 1994 [Catalogue]* (Pottstown, Pa.: Hill School, 1994) 15.
221. Hill School Admissions Office, verbal communication, 21 June 1994.
222. *Hill School : 1994 [Catalogue]* Various pages.
223. "Dress and Appearance," *The Hill School Student Handbook* 27.
224. Medina, Toastmaster's address, 1951.

The Textbooks: Teaching and Learning

1. James A. Michener, personal interview, 24 May 1993.
2. Paul Chancellor, *The History of The Hill School : 1851–1976* (Pottstown, Pa.: The Hill School, 1976) 63.

George School Teaching Years: 1933–1936

1. A. Grove Day, *James Michener*, 2nd ed. (Boston: Twayne, 1977) 17.
2. James A. Michener, *The World Is My Home : A Memoir* (New York: Random, 1992) 123-28 and 447-48.
3. James A. Michener, personal interview, 24 May 1993.
4. James A. Michener, letter to George A. Walton, 15 Jan. 1933, George School Archives.
5. George A. Walton, letter to James A. Michener, 10 Feb. 1933, George School Archives.
6. James A. Michener, cable to George A. Walton, 22 Feb. 1933, George School Archives.
7. James A. Michener, letter to George A. Walton, 24 Feb. 1933, George School Archives.
8. George A. Walton, letter to James A. Michener, 9 Mar. 1933, George School Archives.
9. "Instructors at Meeting," *George School News* 15 May 1935: 1.
10. Michener, personal interview, 24 May 1993.
11. James A. Michener, letter to George A. Walton, 11 Apr. 1933, George School Archives.
12. James A. Michener, letter to George A. Walton, 14 Apr. 1933, George School Archives.
13. John Lester, letter to George A. Walton, 10 Apr. 1933, George School Archives.
14. George A. Walton, letter to John Lester, 18 May 1933, George School Archives.
15. James I. Wendell, letter to George A. Walton, 20 May 1933, George School Archives.
16. John Lester, letter to George A. Walton, 22 May 1933, George School Archives.
17. James A. Michener, letter to James I. Wendell, Undated, George School Archives.
18. James A. Michener, letter to authors, 7 May 1994.
19. Kingdon W. Swayne, *George School : The History of a Quaker Community* (Philadelphia: Society of Friends, 1992) 5.
20. Ibid 10.
21. Ibid 19-27.
22. Kingdon W. Swayne, *George School : The History of a Quaker Community*, Scholars' ed. (Philadelphia: Society of Friends, 1992) 180.
23. Michener, *World Is My Home* 448.
24. Kingdon W. Swayne, personal interview, 4 Nov. 1993.
25. Swayne, *George School*, Scholars' ed., 232.
26. Swayne, *George School* 28-34.
27. *George School : A Quaker, Coeducational Boarding and Day School, Grades 9-12, in Newtown, Pennsylvania [Bulletin]* (Newtown: George School, 1992?).
28. "Vitarelli Stars in Faculty Play 'Phiz the Whiz,'" *George School News* 11 Oct. 1933: 1.
29. George A. Walton, letter to William Wrinkle, 30 July 1936, George School Archives.
30. Michener, personal interview, 24 May 1993.
31. Michener, *World Is My Home* 243.
32. Swayne, personal interview, 4 Nov. 1993.
33. "Marionette Guild Begun," *George School News* 14 Dec. 1933: 4.
34. "Miccelli Marionettes in Shakespearean Scenes," *George School News* 12 Apr. 1934: 1.
35. *1934* (Newtown, Pa.: George School, 1934) 7-8.
36. Ibid 91.
37. Ibid 93.
38. *George School Bulletin : The Georgian* 5.5 (1934) 12-13.
39. "Mr. Michener Possesses Collection Of Old English, Scottish Ballads," *George School News* 16 Mar. 1934: 1+.
40. "Scottish Trip Described," *George School News* 28 Feb. 1934: 3.
41. "Mr. Michener Speaks," *George School News* 23 May 1934: 2.
42. "Coaches Attend Meeting," *George School News* 12 Dec. 1933: 3.
43. "Training Tables Started," *George School News* 12 Dec. 1933: 4.
44. "Faculty Downs Varsity Quintet by Final Rally," *George School News* 28 Feb. 1934: 3.
45. "Michener Chooses Cubs," *George School News* 2 May 1934: 3.
46. "Mr. Michener Recovering," *George School News* 16 May 1934: 1.
47. "Meijer Editor for Next Year; Eastburn, Swayne Associates," *George School News* 12 June 1934: 1.
48. "Teachers Plan Summer to Include Travel, Study at Home and Abroad," *George School News* 12 June 1934: 1+.
49. Michener, personal interview, 24 May 1993.
50. "Faculty Travels Extended to All Parts of World," *George School News* 3 Oct. 1934: 4.
51. "Micelli Marionettes Fill Heavey [sic] Summer Schedule," *George School News* 3 Oct. 1934: 4.
52. Mrs. H. Spenker, letter to George A. Walton, 3 Sept. 1934, George School Archives.
53. James A. Michener, letter to George A. Walton, 8 Oct. 1934, George School Archives.
54. Richard Miller, "Correspondence," *George School News* 18 Oct. 1934: 2.
55. James A. Michener, "Correspondence," *George School News* 24 Oct. 1934: 2.

56. Connie Ernst, "The Prompter : When The Cat's Away," *George School News* 21 Nov. 1934: 2.
57. Ibid.
58. Swayne, *George School* 81.
59. Swayne, personal interview, 4 Nov. 1993.
60. *1935* (Newtown: George School, 1935) 17.
61. Ibid 104 and 106.
62. "Marionettes Will Tour Country During Summer," *George School News* 10 June 1935: 2.
63. "Faculty Quintet Trounces Varsity : Michener High Scorer for Teachers With 13 Points Out of 45-16 Total," *George School News* 30 Jan. 1935: 3.
64. *George School Bulletin : The Georgian* 6.6 (1935) 17-18.
65. "Instructors at Meeting : Shane, Michener, Mohr, Mendenhall Attend Curriculum Conference," *George School News* 15 May 1935: 1.
66. James A. Michener, letter to George A. Walton, 28 Mar. 1935, George School Archives.
67. Michener, personal interview, 24 May 1993.
68. Ibid.
69. *1935* (Newtown: George School, 1935) 15 and 17.
70. "The Prompter," *George School News* 10 June 1935: 2.
71. "L-1937 Students Give Melodrama Of Farm and City . Hummel, Brown, Swayne Star in 'Moral Drama;' Players Sing Between Acts," *George School News* 15 May 1935: 1.
72. "Instructors Will Paint, Play, Ponder, Plod ---at Home and All Over the Map," *George School News* 10 June 1935: 1+.
73. Swayne, *George School* 188.
74. "Faculty Quintet Trounces Varsity," *George School News* 30 Jan. 1935: 3.
75. Swayne, personal interview, 4 Nov. 1993.
76. Ibid.
77. "Instructors Will Paint, Play, Ponder, Plod ---at Home and All Over the Map," *George School News* 10 June 1935: 1+.
78. James A. Michener, letter to George A. Walton, undated [1935], George School Archives.
79. George A. Walton, letter to James A. Michener, 3 July 1935, George School Archives.
80. James A. Michener, letter to George A. Walton, 5 July 1935, George School Archives.
81. Patti Koon, letter to George A. Walton, 5 July 1935, George School Archives.
82. S. P. Koon, letter to George A. Walton, 8 July 1935, George School Archives.
83. George A. Walton, letter to S. P. Koon, 10 July 1935, George School Archives.
84. John P. Hayes, *James A. Michener : A Biography* (Indianapolis: Bobbs, 1984) 51.
85. "Faculty Stages the 'Rivals,'" *The News* 8 Feb. 1936:1.
86. James A. Michener, letter to George A. Walton, 30 Mar. 1936, George School Archives.
87. *1936* (Newtown: George School, 1936) 6 and 68.

Postlude: Colorado State, Harvard, Macmillan, WW II

1. William L. Wrinkle, letter to George A. Walton, 28 July 1936, George School Archives.
2. George A. Walton, letter to William L. Wrinkle, 30 July 1936, George School Archives.
3. James A. Michener, letter to George A. Walton, 17 Nov. 1936, George School Archives.
4. James A. Michener, letter to George A. Walton, 16 Jan. 1939, George School Archives.
5. James A. Michener, et. al., "As They Look Back," *George School Bulletin : The Georgian*. 9.1 (1937) 11-12.
6. A. Grove Day, *James Michener*, 2nd ed. (Boston: Twayne, 1977) 18. George J. Becker, *James A. Michener* (New York: Ungar, 1983) vii.
7. John P. Hayes, *James A. Michener : A Biography* (Indianapolis: Bobbs, 1984) 54. James A. Michener, *The World Is My Home : A Memoir* (New York: Random, 1992) 177.
8. Ibid 176.
9. George A. Walton, letter to James A. Michener, 1 Mar. 1939, George School Archives.
10. Day, *James Michener* 18. Hayes, *James A. Michener* 56. Becker, *James A. Michener* 7.
11. George A. Walton, letter to James A. Michener, 3 Nov. 1941, George School Archives.
12. Michener, *World Is My Home* 268.
13. James A. Michener, personal interview, 24 May 1993.
14. James A. Michener, *The Novel* (New York: Random, 1991).
15. James A. Michener, letter to George Walton, 30 Sept. 1942, George School Archives.
16. George A. Walton, "To Whom It May Concern" letter on Michener's behalf, 1 Oct. 1942, George School Archives.
17. James A. Michener, letter to James I. Wendell, undated [May 1942], Hill School Archives.
18. James I. Wendell, letter to James A. Michener, 17 May 1942, Hill School Archives.
19. Michener, personal interview, 24 May 1993.
20. Michener, *World Is My Home* 278-80.
21. James A. Michener, *Tales of the South Pacific* (New York: Macmillan, 1947).

Afterword

1. Ann Charters, *Kerouac* (San Francisco: Straight Arrow, 1973).
2. John P. Hayes, *James A. Michener : A Biography* (Indianapolis/New York: Bobbs, 1984) 51.
3. James A. Michener, *Memories* Videocassette (George School, 1993).

SOURCE BIBLIOGRAPHY

Becker, George J[oseph]. *James A. Michener.* New York: Ungar, [^c1983 by Ungar]. A biography.

Biddle, Robert, III. Telephone interview. 31 May 1994. Four-page transcription of a taped interview by Joy V. Bliss. Hill School Class of 1933. Michener was not his coach, teacher, or dorm master at The Hill, but he later was a Bucks County, Pennsylvania, neighbor and they played tennis together.

Bissell, Frank. Telephone interview. 22 May 1994. Hill Class of 1933. He taught and coached at The Hill 1947–73. He said Michener was not his dorm master, coach, or teacher. He has had a long association with The Hill.

Bucks County Intelligencer. Doylestown, Pa. Daily newspaper. Spruance Library in the Mercer Museum, Doylestown, has microfiche copies.

Bühler, Walter C. Telephone interview. 26 Apr. 1994. Hill Class of 1932. Michener reviewed his contributions to the *Hill Record*, but Bühler has no memory of Michener while he was a student at Hill. He took a trip to Afghanistan on the strength of Michener's *Caravans.*

Chancellor, Paul [G.], ed.. *A History of Pottstown Pennsylvania.* Pottstown, Pa.: Historical Society of Pottstown, Pennsylvania (Feroe Press), 1953 [^c1953 by Historical Society of Pottstown : Reprint, 1974].

Chancellor, Paul [G.]. *The History of The Hill School : 1851–1976.* Pottstown, Pa.: The Hill School, [^c1976 by The Hill School]. Chancellor taught at The Hill, including during the two Michener years.

Charters, Ann. *Kerouac.* [San Francisco, Calif.: Straight Arrow, ^c1973 by Ann Charters]. A biography.

Close, David P. Telephone interviews. 20 Apr. 1994 and 17 May 1994. Hill School class of 1934. He had Michener as dorm master on 4 East of Middle School in 1930–31. Michener coached Close in far-field football. Close was on the Hill School Board of Trustees from 1965–85; Chairman, 1973–85. Interviewed by Joy V. Bliss. His brother, Walter, who is mentioned in Michener's letter on page 88, was an editor for, and contributor to, the 1929 Christmas issue and Michener's student.

Davis, William P. Telephone interview. 22 May 1994. Hill Class of 1933. He has no memories of Michener as his dorm master or teacher but he is a good source for general information about The Hill. Interviewed by Joy V. Bliss.

Day, A. Grove. *James Michener.* 2nd ed. Boston: Twayne, [^c1977 by Hall]. Michener prefers this biography primarily due to his long acquaintance with Grove Day as author and friend. Day has extensively written about Hawaii.

Doylestown High School. *The Torch.* Doylestown, Pa.: Doylestown High School. Student literary magazine issued every two months during the school year. Copies are found in the library of Central Bucks West High School and in Spruance Library, Mercer Museum.

Ferenbach, Carl. Telephone interview. 20 May 1994. Hill Class of 1933. He wrote for Michener's 1929 Christmas issue and therefore was in Michener's English class as a third former. He has no memories of Michener at the Hill. Interviewed by Joy V. Bliss.

Feroe, Mrs. Melvin. Lancaster, Pa. Telephone interview. 23 Mar. 1994. Interviewed by G. L. Dybwad. The Feroes are still very much interested in Pottstown and Hill School. Besides answering questions, she supplied copies of *The History of Pottstown* by Chancellor and Lester's *A Spelling Review*, both printed by the Feroe Press.

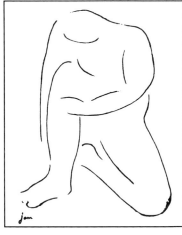

George School Archives. Newtown, Pa. Kingdon W. Swayne, Archivist. Correspondence between James A. Michener and George A. Walton. Correspondence on Michener's behalf. Photographs of Michener when he was a George School instructor. Complete runs of *George School News* and *Bulletin* and the school yearbooks (annuals). The archives contain a painting and a drawing by Michener, most likely while he taught at at George School. Initialed "JAM," both are shown on the right.

George School. *George School : A Quaker, Coeducational Boarding and Day School, Grades 9-12, in Newtown, Pennsylvania [Bulletin].* [Newtown, Pa.: George School, 1992?]. 1992–93 school year prospectus.

George School. *George School Bulletin : The Georgian.* [Newtown, Pa.: George School]. 5.5 (1934): 12-13 "Hobby Groups Active During Year"; 6.6 (1935): 17-18 "A Famous Five," by James A. Michener; 9.1 (1937): 11-12 "As They Look Back" by James A. Michener, et. al.

George School. *George School News.* Newtown, Pa.: George School, 1933–1936. This is the student newspaper. The George School archives contain copies.

George School. *Memories.* Videocassette. Newtown, Pa.; George School, 1993. VHS tape cassette with label: "James Michener Greeting to George School, August 1993." This was Michener's contribution to the George School centennial.

George School. *1934.* [Newtown, Pa.: George School, 1934]. School annual for 1934. The annual was later named *Opus.*

George School. *1935.* [Newtown, Pa.: George School, 1935]. School annual for 1935. The faculty panorama is on page 15. The annual was later named *Opus.*

George School. *1936.* [Newtown, Pa.: George School, 1936]. School annual for 1936. The faculty panorama was taken on the front steps of Main; Michener is in the back row. The annual was later named *Opus.*

George School. *The News.* Newtown, Pa.: George School. 1936. This is the student newspaper with the smaller new format, which replaced the *George School News.* The volume numbers started over with Volume 1 in 1936. George School archives.

Michener's Artwork From George School (Joy V. Bliss photos)

Griffiths, Paul L. Telephone interview. 22 May 1994. Michener was his dorm master in 1930–31 on 4 East of Middle School and his teacher in 1930–31. His recollections of Michener are few. Mentioned in Michener's letter, page 88. Interviewed by Joy V. Bliss.

Hayes, John P[hillip]. *James A. Michener : A Biography.* Indianapolis: Bobbs, [^c1984 by Hayes].

Hill School Archives. Pottstown, Pa. Lauren A. Chapis, Archivist. The archives contain: correspondence between James A. Michener and James I. Wendell, correspondence between James A. Michener and John Lester, correspondence in James A. Michener's behalf, and complete runs of *The Hill School News, The Hill Record, The Hill School Snooze,* and *The Dial* (annual).

Hill School. *Hill : The Hill School Bulletin.* Pottstown, Pa.: Hill School. Hill information magazine with articles by alumni, guests, and faculty.

Hill School. *The Dial : Published by the Class of 1931*. Volume 35. Pottstown, Pa.: Hill School (Press of E. A. Wright Company), 1931. A Hill School yearbook.

Hill School. *The Hill Record*. N.p.: Hill School. A monthly student literary magazine.

Hill School. *The Hill School Alumni Directory : 1991*. Pottstown, Pa.: Hill School, [c1991 by Harris].

Hill School. *The Hill School : Catalogue : For the Year 1929–1930*. Pottstown, Pa.: [Hill School], 1929? Frontispiece is an aerial view of The Hill with legend of major buildings.

Hill School. *The Hill School News*. Pottstown, Pa.: Hill School. A weekly student newspaper published by Hill School students. Bound volumes in the Hill School archives also contain the parody, *The Hill School Snooze*.

Hill School. *The Hill School Snooze*. Pottstown, Pa.: Hill School. This is an occasionally published student spoof on the *News*.

Hilton, James. *Good-bye, Mr. Chips*. N.p.: Little, [c1934 by Hilton].

Lester, John A. *A Spelling Review : For Preparatory Schools and High Schools*. Pottstown, Pa.: Lester, 1922 [c1922 by Lester]. This first edition book was printed by the Feroe Press in Pottstown, Pa.
---- Also found: 12th ed. Chicago: Follett, [c1947 by Follett].

Medina, Standish F. Letters to the authors. 24 Mar. 1994 and 19 Apr. 1994. Medina, Hill School class of 1933, does not remember Michener at The Hill, but has many recollections of school life in the early 1930s. Several Medina family members have attended Hill. Medina's daughter-in-law is Michener's editor at Random House.

Medina, Standish F. Toastmaster's address. 100th Anniversary of Hill School. Pottstown, Pa. 1951. Unpublished seven-page typed manuscript. From Medina's personal papers. The speech contains personal reminiscences and introductions of other keynote speakers for the evening. Michener was in attendance.

Michener, James A[lbert]. Letter to the authors. 7 May 1994. Answers to several pages of questions posed by the authors.

Michener, James A[lbert]. Personal interview. 24 May 1993. This recorded interview at Michener's home office in Austin, Texas, was later transcribed into an unpublished 72-page document. John Kings, Michener's secretary and coordinating editor, and Deborah Brothers, publisher, State House Press also attended the morning session. G. L. Dybwad and Joy V. Bliss conducted the interview.

Michener, James A[lbert]. *Report of the County Chairman*. New York: Random House, [c1961 by James A. Michener]. The author signed this copy and the accompanying letter dated 1962.

Michener, James A[lbert]. *Tales of the South Pacific*. New York: Macmillan, 1947 [c1946, 1947 by Curtis, c1947 by Michener].

Michener, James A[lbert]. *The Fires of Spring*. New York: Random, [c1949 by Michener].

Michener, James A[lbert]. *The Novel*. New York: Random, [c1991 by Michener].

Michener, James A[lbert]. *The World Is My Home: A Memoir*. New York: Random, [c1992 by Michener].

Nicholson, John W. Telephone interview. 31 May 1994. Hill School Class of 1933. He wrote for the *Hill Record* and Michener reviewed his work twice, but he never had Michener for a dorm master, teacher, or coach. He has many crisp memories of his years at The Hill. Medicine was his career. Interviewed by Joy V. Bliss.

Revell, Alexander, III. Letter to the authors. 25 Apr. 1994. Hill School Class of 1943. He taught at The Hill for 37 years and owned a bookstore in Pottstown (now closed). We contacted him about the Christmas issue that Michener's class published in 1930, which we were ultimately unable to locate.

Roe, Edward C. Letters to the authors. 21 Apr. 1994, and 19 May 1994. Hill School class of 1931. He did not take any Michener classes, but has many fond memories and memorabilia of Hill School life. He excelled at boxing and football at The Hill. He went on to Princeton University and played varsity football there.

Roe, Edward C. Personal interview. 14 Apr. 1994. G. L. Dybwad and Joy V. Bliss conducted the taped interview at his home in Santa Fe, New Mexico, and transcribed it to a fifteen-page document.

Stauffer, George K. Telephone interview. 22 May 1994. Hill school class of 1933. He had Michener as an English teacher, and he was Art Editor for the 1929 Christmas issue published by Michener's English class. As a baptismal gift, Dwight Meigs, his godfather, gave him a six-year scholarship to The Hill which Headmaster Wendell did not honor (the school had changed from Meigs family owned to alumni owned).

Swarthmore College. *Halcyon : 1930*. N.p.: Published by The Junior class of Swarthmore College, [c1929 by Richard M. Kain, Editor-in-Chief : Alex. J. McCloskey, Jr., Business manager]. This annual contains data from Michener's senior year.

Swarthmore College. *Halcyon : 1927*. N.p.: Published by The Junior class of Swarthmore College, [c1926 by Girand B. Ruddick, Editor-in-Chief George W. McKeag : Business Manager]. This annual contains data from Michener's freshman year and gives his Doylestown address.

Swarthmore College. *Swarthmore Phoenix*. This is a weekly Swarthmore College student newspaper.

Swarthmore College. *The Portfolio : A Literary Quarterly Published by the Students of Swarthmore College*. N.p.: Swarthmore College. Student literary publication found bound by calendar year at Swarthmore College McCabe Library.

Swayne, Kingdon W. *George School : The History of a Quaker Community*. [Philadelphia, Pa.: Philadelphia Yearly Meeting Religious Society of Friends, c1992 by George School]. George School had this book issued as part of the centennial celebration. Book starts with geological time setting patterned after Michener's epic novels.

Swayne, Kingdon W. *George School : The History of a Quaker Community*. Scholars' ed. [Philadelphia, Pa.: Philadelphia Yearly Meeting Religious Society of Friends, c1992 by George School]. This is a companion book to the Swayne history listed above. The Scholars' edition lists the statistical data relevant to the first 100 years of George School.

Swayne, Kingdon W. Personal interview. 4 Nov. 1993. Kingdon Swayne, George School class of 1937, has come out of retirement several times to aid his alma mater. He is currently historian and archivist at George School. The archives are located in a special room below a 1752 Quaker Meeting House moved to George School from Philadelphia. Interviewed by G. L. Dybwad and Joy V. Bliss at George School.

Sweeney, Michael F. *Mike Sweeney of The Hill : The Autobiography of Michael F. Sweeney*. Ed. W. Reginald Wheeler. New York: Putnum's, [c1940 by Putnum's]. Sweeney became athletic director at The Hill in 1896 and remained there 40 years.

Walton, Richard J. *Swarthmore : An Informal History*. [Swarthmore, Pa.: Swarthmore College, c1986]. Introduction by James A. Michener.

Watling, William B. "Spike". Telephone interview. 19 May 1994. Hill Class of 1933. This interview resulted in a four-page transcription. Watling has an excellent memory for detail. He had Michener as dorm master on 4 East of Middle School for the school year 1930–31, but he did not have Michener as a teacher. Interviewed by Joy V. Bliss.

White, Major Lee. Telephone interview. 22 May 1994. Hill Class of 1933. He did not have Michener for a dorm master, coach, or teacher. He has general Hill memories but does not remember Michener from his time at The Hill. Interviewed by Joy V. Bliss.

BIBLIOGRAPHY OF THE HILL SCHOOL TEXTBOOKS

Baldwin, James. *The Story of Roland.* New York : Scribner's, [^c1883, 1930 by Scribner's; ^c1911 by Baldwin].
   24 cm x 19 cm.   xiv, 347 pages with color illustrations. Black cloth hardcover; color illustration tipped in on the front cover shows two knights in battle; gilt print on spine. The top edge is pink. End papers are color illustrations. Title page is a color lithograph with red, brown, and black print. Color plates are by Peter Hurd of the Brandywine School. Signed by Michener.

Bement, Howard, ed. *The Sir Roger de Coverley Papers : From The Spectator.* Chicago: Laurel, [^c1925, 1930 By Laurel].
   16½ cm x 12 cm.   1 leaf, 301 pages. Dark green cloth hardcover with gilt print. "Laurel English Classics" is blind-stamped on the front cover. The first leaf verso is a frontispiece portrait of Joseph Addison.

Blackmore, Richard Doddridge. *Lorna Doone: A Romance of Exmoor.* Ed. by Albert L. Barbour. 6th ed. New York: Macmillan, 1923 [^c1905 By Macmillan].
   14½ cm x 12 cm.   3 leaves, vii-xix, 642 pages. Dark brown cloth hardcover with gilt print. The frontispiece is titled "The Water Slide."

Boyd, James. *Marching On.* New York: Scribner's, 1927 [^c1927 by Scribner's].
   20 cm x 14 cm.   4 leaves, 3-426 pages. Forest green cloth hardcover with gilt print. The cover title is the same as the title page. Signed by Alfred G. Rolfe.

Dickens, Charles. *Great Expectations.* London: Milford Publisher to Oxford UP, [1907, …1928].
   15½ cm x 9½ cm.   4 leaves, 540 pages with illustrations by Warwick Goble. Dark blue cloth hardcover with gilt cover design and spine print. "The World's Classics CXXVIII" is printed on a leaf before the title page. Marginal marks and character list by Michener.

Drinkwater, John. *The Way of Poetry : An Anthology for Younger Readers.* Boston: Houghton, [^c1922 by Houghton, 1923].
   19½ cm x 13½ cm.   xxx, 1 leaf, 240 pages. Green cloth hardcover; gilt cover design and spine print. Signed twice by Michener. Contains Michener's handwritten poem, "Keats and Shakespeare"; author list; and marginal marks.

Edgar, Henry C. *Sentence Analysis by Diagram : A Handbook for the Rapid Review of English Syntax.* New York: Newson, [^c1915 by Newson].
   19½ cm x 13 cm.   viii, 112 pages. Brown cloth hardcover with dark brown print. Signed by Michener.

Edwards, Boyd and Isaac Thomas, comp. and ed. *Mr. Rolfe of The Hill.* [Pottstown, Pa.: Hill School (Feroe Press)], [1929?].
   20 cm x 14 cm.   4 leaves, 9-134 pages. Tan cloth hardcover with blue print. The last of the four leaves contains an illustration of Rolfe standing behind the desk in his classroom. Presentation copy signed by Alfred G. Rolfe.

Hardy, Thomas. *The Return of the Native.* New York: Modern Library, n.d.
   17 cm x 11½ cm.   ix, 1 leaf, 506, (1) pages. Blue cloth hardcover; gilt cover design and spine print. The dust jacket is light blue-green paper with black print and green border trim. This reprint is Modern Library book number 121. The preface by Hardy is dated July 1895. Signed twice by Michener.

Hawthorne, Nathaniel. *The House of the Seven Gables : A Romance.* Ed. Ernest Rhys. Ordinary ed. London: Dent, n.d.; New York: Dutton, [1907, 1930].
   17½ cm x 11½ cm.   xv, 310, 8 pages. Red cloth cover with gilt spine print. The cover is blind stamped, "J. M. Dent & Sons Ltd." The top edge is stained black. This reprint is Everyman's Library, No. 176. Michener's marks in the margins.

Hawthorne, Nathaniel. *The House of the Seven Gables: A Romance.* N.p.: Burt, n.d.
   19 cm x 13½ cm.   1 leaf, 374 pages, 4 leaves of ads. Maroon cloth hardcover with gilt spine print. This is part of the A. L. Burt uniform "Home Library" series.

Hudson, W[illiam]. H[enry]. *Green Mansions: A Romance of the Tropical Forest.* New York: The Modern Library, Publishers, n.d.
   17 cm x 11½ cm.   ix, 1 leaf, 289 pages. Mauve cloth hardcover reprint with gilt cover design and gilt spine print. This copy has no dust jacket. The top edge is stained mauve. The introduction by John Galsworthy is dated 1915. Signed by Michener.

Lewis, W. D., ed. *Tennyson's Idylls of the King : The Coming of Arthur : Gareth and Lynette : Lancelot and Elaine : The Holy Grail : Guinevere : The Passing of Arthur.* New York: Merrill, [^c1911, 1912 by Merrill].
   17 cm x 11½ cm.   1 leaf, 251 pages. Blue-gray cloth hardcover with black print. At the head of the title: "Merrill's English Texts." The frontispiece is a portrait of Alfred Lord Tennyson. The title page names Lewis as principal of the William Penn High School for girls, Philadelphia. Signed by Michener. Michener's handwritten poem, "Ode to Tennyson"; extensive margin marks; passage underlining; and text notes.

Linn, James Weber, ed. *A Tale of Two Cities by Charles Dickens.* Boston: Ginn (The Athenæum Press), [^c1906 by Ginn].
   19 cm x 13 cm.   1 leaf, xv, (1), 455 pages with illustrations. Purple cloth hardcover with black spine print. The front cover is blind stamped: "Ginn and Company". The frontispiece is a lithograph of Dickens. Signed by Michener.

Miller, George Morey, ed. *The Victorian Period.* New York: Scribner's, [^c1930 by Scribner's].
   17 cm x 11½ cm.   lxxix, 509 pages. Bright red cloth hardcover with gilt print. The top of the title page reads: "English literature." The title page is printed in orange ink. The front and back fly leaf papers are maps of England. Extensive marginal marks for passages Michener memorized.

Reynolds, George F. and Garland Greever. *The Facts and Backgrounds of Literature : English and American.* New York: Century, 1920 [^c1920 by Century].
   17½ cm x 13 cm.   xvi, 425 pages. Dark green cloth hardcover which is blind stamped; the spine has gilt print. Michener's personalized bookplate. On the fore edge is hand-lettered "DHS Michener." Extensive marginal marks and notes in Michener's hand.

Shakespeare, William. *The Merry Wives of Windsor.* Ed. Fred P. Emery. New York: Macmillan, 1928 [^c1913 By Macmillan].
   15 cm x 11 cm.   1 leaf, xx, 157 pages. Olive green cloth hardcover with gilt print. The frontispiece is an illustration of Windsor Castle. The decorative end papers are green. Extensive marginal marks and underlining; contains Michener's untitled and unsigned handwritten poem, character list, and doodle.

Tatlock, John S. P., and Percy MacKaye. *The Complete Poetical Works of Geoffrey Chaucer : Now Put Into Modern English.* New York: Macmillan (Norwood), 1923 [^c1912, By Macmillan].
   20½ cm x 14½ cm.   xii, 1 leaf, 607 pages with illustrations by Warwick Goble. The black cloth hardcover is blind stamped; the spine print is gilt. At the head of the title is printed: "The Modern Reader's Chaucer." Signed by Michener. Endnotes by Michener.

INDEX

-A-

Abraham, Herbert 77
Acting—Chautauqua
  Skidding 31
Acting—Student Years
  "Frankie and Johnnie" 27
  Hamburg Show 27, 28
  "The Hero" 28
  Jim Michener and Co. 27
  Outward Bound (Henry) 27, 28
  Twelfth-Night (Orsino) 28
Acting—Teaching Years
  A Christmas Carol (Marley) 44
  The Dover Road (Dominic) 44
  Hay Fever 80
  The Rivals (Multiple parts) 84
Admissions (Hill) 39, 54
Allgyer, David S. 11
Allgyer, Hazel 14, 92
Archives
  George School 82, 98
  Hill School 54, 98
  Swarthmore College 92
Art by Michener 98
Articles Written by Michener
  "The Beginning Teacher" 7
  "A Famous Five" 81
  Glasgow Herald Essays 79
  "Personal Opinion" 28
  "Progressive Education" 86
  "Ten Best Books" 80
  Untitled Article by Michener 85
Athletic Department (Hill) 36, 39, 41-42, 51, 54
Athletics (George School)
  Facilities and Philosophy 76
  See: Baseball, Basketball, Tennis
Auction: See Oley Auction
Austin, Texas 9, 12, 55, 89, 92
Autobiography (Michener's) 7, 88
Awards
  Doylestown High School 20, 21
  Phi Beta Kappa 30
  Lippincott Fellowship 52
  Swarthmore College 18, 20-21, 24, 26, 30
  Navy 88
Aydelotte, Frank 20, 24, 32

-B-

Baldwin, James 55, 100
Bancroft Hall 76
Barbour, Albert L. 55, 100
Baseball
  Coach Far-fields (Hill) 42
  Coach of Cubs (George School) 79, 81
  Player (Doylestown) 15, 16, 17
Basketball—Student Years
  Doylestown High 15, 16, 17, 18, 19
    Bux-Mont League 17, 20
    Dismissal for Insubordination 17
    Junior Championship 15
  Swarthmore College 25, 26, 28
Basketball—Teaching Years
  Eastern Board of Coaches 79, 81
  George School
    Coaching 79, 81
    Faculty Team 79, 81, 82
  Hill School Faculty Team 44

Becker, George G. 7
"The Beginning Teacher" (article) 7
Bement, Howard 55, 100
Bickel, George 50
Biddle, Robert III 52, 92
Black Cultural Center 32
Blackmore, Richard Doddridge 55, 100
Boarding Students, "Boarders" 39
Bonus Books 65
Bookplate 70-71
Bourns, David 76
Boyd, James 55, 100
"Boyhood Along the Delaware" (speech) 79
Boy's Brigade 15
Boys' Week Speech 20
Breaking College Rules 24
Brothers, Deborah 92
Bucks County 52
Bucks County Historical Society 92
Bucks County Intelligencer 15, 22, 31
Bucks County Jail 90
Bühler, C. Walter 47, 52, 92
Bux-Mont League 17, 20

-C-

Call Chronicle (Allentown) 11
Caravans 52
Carnival Grounds 11
"The Castle of My Dreams" (poem) 17
Centennial Year
  Hill School 48, 53
  Swarthmore College 32
Central Bucks West 15, 92
Chancellor, Paul 37, 38, 50, 51
Chapis, Lauren A. 92, 98
Chautauqua 22, 24, 31, 43
Cherry-Garrard, Apsley 55, 56
Christmas Book, 1929 44, 49
Christmas Book(s), 1930 47, 49
A Christmas Carol (play) 44
Close, David P. 92
Coaches (Hill): See Athletic Department
Colbath, Henry J. 50
Collection Hall 25
Collections 25
Colorado State College 85
*The Complete Poetical Works of Geoffrey
  Chaucer* 72, 100
Conley, Harold 44
Consignors (of textbooks) 14
"Cookie" 89, 91
Coolidge, President Calvin 20
"The Courtship of Miles Standish" (marionette
  play) 77
Cowperthwaite, Robert 50
Cressman, Pam 92
Cross, Robert 32

-D-

Day, A. Grove 7
Day Students 39
Deaccession (of textbooks) 14, 55
Demerits (Hill) 40, 50, 53
Depression 31, 52, 56, 90
Diagramming Sentences 61-62, 90
The Dial 14, 36, 41, 52
Dickens, Charles 57-60, 70, 100
Diplomacy 28, 47, 91
"Diversions in the Student's Life" (speech) 20-21
Doodle 71, 100
Dormitory Master

Colorado State University 85
  George School 77, 83
  Hill School 51, 52, 63
"Dos Sabios" (poem) 25-26
Dougherty, David R. 54
The Dover Road (play) 44
Doylestown High School 7, 15-22
Doylestown Homes
  81 N. Clinton Street 30, 31
"The Dramatists—In Three Acts" (poem) 29
Dress Code
  George School 76
  Hill School 40, 54
Drinkwater, John 60, 100
Durken, Michael 92

-E-

East Wing: See Middle School
Edgar, Henry C. 55, 61, 62, 100
Edwards, Boyd 36, 37, 38, 62, 100
Emery, Fred P. 71, 100
Emmaus, Pennsylvania 11, 12
Endowment Support 29, 32, 90
English Club (Hill) 36
English Department
  George School 75, 76, 77, 78, 80, 81
  Hill School 33, 37, 38, 50, 62
  1929 Faculty List 50
English Honors Course (Hill) 42
English Proficiency Exam 39
Europe 9, 14, 31, 52, 73
Evans, Howard Vick 53

-F-

The Facts and Background of Literature 14, 70,
  71, 100
"A Famous Five" (article) 81
Far-fields Sports 42, 53
Fell, Margaret 23
Feroe, Melvin 49, 92
Feroe, Robert A. 49
Feroe, William 49
Feroe Press 49, 63, 92
Field Trips 51
The Fires of Spring 22, 30
Fletcher, Stevenson 79, 81
Football 15
  Far-fields Coach 53
  Touch Player 53
Forms 36, 39
Fox, George 23
"Frankie and Johnnie" (play) 27
Fraser, David 32
Fraternity: See Phi Delta Theta
  Views on 25
Friend, Theodore III 32
Fuller, Ed 92

-G-

Gardy, J. Allen 15, 16
Garner, Catherine Roth 20, 30
George, John Malin 75
George School 7, 12, 31, 66, 73-84
  Annuals 78, 81
  Campus Map Today 76
  Comparison with Hill School 77
The George School Bulletin 78
  "A Famous Five" by Michener 81
  Untitled Article by Michener 85
George School News 77
  Faculty Advisor 79

The Georgian: See *The George School Bulletin*
Gifts 32, 90
Glasgow Herald (Michener's essays) 79
Gogol, Nikolay 66
"Gold" (Michener's original play) 28
Good-bye Mr. Chips 36
Graduation
    Doylestown High School 18, 20-21
    Swarthmore College 29-30
"The Grand Army of the Class of 1925" 20
Great Expectations 55, 57, 100
Greeley, Colorado 85
Green Mansions 65, 100
Greever, Garland 70, 100
Gregorie, Jeffrey 90
Guarded Education (Quaker) 23, 75

-H-

Halcyon 30
Hall, Edward T. 53
Hamburg Show 27, 28
Hardy, Thomas 57, 63, 100
Harris, Leo John 92
Harvard University 46, 85, 86, 87
Haverford College 33
Hawthorne, Nathaniel 64, 100
Hayes, John P. 7
"The Heart of the Boy" (speech) 20
"The Hero" (play) 28
Hicksite 23, 75
High Street 48
Highest Honors (*summa cum laude*) 30
Hill School 7, 9, 31, 33-54, 55
    Aeroplane view 1929 39
    Campus Map 1993 54
    Catalog 39, 41
    Comparison with George School 77
    History 35-38
    Honors Program 42, 54, 74
    Job Interview 33
    Job Offer 34
    Michener's Campus Sketch 48
    Students Serving in WW II 88
The Hill School News 35, 36, 41, 54
The Hill School Snooze 43, 54
Hilton, James 36
The History of The Hill School 37
History Teaching 81, 83, 84
Hoenstine, John 31, 92
Hollowell, Benjamin 23
Hollowell, Thomas 28
Honor Rank (Doylestown) 20
Honors Program
    Hill School 42, 54, 74
    Swarthmore College 24, 26, 27, 31, 32, 74
The House of the Seven Gables 64, 100
Hudson, William Henry 65, 100
Humanist 74, 90

-I-

Idylls of the King 56, 67-68
Intelligence Quotients 37, 74
Irresponsibility 85
"Ivy Oration" (speech) 29-30

-J-

James A. Michener Art Museum 90, 92
"Jim Michener and Co." 27
Johnson, Lindsay 17

-K-

Katsiff, Bruce 92
"Keats & Shakespeare" (poem) 60-61
Kempton, Herbert "Fido" 41, 42
Kerouac, Jack 90
Kings, John 9, 89, 92
Kogel, Chris 41
Koon, Patti 82, 83, 84, 85, 87, 90
Koon, Rev. S. P. 83, 84

-L-

Lavertu, Francis L. 51
Leeds Room 80
Lefever, Odie 92
Lehigh Valley 11
Lester, John A. 33, 34, 38, 42, 43, 62, 69, 73, 74, 75, 77
Lewis, W. D. 67, 100
Linn, James Weber 70, 100
Lippincott Fellowship 52, 73
The Little Theater Club 27
Long, H. M. 85
Lorna Doone: A Romance of Exmoor 55, 100

-M-

MacKaye, Percy 72, 100
Macmillan Publishing 86-87, 88
Macpherson, Gilbert 47
Magill, Edward 23, 24
Main
    George School 75, 80
    Swarthmore College 23
Marching On 14, 55, 100
Marks (Hill) 40, 53
Marionettes
    Chautauqua 31
    George School Marionettes 80, 84
    Guild 77
    Micelli or Miccelli 77, 78, 79, 80, 81
    Productions 77
        "The Courtship of Miles Standish"
        "A Midsummer Night's Dream"
        "Phiz the Whiz"
    Stage in Storage 77
Maris, George 76
Marriage 83, 84, 90
Master: See Dormitory Master
Master Builder 35
Master-Student Relations (Hill) 42
Master's Degree 85
Mathematics 21, 62, 86, 87
Mauve Decade Party 43
McFeely, Richard H. 76, 86
Medical Department (Hill) 39, 40
Medina, Harold R. 41
Medina, Standish F. 41, 53, 92
Meigs, Dwight 36, 37
Meigs, John 35-36
Meigs, Marion Butler 36
Meigs, Mary 35
Meigs, Matthew 35
Memoirs: See *The World Is My Home*
Mendenhall, Birkenshaw 81
The Merry Wives of Windsor 71, 100
"Mi Proprio Amo" (poem) 16-17
Micelli (or Miccelli) Marionettes: See Marionettes
Michener for Congress Committee 13

Michener, James A.
    Acting: See Acting
    Art 98
    Articles: See Articles Written by Michener
    Attributes
        Attentive to detail 28
        Diplomatic 28, 47, 91
        Generous 32, 90
        Humanist 74, 90
        Independent 15, 24, 25, 26, 73, 88
        Insubordinate 17
        Irresponsible 85
        Modest 19
        Non-doodler 71, 100
        Quaker Ideals 73, 74-75, 90
        Tardy 17, 85
    Awards: See Awards
    Fraternity Member 25, 26
    Marionette Plays: See Marionette
    Letters Reproduced 13, 33, 34, 46, 73, 74, 80, 82, 83, 84, 86, 87, 88
    Notes on The Hill Textbooks
        "Analyzing a Sentence by Diagramming" 62
        "The Bonus Books" 65
        "The Essential Dickens" 57
        "Graduate Course" 63
        "The Missing Jewel" 55
        "My Failure" 68
        "Reading Should Be Fun" 71
    Plays: See Acting
        "Gold" (original script) 28
    Poems
        Doylestown High School: See *Torch*
        Swarthmore College: See *Portfolio*
        Textbook: See Poems in Textbooks (unpublished)
        George School "The Princess Who Could Not Dream" 77
    Speeches: See Speeches
    Sports: See Baseball, Basketball, Far-fields, Football, Tennis, Walking
    Views on Education: See Views on Education
    Views on Sports and Academia
        American Tragedy 51
        Letter to the Editor 28
        Ivy Oration 29-30
Michener, Mabel Haddock 45, 57, 91
Michener, Mari 91
Michener-Worthington Reunions 22
Middle School Residence (Hill) 40, 46-47, 48, 49, 52
"A Midsummer Night's Dream" (marionette play) 77
Mike Sweeney of The Hill 50
Miller, George Morey 70, 100
"Mind the Light" 75
Mr. Rolfe of The Hill 14, 36, 62-63, 100
Montgomery, Archibald R. III 53
Murray, George 15
Music
    Influence on Prose 90
    Music Hobby Group 84
    Record Collection 47, 51, 52
    Red Seal Records 51
    Scottish Ballads 79

-N-

NASA 87
Nason, John 32
National Council of Social Studies 7

Naval Reserve 88
    Rank 88
    Service History by Michener 88
Nazi Regime 86
Newtown, Pennsylvania 75
Niantic, Pennsylvania 14
"The Night After Christmas" (poem) 16
The Novel 48, 87

-O-

"Ode to Tennyson" (poem) 67-68
"An Old, Old Theme" (poem) 19
Oley Auction 11, 55, 90, 92
    Stubs and Receipts 12
Oley, Pennsylvania 11, 14
Open Scholarships 24
Outward Bound (play) 27

-P-

Paradise Park 22
Parrish, Edward 23
Parrish Hall 23
Pearson, Paul M. 24
Peterson, Brian 92
Ph.D. Degree 86
Phi Beta Kappa 30
Phi Delta Theta 25, 26
"Phiz the Whiz" (marionette play) 77
"Pirate Gold" (poem) 25-26
"The Player's Soliloquy" (poem) 17
Plays: See Acting; See Marionettes
Poems in Textbooks (unpublished) 9, 55, 60, 61,
    67, 68, 71
    "Keats & Shakespeare" 61
    "Ode to Tennyson" 68
    [Untitled] 71
Poetry—Influence on Prose 71, 90
Politics 41, 85
The Portfolio (Swarthmore College)—Michener's
    Contributions
    "Dos Sabios" 25-26
    "The Dramatists—In Three Acts" 29
    "Pirate Gold" 25-26
    "Spring Virtue" 26-27
    "The Wizardry of Dis" 26
Potts, Marjorie 38
Pottstown 7, 9, 33, 34, 39, 49, 53
Presbyterian 35
"The Princess Who Could Not Dream" (poem)
    77
Progressive Education 37, 38, 42, 73, 81, 86
"Progressive Education" (article) 86
Pulitzer Prize 88

-Q-

Quaker 23, 24, 31, 73, 90
    Competitive Sports 76
    Guarded Education 23, 75
    Meeting House 23, 75

-R-

Random House 12
The Record (Hill) 36, 41, 52
Report of the County Chairman 12, 13
The Return of the Native 63, 100
Reviews by Michener
    One-Act Plays (Swarthmore College) 28-29
    The Record (Hill) 45, 47-48
Reynolds, George F. 70, 100
Rhodes, Lawrence 36
Rhodes Scholarship 52

Rhys, Ernest 64, 100
Rice, Leonard A. (Bill) 43, 44, 50, 51
The Rivals (play) 84
Robins, George Douglas 51
Robinson House 32
Roe, Edward C. 42, 92
Rogers and Hammerstein 88
Rolfe, Alfred G. 12, 14, 36, 37, 41, 50, 55, 63,
    100
Ross, Principal 17
Rubendahl, Howard L. 53

-S-

Salary 33, 46, 76, 83, 85
Saunders, A Peirce 50
Scholarship Award (Swarthmore College) 18,
    20-21, 24, 30
School Rules and Orders 40
Schuylkill River 39
Scotland 73, 78, 79
Scott, Robert Falcon 56, 57
Senior Class Trip 20
Sentence Analysis by Diagram 61, 100
Shakespeare, William 71, 100
Shrigley, George A. C. 50, 52
"Silly Sentimentalities" (poem) 16
The Sir Roger de Coverley Papers 55, 100
Skidding (play) 31
Smith, Constance 81
Smith, Courtney 32
Social Science Department 85
Society of Friends 23, 73
Sousa, John Philip 22
South Pacific 88
South Pacific (musical) 88
Speeches by Michener
    "Boyhood Along the Delaware" 79
    "Diversions in the Student's Life" (Doylestown
        Class President) 20-21
    Easter Vacation (Swarthmore College) 25
    For Endowment (Swarthmore College) 29
    "The Heart of the Boy" (Boys' Week) 20
    "Ivy Oration" (Swarthmore Baccalaureate)
        29-30
    Pre-game School Spirit Speech (Swarthmore
        College) 28
*A Spelling Review : For Preparatory Schools
    and High Schools* 38, 92
Spenker, Mrs. H. 80
"Spring Virtue" (poem) 26-27
Stahl, Jasper Jacob 50
Stock Market Crash of 1929 34, 41, 46
The Story of Roland 11, 12, 55, 100
Strachan, Malcolm 50, 52
Swain, Joseph 24
Swarthmoor Hall 23
Swarthmore College 7, 23-32
Swarthmore Phoenix 23, 27
Swayne, Kingdon 82, 92, 98
Swayne, Norman 82
Sweeney Gymnasium 38
Sweeney, Michael 36, 37, 41, 50, 54
Syntheses of Disciplines 81, 82

-T-

A Tale of Two Cities 70, 100
Tales of the South Pacific 7, 88
Taras Bulba 66, 80
Tardiness 17, 85
Tatlock, John S. P. 72, 100
"Ten Best Books" 80

Tennis 15, 25, 52, 79
Tennyson, Alfred Lord 56, 100
Tennyson's Idylls of the King 56, 67
Tess of the d'Urbervilles 63, 80
Thomas, Isaac 50, 51, 62, 100
The Torch (Doylestown High School)—
    Michener's Contributions
    "The Castle of My Dreams" 17
    "Mi Proprio Amo" 16-17
    "The Night After Christmas" 16
    "An Old, Old Theme" 19
    "The Player's Soliloquy" 17
    "Silly Sentimentalities" 16
Torch Staff 15, 16, 18
The Town and the City 90
Triple Threat 87
Tuition
    George School 76
    Hill School 39, 54
    Swarthmore 24, 32
Turner, Luther (Pop) 50
Twinning, Edward 15
Typewriter 55, 89
Tyson, Martha 23

-U-

Unit in Social Studies 85
U.S. Army 87
University of Chicago 46
University of Miami 12, 13, 89
University of Texas-Austin 89
University of Virginia 82
[Untitled] (poem) 71

V

The Victorian Period 70, 100
Views on Education 31, 49, 51, 62, 63, 65-67,
    80, 82, 89
Vitarelli, William 77, 78, 79, 80, 81, 84

-W-

WAACS (Patti Koon) 87
Walking 15
Walton, George A. 31, 73, 75, 76, 80, 81, 82,
    83, 85, 86, 87
Walton, Joseph 76
Warton Club 28
Watling, William B. 53, 92
Watson, Charles C. 53
The Way of Poetry 60, 100
Wendell, James I. 33, 34, 37-38, 40, 46, 47, 50,
    52, 53, 75, 88
"Why Girls Leave Home" 43, 44
Willow Grove, Pennsylvania 22
"The Wizardry of Dis" (poem) 26
The World Is My Home 15, 34
World War II 32, 73, 88, 90
The Worst Journey in the World 49, 55, 56
Wrinkle, William L. 85
Writing Associates Program 32
Wyeth, N. C. 54

ℬℬℬℬ

Published by

The Book Stops Here
1108 Rocky Pt. Ct. NE
Albuquerque, NM 87123

The manuscript for this book was laser
printed in Arial and New Times Roman
type, 5pt to 48pt. The text is 10 pt New
Times Roman. Photo illustrations are 150-
line screen halftones. The text paper is 80
pound Sterling satin. The spine is Holliston
Roxite C Maroon vellum, the board
covering Rainbow Birch A, and the end
papers Rainbow Crimson D.

Printed by

BookCrafters
613 E. Industrial Drive
Chelsea, Michigan 48118

ℬℬℬℬ